SAGE was founded in 1965 by Sara Miller McCune to support the dissemination of usable knowledge by publishing innovative and high-quality research and teaching content. Today, we publish over 900 journals, including those of more than 400 learned societies, more than 800 new books per year, and a growing range of library products including archives, data, case studies, reports, and video. SAGE remains majority-owned by our founder, and after Sara's lifetime will become owned by a charitable trust that secures our continued independence.

Los Angeles | London | New Delhi | Singapore | Washington DC | Melbourne

MUSLIMS IN INDIAN LABOUR MARKET

MUSLIMS IN INDIAN LABOUR MARKET

ACCESS AND OPPORTUNITIES

JAVAID IQBAL KHAN

Los Angeles | London | New Delhi
Singapore | Washington DC | Melbourne

Copyright © Javaid Iqbal Khan, 2019

All rights reserved. No part of this book may be reproduced or utilized in any form or by any means, electronic or mechanical, including photocopying, recording or by any information storage or retrieval system, without permission in writing from the publisher.

First published in 2019 by

SAGE Publications India Pvt Ltd
B1/I-1 Mohan Cooperative Industrial Area
Mathura Road, New Delhi 110 044, India
www.sagepub.in

SAGE Publications Inc
2455 Teller Road
Thousand Oaks, California 91320, USA

SAGE Publications Ltd
1 Oliver's Yard, 55 City Road
London EC1Y 1SP, United Kingdom

SAGE Publications Asia-Pacific Pte Ltd
18 Cross Street #10-10/11/12
China Square Central
Singapore 048423

Published by Vivek Mehra for SAGE Publications India Pvt Ltd. Typeset in 10/12.5 pt ITC Stone Serif by Zaza Eunice, Hosur, Tamil Nadu, India.

Library of Congress Cataloging-in-Publication Data Available

ISBN: 978-93-532-8645-3 (HB)

SAGE Team: Abhijit Baroi, Safia Hassan, Kumar Indra Mishra and Kanika Mathur

To
Those who do not see religion as an identifier in social and economic spaces
The Indian youth who is breaking the glass ceiling of stereotyping to emerge better in different sociopolitical and economic spaces
and
Laiebah, my daughter

Thank you for choosing a SAGE product!
If you have any comment, observation or feedback,
I would like to personally hear from you.

Please write to me at **contactceo@sagepub.in**

Vivek Mehra, Managing Director and CEO, SAGE India.

Bulk Sales

SAGE India offers special discounts
for purchase of books in bulk.
We also make available special imprints
and excerpts from our books on demand.

For orders and enquiries, write to us at

Marketing Department
SAGE Publications India Pvt Ltd
B1/I-1, Mohan Cooperative Industrial Area
Mathura Road, Post Bag 7
New Delhi 110044, India

E-mail us at **marketing@sagepub.in**

Subscribe to our mailing list
Write to **marketing@sagepub.in**

This book is also available as an e-book.

Contents

List of Illustrations ix
List of Abbreviations xi
Acknowledgements xiii

Introduction 1

Chapter 1. Revisiting Discourses on Labour
and Labour Markets 26

Chapter 2. The Muslim Question: Re-examining History,
Politics and Employment Structures 50

Chapter 3. Dynamics of Muslim Participation in Indian Labour
Market 74

Chapter 4. Examining Employment Opportunities Using
the Human Opportunity Index Framework 108

Conclusions and Policy Suggestions 152

Appendix 163
References 244
Index 267
About the Author 271

List of Illustrations

Figure

4.1 Conceptual Framework of HOI Approach   117

Tables

I.1 Description of Household and Demographic Characteristics of Respondents along with Codes as Recorded in Schedule 10 of the Employment–Unemployment Surveys 2004–2005 and 2011–2012   13

2.1 Percentage of Muslims Appointed to Public Service in 1871 Compared with Percentage of Muslim Population   64
2.2 Judicial and Executive Positions in the Uncovenanted Civil Service, 1887   65

3.1 LFPR (2011–2012 and 2004–2005 UPSS)   80
3.2 Workforce Population Ratios 2004–2005 and 2011–2012 (UPSS)   87

3.3	Result of Logit Regression for Participation in Employment 2004–2005 and 2011–2012	100
4.1	Tabular Construct of the Model for Estimation of Human Opportunity for the Indian Labour Market	129
4.2	HOI in Employment Controlled for SRC Status	132
4.3	HOI in Employment for the Age Group 15–24 Years	135
4.4	HOI in Employment for the Age Group 25–39 Years	137
4.5	HOI in Employment for the Age Group 40–64 Years	140
4.6	HOI for Levels of Educational Attainment 2011–2012	145
4.7	HOI for Levels of Educational Attainment 2004–2005	147

List of Abbreviations

AEC	Adult Education Centre
EGS	Education Guarantee Scheme
FC	forward caste
GNP	gross national product
GSCR	Gopal Singh Commission Report
HOI	Human Opportunity Index
ICS	Indian Civil Services
KCR	Kundu Committee Report
LFPR	labour force participation rate
LPM	Linear Probability Model
MLE	maximum likelihood estimation
MOHA	Ministry of Home Affairs
NAR	net attendance ratio
NFEC	Non-formal Education Courses
NSS	National Sample Survey
NSSO	National Sample Survey Office
OAE	own account enterprise
SCR	Sachar Committee Report
SCs	Scheduled Castes

SER	student enrolment rate/ratio
SLM	segmented labour markets
SRCs	socio-religious communities
SSA	Sarva Shiksha Abhiyan
STs	Scheduled Tribes
TACs	traditional arts and crafts
TLC	Total Literacy Campaign
UC	upper caste
UPSS	Usual Principal and Subsidiary Status
UR	unemployment rate
WEIGO	Women in Informal Employment: Globalizing and Organizing
WFPR	workforce participation rate
WPR	worker population ratio

Acknowledgements

This book would not have been possible without the support and encouragement of several institutions and individuals. I am especially indebted to Professor Effat Yasmin, Head of the Department of Economics, University of Kashmir, who has been supportive of my career goals. She has been an inspirational teacher, guide and a wonderful critic.

I am grateful to all of those with whom I have had the pleasure of working during this project. I would especially like to thank Dr Abhay Kumar and Abhishek Kumar for engaging in discussions and providing suggestions to address specific research issues of this book. Their feedback and critical comments during data extraction and formatting have gone a long way in enhancing my understanding of National Sample Survey Office (NSSO) data sets. An essential part of this book builds upon large NSSO data sets. I would like to express my gratitude to the colleagues at NSSO for providing me such data sets besides responding to all my queries regarding data. Special thanks to Jyoti Ranjan Mujumdar and Rashmi Sharma from the computer centre of NSSO, New Delhi, for their invaluable support and cooperation. Professor Ashok Pankaj, Dr Mondira

Bhattacharya and Rajinder Singh of the Council for Social Development, New Delhi, have been a great team to work with.

There are many people who provided useful comments during discussions on different aspects of this work. Professor Mohamad Sultan Bhat from the Department of Jamia Millia Islamia, New Delhi, deserves a special mention. Professor Bhat has been gracious enough to go through the final draft of this work. His suggestions regarding theoretical and philosophical aspects of this study have strengthened its theoretical foundation. Professor S. Madheshwaran from Centre for Economic Studies and Policy, Bangalore, has been a great teacher and a wonderful friend. Apart from his own work in the area of labour market and religious minorities, his positive attitude towards life has been inspiring.

I am especially indebted to Dr Tariq Masood and Dr Mohammad Abdullah from Aligarh Muslim University (AMU) for providing suggestions regarding the identification of relevant variables and the empirical strategy. Special thanks goes to Dr Sheikh Fayaz with whom I have had good times since childhood, particularly during my stay at the Jawaharlal Nehru University (JNU), New Delhi, during the crucial stage of this project. His support and comments have been wonderful all along and continue to be so. The effort he put in during the early drafting of this work and the valuable insights he offered for the final draft have been highly beneficial. Thanks are due to Dr Sohail Masoodi, Dr Irfan Ahmad Sofi, Dr Ajaz Ahmad Khaki and Dr Tanveer Ahmad Darzi for support and encouragement, Dr Sajad A. Darzi for valuable inputs on medieval history, and Dr Sumeer Gul for support, encouragement and guidance. My students and research scholars at the Department of Economics, University of Kashmir, have been a great source of support, inspiration and motivation. All of them deserve a mention and acknowledgement. Participants of various seminars, conferences and workshops that I have attended over the course of writing this book have contributed a lot to my understanding of critical issues relevant to this work and beyond. I thank all of them.

Institutional support is the most important input to any kind of research output. This book would have not at all been possible except for the wonderful support provided by such institutions of excellence as JNU, New Delhi; AMU, Aligarh; V. V. Giri National Labour Institute, Noida, and my alma mater, the University of Kashmir. My stay at JNU and AMU, access to resources at the respective central libraries provided by the respective librarians, Dr Ramesh C. Gaur and Dr Nabi Hasan, proved instrumental in timely completion of this work. Special thanks to the entire staff of all these wonderful institutions for being courteous and helpful.

My deep love and gratitude goes to my parents for their perseverance and unconditional love and support in all circumstances. You have been inspiration unparalleled. The vision of my father has always been a driving force for me in all endeavours, academic and otherwise. You have been a wonderful teacher, a living example of accomplishments and doing something big in life, irrespective of all odds. My in-laws have contributed in no lesser a way. Their moral support, encouragement and admiration of my work have always been encouraging.

I am extremely grateful to Reenu, my wife, for her endurance, unconditional support over the course of our married life in general and during the completion of this work in particular. She has been a guide, a critic and a friend.

Arshid, my brother; Gazala, my sister; and Afak and Sajid, my brothers-in-law, deserve appreciation for being there to 'nudge' me to complete this work well ahead of the deadline.

Last but not least, my little angel, my daughter, who is yet to understand what she means to me, deserves the best of compliments for being the way she has been. Just at the age of 4 she has given an unexplained meaning to my life and being. This one is for you, Laiebah Javaid Khan.

Introduction

The discussion vis-à-vis the relationship between religious identity, economic behaviour and prosperity is not one of the recent origins. One could actually discern a comprehensive discussion in the writings of Karl Marx (1859). 'The mode of production of material life', contends Marx, conditions the general process of social, political and intellectual life. And he further asserts, 'It is not the consciousness of men that determines their existence, but their social existence that determines their consciousness' (Marx, 1859, p. 11–12). From Marx's writings, one could easily ascertain the emphasis he has put on the impact of socio-economic system on individual behaviour and by negating a two-ways causal connection. To Marx, it is the sociocultural and economic system that effects and shapes the individual outcomes and not the other way around. On the opposite side of this understanding lies the Weberian thought outlined in 'The Protestant work ethic' proposition. Weber upholds the opinion that the Reformed Protestantism had the tendency to nurture strong preference for hard work and prudence that eventually led to the greater economic gains. Weber argues, 'As far as the influence of the Puritan outlook extended, […] it favoured the development of a rational bourgeois economic life […] It stood at the cradle of the modern economic man' (Weber, 1904, p. 174). Religion leads individuals to such virtues, asserts Weber, which to him would enable them achieve better life outcomes.

This thread of arguments completely negates what was earlier brought to fore by Marx. As flagged above, Marx believes in the impact of social structure on economic behaviour and undermines the impact of religious adherence on the economic outcomes while Weber on the other hand emphasizes the impact of religious adherence on economic outcomes and delineates on a two-way relationship.

Much before Weber and Marx, Adam Smith has also made some references with regards to social values and economic outputs, but a clear explication of his understanding is wanting and is yet to be conclusive. He further writes,

> [S]elf-interest motivates clergy just as it does secular producers; that market forces constrain churches just as they constrain secular firms; and that the benefits of competition, the burdens of monopoly, and the hazards of government regulation are as real for religion as for any other sector of the economy. (Smith, 1776, pp. 740–766)

While further investigating the causal relationships between the above mentioned values and the economic outputs, Cantoni (2010), in a recent study on economic prosperity (as measured by city growth) in 19th-century Prussia, does not report any effect of Protestantism on the outcome variable. Nonetheless, a positive effect of Protestantism on economic prosperity in Prussia is reported by Becker and Woessmann (2009) in a separate study.

Race, class, gender and other social categories when understood as a subset of religious affiliation (following both Marx and Weber) at an individual level, it emerges, are bound to shape attitudes, beliefs and behaviours. But the question which has remained unanswered thus far is how does this interaction affect the actual life outcomes. How religious identity and affiliation assumes causation in religion's relationship with a host of outcomes especially those concerning with employment and labour market outcomes is still an unsettled debate. Labour market outcomes within the confines of religious affiliation and religion-based identity at the individual level as well as at the societal or national level are highly intricate to understand. As observed above, it has not only baffled great many scholars but has also leads to an ambiguous discourse.

This book is aimed at revisiting the above discourses with a completely new approach. It discusses labour market outcomes of Muslims in India. Their participation in the labour market, work behaviour and absorption as well as the type of work they do are presented in the book. The motivations for studying Muslims are manifold. Muslims form the largest religious minority in India. Their historical antecedents, and the present socio-religious positioning within the Indian economic setup, have become a matter of public debate. Their religious identity as is argued by many is directly linked with their relative depravity on socio-economic indicators. Empirical evidence with regards to this line of argument is provided by the findings of 'Prime Minister's High Level Committee (Sachar Committee) on Social, Economic and Educational Status of the Muslim Community in India' commissioned by the Government of India in 2005.

The Sachar Committee was appointed with the main objective of assessing the social, economic and educational status of Muslims in the states, regions, districts and blocks that they live in, their livelihood activities, their levels of socio-economic development and their asset base and income levels relative to other groups. Prior to this committee, the Gopal Singh Committee was appointed by Government of India to study 'Economic condition of minorities, scheduled castes and tribes'. However, the report was not at all presented to the people until 1990, when it was tabled in the parliament with no follow up.

The Sachar Committee Report (hereafter SCR), submitted in November 2006, has become a landmark in documenting the social, economic and educational status of Muslims, based on pooling together extensive information hitherto scattered across different sources. This committee, the first of its kind as far as the comprehensiveness of the report and its acceptability in the policy and academic circles is concerned, submitted a report spread over 404 pages with report's tables and technical notes running into 130 pages. These numbers are an indication of the coverage of the report and the comprehensiveness of analysis. One of the major highlights the committee finds in the report is that Muslims are generally worse off than most other communities in terms of their access to public and private sector jobs, education, infrastructure and credit, and that the gap between Muslims and other communities has failed to close or has even increased on some dimensions over the past few decades (Sachar Committee, 2006, pp. 40–42). The SCR also maintained that the Muslim community exhibited 'deficits and deprivation in practically all dimensions of development' (p. 237). Beginning with the perceptions of the Muslim community on identity and security, which capture the pervasive feeling of insecurity, deprivation and discrimination, the SCR focused on the issue of equity, and probed the question of whether different socio-economic categories in India have had an equal chance to reap the benefits of development. The SCR felt strongly that 'policies to deal with the relative deprivation of the Muslims in the country should sharply focus on inclusive development and 'mainstreaming' of the community while respecting diversity' (p. 237). An evaluation report occasioned upon the Sachar Committee (the Kundu Committee Report [KCR]) in 2012 reported the continuance of dismal performance of Muslims in the sphere of access to employment.

Conclusions drawn by KCR pointed towards a perpetual low participation of Indian Muslims in the labour market. However, both the above-mentioned reports were unable to explain the causative factors of this perpetual phenomenon. No plausible explanation(s) has been provided for low participation of Muslims in the labour market. This book is aimed at addressing this issue in some detail. Why do Muslims report in less numbers at the labour market? Do Muslims face certain types of 'glass ceilings' at the labour market? What is the nature and content of labour force participation of Muslims in the labour market? All these questions and many others are discussed in the following chapters. Broadly speaking, this work envisages the labour market participation dynamics on the socio-religious plane. Intricacies involved in labour market positioning of individuals are evaluated alongside their socio-religious status. A focused analysis of labour market outcomes of Indian Muslims is carried out within a relative framework. Muslim posturing in labour markets is compared with other socio-religious categories. These include the Scheduled Castes (SCs), Scheduled Tribes (STs) and Hindus (General category as well as Upper Caste [UC]). Identification and analysis of causative factors of differences in employment and employability among individuals based on their socio-religious affiliations is the central theme of this book. A broad focus on the distribution of employment opportunities, their coverage and individual access to them are also discussed. This discussion on access of individuals to prevalent employment opportunities conditional upon their socio-religious status makes a departure from earlier works on Muslims and their labour force participation. This departure explains the nuances of perceived discrimination and depravity of a group. The underlying hypothesis over here is that if opportunities of employment are fairly distributed within an egalitarian framework, after controlling for circumstances of individuals, then differentials in outcomes cannot be attributed to discrimination, otherwise they can be. Fairer distribution of employment opportunities translates into egalitarian access to them.

The Plan

General introduction to the basic premise of this book is discussed in this chapter. The next part of this chapter also provides an overview of the methods, methodology as well as data sources, concepts and definition used in this book. Chapter 1 attempts a general understanding of representative literature concerned with labour markets, labour market analysis and religion dimension in labour markets. Labour markets of developing economies in general and the Indian labour market in particular are largely informal. Understanding of labour market structure especially the nuances of the informal labour market are dealt with in this chapter. Selected studies on 'economics of religion' are discussed to put the 'Muslim question' into a theoretical perspective. This is followed by a discussion on studies which address the question of socio-religious minority affiliation and labour market interactions with a particular focus on Muslims in India. Insights drawn from these studies provide an excellent feedback, used as the basis for the present work in a strong theoretical framework.

Data sources, concepts, definitions and methodology regarding the empirical analysis carried out in this book is presented in the next part of this chapter. Descriptions of all the variables used in the empirical model are presented. Operational definitions of all concepts and variables used are provided. Methodology used to evaluate human opportunity in the Indian labour market is however not reported in this chapter. This is intentionally done to conserve space and maintain coherence of thought and presentation. The same is provided in the relevant chapter.

Chapter 2 presents a detailed overview of the socio-economic positioning of Indian Muslims in a historical context. Deriving from a variety of historical studies, it attempts to situate the Indian Muslims in the current debate vis-à-vis employment. An attempt is made to trace their origins, rise, fall and efforts targeted to their revival into the dominant sociopolitical and economic discourse in India. Muslim employment and their relative position at the advent of British rule is the benchmark. This is followed by an analysis of the events that took place during the company rule leading up to the revolt of 1857. As is reported in the chapter, events leading to 1857 had a profound impact upon the socio-economic wellbeing of all Indians in general and Muslims particularly. The 'demoralization thesis' takes root during this period and hence is analysed in detail. Developments that took place under the crown (direct rule of the British monarchy) up until 1947 are presented. The vagaries of partition and its impact on Indian Muslims within the labour market as also outside it are vividly discussed. From the analysis as presented in this chapter, it becomes clear that the relative position of Muslims in the labour market did undergo a change, and they ended up into depravity and oblivion while political power was changing hands at the highest level. Transfer of power from Mughals (Muslims) to British (Christians) and then to Congress (predominantly Hindu) witnessed a perpetual decline in Muslim participation in the social milieu of the country in general and in the labour market in particular.

Chapter 3 presents a detailed analysis of Muslim participation in the labour market from 2004–2005 to 2011–2012.[1] Labour market participation ratios are an important benchmark for employment outcomes both at the individual and at the community level. A detailed analysis of labour force participation rate (LFPR), workforce participation rate, the unemployment rate (UR) as well as the student enrolment rates/ratios (SERs), across age and educational attainment, is discussed. This is done for all the classified socio-religious groups in order to account for the existing differences across them. Activity status of Indian workforce in broad-based categories of self-employment and regular and casual work is discussed. Industry-based classification of the labour force engagement and distribution of socio-religious categories into formal and informal work is also presented. This chapter presents a vivid positioning of Muslims in relation to other socio-religious communities (SRCs) in the labour market. A logistic regression is also reported in this chapter to validate the descriptive statistics. Effects of various socio-religious characteristics upon labour force participation are also discussed. Results of regression analysis, both in the form of logit modelresults and the logistic, are presented.

There exists a general perception of discrimination against Muslims in India in all walks of life. However, these perceptions could never be, either proved or refuted on empirical basis (Sachar

---

[1] Last two quinquennial rounds of National Sample Survey Office (NSSO) were carried out during these years. Empirical analysis of this book is based on these data sets.

Committee, 2006, pp. 239). It is to be noted that the perception of discrimination against Muslims is indeed complex and encompasses all walks of life (2006). More importantly, it is alleged that discriminatory approach against Muslims has occasioned for them a perpetual inequality of opportunity in access to and realization of public services in general and enhancement of their capabilities in particular. It is in this backdrop that Chapter 4 of this book divulges into the perception of discrimination against Muslims and the resultant alleged inequality of opportunity. This chapter presents a new approach to analysis of discrimination in labour markets. The concept of opportunity of employment and access to existing opportunities in the labour market is invoked. Rigorous theoretical, conceptual and empirical frameworks are reported for the pursuit of the same. Socio-economic circumstances prevalent in the Indian labour market are untangled, and, at the same time, an attempt is made to understand the characteristic features of people who are seeking and are available for work. Equating the two allows an understanding of the labour market circumstances and access to employment simultaneously. This allows us to underline and understand the labour market with some novelty of idea and purpose. To this effect, a Human Opportunity Index (HOI) for Indian labour market is constructed. An attempt to place the SRCs within the same framework is made. Relative position of the Indian Muslims vis-à-vis other SRCs and the total population is then reported.

The last chapter of the book documents summary and conclusions. It reports major findings as well as a series of policy implications for the future of development strategies, both in public policy and in applied research.

Data Sources

Consistency and comparability both over time and space are the primary requirements for the selection of data sets for temporal and comparative analysis. In the Indian context and in complementarities with objectives of this book, there are two data sources that fulfil this criterion: (a) the data collected during the population census and (b) the household survey data collected by the NSSO, Government of India. The census data was first collected during 1871–1872, but the true beginning was made in 1881. Since then, the census data is collected decennially. The census data is available for almost entire country, divided into states and union territories. The latest Census 2011 covers all the 35 states and union territories. The decadal census of India includes data on employment, and allows the identification of workers and non-workers. In 1951 census, a worker was defined as one 'gainfully employed or one working for a livelihood, excluding unpaid family workers'. In 1961 census, the position was however reversed. The basis of work was considered to be satisfied if a person had some regular work of more than one hour a day throughout the greater part of the working season. As a result, many persons were classified as workers. A more rigorous and meaningful definition of worker was adopted in the 1971 census. A worker was defined as 'one whose main activity has been productive participation in any economically productive work by his/her physical or mental activity'. The 1981 census, while adopting the definition of worker as provided in the 1971 census, made a further classification of workers into 'main workers' and 'marginal workers'. It defined main workers as those who have worked in some economic activity over a period of 6 months or more, that is, 183 days or more. Marginal workers, on the other hand, were those who had not worked for a major part of the year, that is, less than six months or 183 days. On the other hand, those who were not engaged in any form of activity were termed as 'non-workers'. These changes in the definition of workers have rendered the participation rates of workers in 1981 almost incomparable with the earlier censuses. However, the 1991, 2001 and 2011 censuses adopted almost the same definition and concepts of workers—main and marginal—used in the 1981 census, thus enabling the direct comparison of the results possible.

The second source of data is collected from the NSSO. It was initiated in the year 1950 and was initially known as the National Sample Survey (NSS). It is a nationwide, large-scale, continuous survey operation conducted in the form of successive rounds. It was established on the basis of a proposal from P. C. Mahalanobis to fill up data gaps for socio-economic planning and policymaking through sample surveys. In March 1970, the NSS was reorganized and all aspects of its work were brought under a single government organization, namely, the NSSO, under the overall direction of governing council to impart objectivity and autonomy in the matter of collection, processing and publication of the NSS data. The NSSO collects data on various socio-economic and demographic aspects and generally covers almost the entire territory of India. Although survey of the households in India started in the early 1950's, it was limited in its scope and coverage. However, since 1973, the data collection through sample surveys were streamlined with two types of surveys: large sample or quinquennial rounds of survey and then sample survey between two quinquennial rounds. The quinquennial rounds of NSSO are the only secondary sources on employment that allow identification of the respondents on the basis of religion. It is this aspect of the data set that makes it suitable for presenting my analysis. To estimate the employment and unemployment status, data recorded in Schedule 10 are excessively relied upon.[2]

The household level or unit record data on employment and unemployment collected by the NSSO is used in the book. The household information in these surveys is collected using a two-stage stratified sampling design technique. Therefore, weights are a natural part of the NSSO data sets. In the quinquennial rounds of survey, detailed information on place of residence, economic activities, social and demographic characteristics and household assets and expenditure are collected from diverse

---

[2] Schedule 10 is a comprehensive questionnaire served by the field staff of the NSSO to the respondents during the course of the survey. It contains detailed questions on household characteristics, such as household size, religion, social group, land possessed, land cultivated, demographic particulars and various aspects of economic activity and time disposition.

households covering different individuals at the all India level. The data includes the NSSO survey during the 61st and 68th rounds which correspond to year 2004–2005 and 2011–2012, respectively. The choice of the study period largely corresponds to the latest census surveys of 2001 and 2011. Thus, the period that would be covered in this book would be from 2004–2005 to 2011–2012. The basic difference between the census and NSSO sources of data are the information content. While from the census we only get basic demographic information about different population groups, NSSO data has information on several easily quantifiable indicators. More so, the identification of individuals on the basis of their location, religious affiliation and social group (recorded in Block 3, Schedule 10) makes the NSSO data set of extreme importance to the analysis. It is in this backdrop that I will rely mostly on NSSO data, given the fact that this is the only detailed data that is available to researchers to analyse labour market outcomes at the individual level alongside recording their religion and socio-economic status.

Concepts

In recent Indian censuses, work is defined as participation in any economically productive activity with or without compensation, wages or profit. Such participation may be physical and/or mental in nature. Work involves not only the physical work but also supervision and direction given to other workers. Work is taken as basis to identify workers. In 1961, the concept of work was introduced in the Indian census. Those who have worked any time in the last one year were categorized as workers, and those who did not work at all were classified as non-workers. In 1971, workers were categorized into main and marginal workers, rendering the respective censuses incomparable. Since 1981, the census definition of work has remained unchanged. Emphasis on detailed profile of the working characteristics of the population and on usual status of the work instead of the current status of the work started from the 1981 census.

The quinquennial national surveys on employment and unemployment are aimed at measuring the extent of employment and unemployment in quantitative terms disaggregated at household level and population characteristics. The household characteristics are recorded in Block 3 and demographic characteristics are recorded in Block 4 of Schedule 10. Household characteristics include location (rural/urban) alongside type of employment as well as religion and social groups. The demographic characteristics of members of the household recorded in Block 4 include sex, age, marital status, educational level, status of attendance and likewise. Activity statuses of the surveyed persons are presented in Block 5.1 (usual principal economic activity) and Block 5.2 (usual subsidiary economic activity) alongside a detailed account of time disposition of the respondents during the preceding week, recorded in Block 5.3. The description of household characteristics and demographic characteristics of household members along with codes as recorded in Schedule 10 are presented in Table I.1.

Data recorded in Blocks 3, 4, 5.1 and 5.2 has been used. After identifying the parameters as recorded in Block 3 and corresponding matching of the respondents to their demographic characteristics in Block 4, individuals are classified into various activity categories based on the activities pursued by them.

The activity of an individual is recorded for the reference period with regards to his/her participation in any economic or non-economic activity and is referred to as his/her activity status. An individual could, therefore, be under any of the following three broad activity statuses during a reference period:

1. Working or engaged in any economic activity
2. Not working/engaging in any economic activity but making 'tangible' efforts to seek work or being available for work if the work was available
3. Not being engaged in any economic activity and also not being available for the work

The individuals in the broad Activity Status 1 and 2 are classified as being in the labour force while those in Activity Status 3

TABLE I.1 *Description of Household and Demographic Characteristics of Respondents along with Codes as Recorded in Schedule 10 of the Employment–Unemployment Surveys 2004–2005 and 2011–2012*

Identifier	Subcategory	Description with NSSO Code(s)
Household type	For rural areas	Self-employed in agriculture–1, non-agriculture–2, regular wage/salary earning–3, Casual labour in agriculture–4, non-agriculture–5; others–9
	For urban areas	Self-employed–1, regular wage/salary earning–2 Casual labour–3, others–9
Religion		Hinduism–1, Islam–2, Christianity–3, Sikhism–4, Jainism–5, Buddhism–6, Zoroastrianism–7, others–9
Social group		Scheduled tribe–1, scheduled caste–2, other backward class–3, others–9
Gender		Male–1, female–2
Age		Recorded in years
Educational level	General	Not-literate–01, literate without formal schooling: EGS/NFEC/AEC–02, TLC–03, others–04; Literate: below primary–05, primary–06, middle–07, secondary–08, higher secondary–10, diploma/certificate course–11, graduate–12, postgraduate and above–13

(Continued)

TABLE I.1 *(Continued)*

Identifier	Subcategory	Description with NSSO Code(s)
	Technical	No technical education–01
		Technical degree in agriculture/engineering/technology/medicine, etc.,–02,
		Diploma or certificate (below graduate level) in: agriculture–03, engineering/technology–04, medicine–05, crafts–06, other subjects–07
		Diploma or certificate (graduate and above level) in: agriculture–08, engineering/technology–09, medicine–10, crafts–11, other subjects–12
Status of current attendance	Currently not attending	Never attended: school too far–01, to supplement household income–02, education not considered necessary–03, to attend domestic chores–04, others–05
		Ever attended but currently not attending: school too far–11, to supplement household income–12, education not considered necessary–13, to attend domestic chores–14, others–15
	Currently attending	EGS/NFEC/AEC–21, TLC–22, pre-primary (nursery/kindergarten, etc.)–23, primary (From class I to IV/V)–24, middle–25, secondary–26, higher secondary–27,
		Graduate in: agriculture–28, engineering/technology–29, medicine–30, other subjects–31
		Postgraduate and above–32,
		Diploma or certificate (below graduate level) in: agriculture–33, engineering/technology–34, medicine–35, crafts–36, other subjects–37
		Diploma or certificate (graduate level) in: Agriculture–38, engineering/technology–39, medicine–40, crafts–41, other subjects–42
		Diploma or certificate in post graduate and above level–43

Source: Authors own compilation from NSSO Schedule 10.0 of the E&US, 2011–2012.

are classified as being out of the labour force. The description of the activity status with the activity codes (given in bracket) that is recorded in Schedule 10 of the employment and unemployment surveys and used in the analysis is as follows:

1. Worked in household enterprise-self-employed
   a. Own account worker (11)
   b. Employer (12)
2. Worked as helper in household enterprise/unpaid family worker (21)
3. Worked as regular salaried/wage employee (31)
4. Worked as casual labour in
   a. Public works (41)
   b. Other types of work (51)
5. Did not work but was seeking and/or available for work (81)
6. Attended educational institutions (91)
7. Attended domestic duties only (92)
8. Attended domestic duties and was also engaged in free collection of goods (vegetables, roots, firewood, cattle-feed, etc.), sewing, tailoring, weaving, etc., for household use (93)
9. Renters, pensioners, remittance recipient, etc. (94)
10. Not able to work due to disability (95)
11. Others (including begging, prostitution, etc.) (97)
12. Did not work due to sickness (for casual workers only) (98)

Definitions

Labour markets in developing economies like India consist of a myriad of sectors, subsectors as well as activities. As such, any survey conducted to account for the employment/unemployment situation in such markets requires conceptual clarity as well as a well-defined nomenclature for various issues to be brought to light. To understand the context and content of this book, definitions of important variables used are provided here.

1. Persons who worked in household enterprise-self-employed are further categorized. *Self-employed*: Persons who worked in household enterprise-self-employed are further categorized.

a. *Own account workers*: Those self-employed persons who operated their enterprises on their own account with one or a few of their partners, and who during the reference period, by and large, ran their enterprises without hiring any labour. They could, however, have had unpaid helpers to assist them in the activity of their enterprise.
b. *Employers*: Those self-employed persons who worked on their own account or with one or a few partners and, who had been, by and large, ran their enterprise by hiring labour.
c. *Helper in household enterprise*: Those self-employed persons, mostly family members, who were engaged in their household enterprises, working full or part time and did not receive any regular salary or wages in return for the work performed. They did not run the household enterprise on their own but assisted the related persons living in the same household in running the household enterprise.
2. *Regular salaried/wage employee*: Those persons who worked in others' farm or non-farm enterprises, both household and non-household, and in return received wages or salary on a regular basis and not based on daily or periodic renewal of work contract. It also included persons receiving piece wage or salary and paid apprentices, both full time and part time, and not only persons getting time wage.
3. *Casual wage labour*: Those persons who were causally engaged in others' farm or non-farm enterprises (both household and non-household) and in return received wages in accordance to theterms of the daily or periodic work contract were classified as casual wage labour.
4. *Activity status*: To ascertain the activity status of a person, three distinct status categories are used by NSSO. They include the usual status, current weekly status and current daily status. These three different activity statuses have been used with respect to three distinct reference periods, namely, a year, a week and a day. According to the NSSO, each individual has been classified into one of the three possible categories on the

basis of the 'time criterion', namely, (a) at work or gainfully employed, (b) unemployed (seeking for work and or available for work) and (c) out of the labour force. The first two categories have constituted the labour force.

The usual activity status of a person is determined regarding a major time criterion during the reference period of 365 days preceding the date of survey. Accordingly, a person is considered as 'working or employed' if engaged for a relatively longer period during the past year in any one or more work-related activities or economic activities, including seeking or being available for work. A person was considered as 'seeking or available' for work or 'unemployed' if the person was not working but was either seeking or available for work for a relatively longer time during the past year. If a person was engaged in any 'non-economic activity' for a relatively longer time of the reference year, that particular individual was considered 'out of the labour force'. The specific activity category was determined on the basis of time spent criterion. In other words, the activity on which major time was spent was assigned as the usual activity status. A person categorized as 'worker' or 'employed' on the basis of the usual principal status was called a 'principal status worker' or 'principal status employed'. For those reporting unemployment or out of the labour force activity status within the usual principal status category, a 'subsidiary status' has been recorded with respect to whether they were at work more or less regularly but not on major time basis. In other words, the 'subsidiary economic status' of a person is defined as his/her principal usual status determined on the basis of the major time criterion pursuing some economic activity for a relatively shorter or minor time period during the reference period of 365 days preceding the date of survey. A non-worker by usual principal status may have pursued some economic activity for a relatively shorter period of time (minor time) during the reference period of 365 days preceding the date of survey. The status of such economic activity pursued was the subsidiary economic activity status of the person. It may be noted that engagement in work in a subsidiary capacity could arise out of the following two situations:

a. A person could be engaged for a relatively longer period during the last 365 days in one economic/non-economic activity and for a relatively shorter period in another economic activity

b. A person could be pursuing one economic/non-economic activity almost throughout the year in a usual principal status activity and simultaneously pursuing another economic activity for a relatively shorter period of time.

A person who pursued some economic activity in a subsidiary capacity and s/he was called a 'subsidiary status worker' or a 'subsidiary status employed'. These two groups, namely, principal status workers and subsidiary status workers, together constitute all workers according to the usual status classification. The Usual Principal and Subsidiary Status (UPSS) criterion is followed in the present work. It is the most comprehensive of all activity statuses and captures work of all time durations.

The current weekly status of a person is defined as the activity status in which a person is found during a reference period of seven days preceding the date of survey. A person is considered working or employed by current weekly status if s/he had worked for at least one hour on any one or more days during the seven days preceding the date of survey. Having decided the broad current weekly activity status of a person on the basis of a 'priority' criterion, the detailed current activity status of a person is decided on the basis of 'major time' criterion, if a person is pursuing multiple economic activities.

A person who had not worked for even one hour on any one day of the week, but had been seeking employment or had been available for work at any time for at least one hour during this period is deemed to be 'seeking/available for work' or unemployed. Others were considered as 'not available for work' or out of the labour force. These two major classifications are the stock measure of employment and measure the number of workers. The current daily status, on the other hand, has a flow measure of employment and measures the number of days worked. The current daily activity status of a person was determined on the basis of his/her activity status on each day of the reference week using a priority cum major time criterion. NSSO looks upon each day of the reference week as comprising of either two half days or one full day for assigning the activity status. The unit of classification as such becomes half a day under the current daily status. A person has considered working or employed for the entire day if s/he had worked for four hours or more during the day. If a person who works for one hour but less than four hours were considered to be working (or employed) for half a day, and seeking or available for work (or unemployed) or not available for work (or out of the labour force) for the other half of the day depending on whether s/he was seeking or available for work. If, on the other hand, a person was not engaged in any work for even one hour a day but was seeking or available for work for four hours or more, s/he was considered unemployed for the entire day. If s/he was available for work for less than four hours only, s/he was considered unemployed for half day and not in the labour force for the other half of the day. A person who neither had a work to do nor was available for work even for half of the day was considered not in the labour force for the entire day. The aggregate of person-days classified under the different activity categories for all the seven days gave the distribution of person-days by activity category during an average week over the survey period of one year.

The NSSO assigns an activity status to every individual in its employment and unemployment surveys based on these definitions and concepts. Thus, a worker can be classified as a worker or employed and unemployed or out of the labour force accordingly.

5. *Economic activity*: Any activity which resulted in the production of goods and services that add value to the national product is considered an economic activity. Also included as economic activity is the production of only primary goods for own consumption. However, processing of primary goods for own consumption is not considered an economic activity by the NSSO.

6. *Workers or employed*: Persons who were engaged in any economic activity or who were temporarily absent or abstained from work due to illness, injury or other physical disability, bad weather, festivals, social or religious functions, despite their attachment to economic activity, constituted workers or the employed. Unpaid helpers who assisted the operation of an economic activity of the household farm or non-farm activities were also considered as workers. Activity status codes 11 to 51 are assigned to persons in this category.
7. *Workforce participation rate (WFPR)*: It includes the proportion of the total number of persons in the work force to the total population aged 15 years and above. Work force consists of persons who were either working or employed.
8. *Unemployed or seeking or available for work*: Persons, who owing to lack of work had not been working but sought work by making applications to prospective employers or employment exchanges or expressed their willingness to and availability for work under the prevailing conditions of work and remuneration, constituted the unemployed or those persons who are seeking or available for work. Activity status code 81 was assigned to those individuals in this category.
9. *Labour force*: Persons who were either working or employed or seeking or available for work or unemployed constituted the labour force. Activity status codes from 11 to 81 constituted the persons in the labour force.
10. *LFPR*: It is defined as the ratio of labour force to working age population (15–64 years) expressed as a percentage. The labour force is the sum of the number of persons employed and the number of persons unemployed during a particular period of time, preferably a year
11. *Not in the labour force*: Persons who were neither working nor seeking or available for work during the reference period were considered to be out of the labour force. Persons under this category generally include students, individuals who were engaged in their domestic duties, renters, pensioners, those living on alms, infirmed or disabled persons and casual labourers not working due to illness.

12. *Education level*: A person was considered literate if s/he was able to read and write a simple message with understanding in at least one language. The highest level of education successfully completed by each member of a household was decided by considering his/her general/technical/vocational educational level which was recorded under the following categories:
    a. Not-literate,
    b. Literate without formal schooling: (a) Education Guarantee Scheme (EGS)/Non-formal Education Courses (NFEC)/Adult Education Centre (AEC), (b) Total Literacy Campaign (TLC) and (c) Others
    c. Literate but below primary
    d. Middle
    e. Secondary
    f. Higher secondary
    g. Diploma/certificate course
    h. Graduate
    i. Postgraduate and above.

    The category 'diploma/certificate course' implied diploma or certificate courses in general education, technical education or vocational education which is below the graduate level. Diploma or certificate courses in general education, vocational education and technical education equivalent to graduate-level education were considered under the category of graduate. Likewise, for the diploma or certificate courses equivalent to postgraduate-level education was considered under the category of postgraduate and above.

In the present analysis, level of education is reclassified to literate but below primary to include literates without formal schooling. In all other cases, the original classification is maintained.

The Choice of Model

When the dependent variable is binary (categorical) in nature, we use a class of binary response models. The Linear Probability

Model (LPM) is the easiest and most straightforward to estimate, although it has some drawbacks. The three main disadvantages are that the fitted probabilities can lie outside (0–1) range; the variance of the disturbance term is heteroscedastic; and the observed value of the regressor is not normally distributed but rather exhibits binomial distribution. A model with multiple independent variables is shown as

$$y_i = \alpha + \beta_1 x_1 + \beta_2 x_2 + \cdots + \beta_k x_k + \varepsilon_i$$

where x is the independent variable ($i=1,\ldots, k$); α is the predicted probability of the individual's employment when all xj's are equal to zero; β is a vector of coefficients ($kx1$) which measures the probability of participation when xj changes, holding other variables fixed; ε_i is the disturbance term ($E(\varepsilon_i)=0$); and $y=1$, when a respondent participates in the labour force and 0 otherwise.

$$yi = \begin{pmatrix} 1 \text{ for participant} \\ 0 \text{ Otherwise} \end{pmatrix}$$

When the dependent variable y is categorical, it is certainly true that the probability of labour force participation is the same as the expected value of y, that is, $P(y=1|x=E(y|x)$. Hosmer and Lemeshow (1989, p. 6) refer this probability $\pi(x)$. Consequently, this gives the following equation:

$$\pi(x) = E(y|x) = P(y = 1|x = \alpha + \beta_1 X_1 + \beta_2 X_2 + \cdots + \beta_k X_k + \varepsilon_i$$

'These limitations of the LPM can be overcome by using more sophisticated binary response models' (Wooldridge, 2009).

The Logistic Model

To overcome the foregoing disadvantages, many authors have suggested several procedures, (e.g., Hosmer and Lemeshow, 2000; Long, 1997; Wooldridge, 2009). To eliminate the probability that probability of employment is outside the (0–1) limit, a logistic regression is recommended. Logistic regression (also known as logit regression) is one appropriate method for analysing binary outcome data (e.g., DeMaris, 1992; Long 1997; Menard, 1995). The logistic transformation of probability of employment p is $\log p/(1-p)$, which is written as logit (p), where $p/(1-p)$ is the odds of employment, which converts the $\log(p)$ in the limit of $(0-1) to -\infty$. If p is the probability of employment, then $p/(1-p)$ is the odds of employment. In this case, the odds are shown as

$$\frac{P(y=1|x)}{P=(1|x)} = \frac{P(y=1|x)}{1-P(y=1|x)}$$

Here, $(y=1)$ indicates the odds of employment compared to $(y=0)$, the odds of not being employed. The linear logistic model for the relationship between the dependent variable (*Emp*) on $k+1$ explanatory variables is

$$\text{Logit}(pi) = \alpha + \beta_1 x_1 + \beta_2 x_2 + \cdots + \beta_k x_k$$

The equation can also be written as

$$\frac{\exp(\alpha + \beta_1 x_1 + \beta_2 x_2 + \cdots + \beta_k x_k)}{1 + \exp(\alpha + \beta_1 x_1 + \beta_2 x_2 2 + \cdots + \beta_k x_k)}$$

First, the $k+1$ unknown parameters $\alpha + \beta_1 + \beta_2 + \cdots + \beta_k$ are predicted using the maximum likelihood estimation (MLE) which is given by

$$L(\beta) \prod_{I+1}^{n} p_i^{y_i} (1-pi)^{1-yi}$$

For the calculation of the contribution of different factors to employment, it was assumed that employment is a phenomenon that is affected by a set of factors that could explain the outcome. Based on these considerations, we define a binary variable y that takes values $y=1$ if individual is employed,

$y=0$ otherwise. This binary variable was then regressed on a set of explanatory variables that includes various individual and household characteristics. Such a specification of an econometric model has been extensively used in the literature. It is to be noted, however, that, since the dependent variable is binary, we cannot use least squares method to estimate the coefficients. Instead, we would use MLE techniques to calculate the coefficients. The issues involved in specification and estimation of these models are discussed at length in Johnston (1984), Kmenta (1985), Amemia (1985), Johnston and DiNardo (1997), and Greene (1997).

Logistic regression as a predictive model is used over here, because the dependent variable is dichotomous. Using linear regression would be inappropriate due to response values that are not measured on a ratio scale, and there is no requirement for normal distribution of error terms (Hosmer & Lemeshow, 2000). The dependent variable is the alternative (binary) variable, employment (*Emp*). It represents a self-defined current economic status, which according to NSSO refers to

> Persons who were engaged in any economic activity or who, despite their attachment to economic activity, abstained themselves from work for reason of illness, injury or other physical disability, bad weather, festivals, social or religious functions or other contingencies necessitating temporary absence from work, constituted the employed or workers. Unpaid helpers who assisted in the operation of an economic activity in the household farm or non-farm activities were also considered as workers. (NSSO, 2012)

The variables 'employment' and 'gender' are bivalent while 'education' and 'age' are considered as ordinary variables. However, in the process of the analysis, the reduction of ordinary variables in the nominal scale was performed.

A logistic regression model allows for quantifying the chances of modelled value occurrence depending on the values of the explanatory variables. In our model, employment represents the dependent variable (log of the odds ratio) regressed against explanatory variables. Therefore, we used a logit model to quantify the chance of being employed, given selected variables chosen from the NSSO surveys, namely, gender, region, age, education, social status, land ownership and education of the household head, in the years 2004–2005 and 2011–2012 in India.

A priori, we consider the logit model.

$$P(y = 1 \mid x_i \beta) = \frac{e^{x_i \beta}}{1 + e^{x_i \beta}}$$

x_i—the ith row of the regression matrix X containing the explanatory variables in columns; β—the estimated vector of regression coefficients; y—the column vector of dependent binary variable; $y=1$ if the person is employed, $y=0$ if the person is unemployed.

The final equation which estimates Employment in India is

$Emp = \alpha + \beta_1(\text{Location}) + \beta_2(\text{gender}) + \beta_3(\text{age})$
  $+ \beta_4 (\text{Primary\_Edu})$
  $+ \beta_5 (\text{Secondary Edu}) + \beta_6 (\text{Higher secondary\_/Diploma})$
  $+ \beta_7 (\text{Graduate \& above}) + \beta_8 + (\text{SC/ST})$
  $+ \beta_9 (\text{Hindu\_OBC})$
  $+ \beta_{10} (\text{Muslim\_OBC}) + \beta_{11}(\text{Muslim\_General})$
  $+ \beta_{12}(\text{Other\_Minorities})$
  $+ \beta_{13}(\text{Ownership of Land}) + \beta_{14} (\text{Primary\_Edu}_{\text{Head}})$
  $+ \beta_{15} (\text{Secondary\_Edu}_{\text{Head}})$
  $+ \beta_{16} (\text{Higher secondary/Diploma\_Edu}_{\text{Head}})$
  $+ \beta_{17}(\text{Graduate \& above\_Edu}_{\text{Head}}) + \varepsilon_i$

Revisiting Discourses on Labour and Labour Markets

> Labour, it must always be remembered, and not any particular commodity, or set of commodities, is the real measure of the value both of silver and of all other commodities.
>
> —Adam Smith

The Context

Approaches to the study of labour markets are traditionally based on an understanding of the classical, neoclassical and the institutional schools of thought. Labour economics, being the larger domain of economic research, has been at the centre stage. Classical economists laid stress on maximizing behaviour by individuals and firms. From this follows the assertion that rational economic agents relentlessly strive for maximization of economic well-being. Individuals pursue utility maximization in accordance to their own assessment of economic good. The neoclassical labour economists emphasized upon the validity of the marginal productivity theory of demand on the basis of profit maximizing behaviour of employers and a supply theory on the basis of utility maximization by workers. Their labour supply theory accentuates issues related to individual productivity and decisions on investment in human capital and leisure choices, which determine the amount of one's labour supply. Following this, the wage structure is then taken as given, differentiated by worker attributes, which are believed to be different as determined by a myriad of sociocultural and economic factors. Neoclassical theory assumes that individual workers can freely make a choice among a wide range of job options in the labour market on the basis of their personal tastes, preferences, abilities and skills, and thereby receive rewards (wages) on the basis of their human capital endowments. Therefore, the crux of the arguments proposed by the aforementioned three schools of thought is that wages in the labour market mechanism are a 'control tool'. Endogenous changes in tastes of individuals and details of the institutional framework of various markets are largely overlooked. The ignorance of the same forms the basis of the institutionalist approach. From a synthesis of the institutionalist approach and the emergence of the wage differentials arising from differential abilities is derived the genesis of human capital theory.

Over the last two–three decades, we have noticed a surge in the literature attempting to bring a vertical and horizontal integration into the approaches to the study of labour economics. Also, attempts are made to investigate labour markets under the umbrella of the segmented labour markets (SLM) theory. SLM theories were initially developed into internal labour market by Kerr (1954) and Dunlop (1957) and later well articulated by Doeringer and Piore (1971) and Adnett (1996). The basis of segmentation theory is its objection to the existence of a direct linkage between the productive capacities of an individual and his/her wage as well as the allocation of that individual across jobs, implicit in the neoclassical and human capital version of labour market theory. Within the SLM framework, maximizing behaviour is relatively unimportant. Segmentation theory derives from the multilayer character of the labour market and the heterogeneity within it. The institutional barriers do not allow all parts of the populace from benefiting alike from education and training. Sociocultural, economic and geographic factors dictate the labour market outcomes. Vulnerable groups as defined within these parameters get trapped in the lower strata/segment of the labour market, thus limiting the upward mobility of these segments. This makes the wage differential persistent as the excess demand pressures do not get competed by continuous influx of labour from the lower segments.

The amount of research produced on labour market outcomes by the aforementioned schools of thought is very huge. As such, a thorough review of the entire literature in this area will not be possible. However, I have deliberately divided the representative and relevant literature into six sections. The second section deals with conceptual underpinnings of labour and labour markets, followed by an understanding of labour market structure in the developing economies in the third section. Studies concerned with religious affiliation and its relationship with labour markets are dealt in the fourth section. Studies concerned with labour market positioning of Muslims are discussed in the fifth section. The sixth section reaffirms the aim and objectives of this book in the light of major reflections from the literature.

Labour and Labour Markets

Labour is the most standard factor of production and perhaps the most important input in a conventional production function. Defined in terms of the 'people's capacities to carry out work', its inherent inseparability from the human mind and body becomes as important a subject of enquiry as the study of all sciences, arts and social sciences. As noticed by Marx (1933, 1996) and Polanyi (1957), it is inseparable from its bearer.[1] For Polanyi (1957), labour is a 'fictitious' commodity

---

[1] If, in the labour market, labour power is not the property of its bearer, slavery is the proper notion. Marx (1933, pp. 19–20; 1996,

because commodities are, in his view, 'objects produced for sale on the market'. Like land and money, it is not produced for that purpose, and therefore the conclusion is that all three have a fictitious characteristic. Although not being genuine commodities, they are nevertheless 'actually bought and sold in the market'. Linking up with the analysis by Polanyi (1957), Offe has argued that labour power must be considered a 'fictive' commodity, because, in contrast to conventional commodities, it is characterized by a 'marked variability and plasticity' (Offe & Keane, 1985).[2] Furthermore, he has suggested that labour power is not 'clearly separable from its owner'. Labour power is the object for the transactions in the labour market, or, to use Karl Marx's terminology from Volume 1 of *Capital*, it is 'the aggregate of those mental and physical capabilities existing in a human being, whom he exercises whenever he produces a use value of any description' (Marx, 1887, pp. 119). The concept, evolution, usage and economic significance of labour and

---

p. 178) expresses this very clearly by contrasting the modern free labour market with the slave market. Through a straightforward and vivid comparison, he demonstrates the crucial differences between the two systems. The slave owner controls both, the labour power and its bearer, and can sell the whole package to labour markets prospective buyer. Accordingly, the slave is not free and cannot offer his capacities for work to an employer any more than an ox can do it to a peasant: 'He himself is a commodity, but his labour-power is not his commodity' (Marx, 1933, p. 20). In a modern labour market, however, the individual is free to market his/her capacities to anyone who wants to make use of them. A prerequisite is that labour power is made available for the owner of money only temporarily, for a limited period of time, otherwise the worker will be converted 'from a free man into a slave, from an owner of a commodity into a commodity' (Marx, 1996, p. 178). Still, there is a limit to the freedom of the 'free' labour market; the individual has to be available unless he/she can support himself/herself in some other way, for example, through ownership of a fortune or through family relationships.

[2] Plasticity refers to the ability of the living to change their biology or behaviour to respond to changes in the environment, particularly when these are stressful. Humans are, perhaps, the most plastic of all species, and hence the most variable.

labour power (used interchangeably hereafter) can be analysed along different dimensions.

Notwithstanding the fact that all the latest textbooks on labour economics and the academic/non-academic investigation have taken the word 'labour' as self-explanatory and seek to understand the underpinnings of what goes into the making of efficient/inefficient, productive/unproductive labour, but what is wanting is the proper conceptualization of labour itself. With emphasis ranging from (a) biological capacities of individuals (their physical strength, speed, endurance and concentration) to (b) their qualifications[3] (i.e., all types of skills and knowledge applied in the production of goods and services) and (c) to motivation or willingness to work,[4] the search for an explanatory factor for improving labour efficiency and productivity and explanations for the differences therein continues to be an enduring literary task. Of the most important strands of literature aiming at an understanding, the dynamics of efficiency of labour, and as an answer to the exhibits at the market place, the most dominant has been the emphasis on developing human capital. This is owing to its roots to the concept of physical capital generally associated with all other factors of production except labour. The concept of human capital, and its role in improving the productivity and efficiency of labour in the modern market place,[5] has been established beyond

---

[3] Over the last decades, a great deal of attention has been paid to the changes regarding skills and qualifications in modern economies (e.g., Kerr et al., 1960; Blauner, 1964; Gallie et al., 1998, Ch. 2; Kern & Schumann, 1990; Knights & Willmott, 2016; Piore & Sabel, 1984). Some argue that most jobs now demand much more qualified workers than ever before; for them, upgrading is the major trend, and, among other things, they refer to the fact that people stay longer in the school system.

[4] An aspect dealt with in numerous research publications (e.g., Gellerman, 1963; Kleinbeck & Fuhrmann, 2000; Maslow, 1962; McGregor & Borooah, 1992; Vroom, 1964). Workers' motivation is a matter of commitment, either to the work itself or to the employing organization (e.g., Lincoln & Kalleberg, 1996, pp. 39–59).

[5] There is little doubt that education and wages are positively related in the modern sector. However, relationship between education and

reasonable doubts. Its role in the development process (both at the individual level and for the macroeconomy) has been at the centre of economic analysis since the seminal contributions of Becker (1962, 1964), Schultz (1963) and Welch (1970). Of late, growth theorists such as Romer (1986, 1990), Lucas (1988, 1993), Stokey (1988) and others like Azariadis and Drazzen (1990), Ciccone (1994) have identified accumulation of human capital as a means to sustain long-term growth. Empirical support provided by the work of economic historians such as Fogel (1990) and from macroeconomic regression analysis emphasizing the positive role of education on growth by Mankiw, Romer and Weil (1992) and Barro and Sala-i-Martin (1992, 1995) have strengthened the literary tradition of human capital and its impact on life outcomes in general and employment outcomes in particular. At the individual level, human capital plays a more powerful role for economic development. Jamison and Lau (1982) and Psacharopoulos and Tzannatos (1989) provide a brilliant review of surveys in this regard. With education and skill development taking the central place in creation of human capital, there is a general agreement among contemporary theorists that education provides both productive capacities to individuals and their signals to potential employers. Hence, attained qualifications are a main asset in worker competition for jobs available on the labour market (Gangl, 2000).[6]

---

farm productivity remains a contentious issue. Lockheed, Jamison and Lau (1980) summarize 39 regressions from 18 different studies in 13 countries and conclude that education has a positive effect on farm productivity. This positive relationship varies across geographical areas (Phillips, 1987). Studies from Asia support the positive and significant relationship between education and farm efficiency, but the evidence from Latin America and Africa is mixed.

[6] A considerable amount of literature, for example, Mincer, (1958, 1974), Glewwe (1996), Gangl (2000, 2001), Hauser (2002), Margolis and Simonnet (2003) Tansel & Tasci (2004), Pascarella and Terenzini (2005), Goldberg and Smith (2008), Noll (2011) and Edgerton et al. (2012), has been published on the relationship between education and labour market outcomes.

Literature on the *construct of the labour market* broadly draws upon the supply of and demand for labour. As regarding the supply of labour and the determinants thereof, one can trace the literary developments back up to the mercantilist era.[7] The explanations for labour force participations are varied and range from the seminal works of Jevons (1888) to Robbins (1930), Hicks (1932) followed by Douglas (1934) up to Mincer (1962a). Jevons on his part laid the foundations of many latter developments in the field of supply of labour and reported that the labour supply function was negatively sloped with respect to wages (Wood, 1988). This idea is embedded into what Jevons wrote:

> Supposing that circumstances alter the relation of produce to labour, what effect will this have upon the amount of labour which will be exerted? There are two effects to be considered. When labour produces more commodity, there is more reward, and therefore more inducement to labour. If a workman can earn nine pence an hour instead of six pence, may he not be induced to extend his hours of labour by this increased result? This would doubtless be the case were it not that the very fact of getting half as much more than he did before, lowers the utility to him of any further addition. By the produce of the same number of hours he can satisfy his desires more completely and if the irksomeness of labour has reached at all a high point, he may gain more pleasure by relaxing that labour than by consuming more products. The question thus depends upon the direction in which the balance between the utility of further commodity and the painfulness of prolonged labour turns. In our ignorance of the exact form of the functions either of utility or of labour, it will be impossible to decide this question in an a priori manner .... (Jevons, 1888, pp. 179–180)

Taking lead from Jevons (1888), Robbins (1930) asserted that constrained utility maximization yields abstruse implication

---

[7] References cited in Douglas (1934, p. 270) give an idea on this long literary tradition about labour supply.

about the wage slope of the labour supply curve. Robbins (1930) had vividly demonstrated the conditions under which individuals' labour supply curves were positively or negatively sloped. This indeed was a break from the earlier view of most of the economists who had argued for short-run labour supply curves to be always negative. Prior to Robbins, it was believed that 'rational' men would always reduce their hours of work when their wages increase. Robbins (1930) was followed by John Hicks' theoretical work with the title *The theory of wages*. The purpose of the book as Hicks stated was to restate 'the theory of wages in a form which shall be reasonably abreast of modern economic knowledge' (Hicks, 1932).

Paul Douglas' *The Theory of Wages*, considered the first and a significant contribution to examine the wage slope of the labour supply curve in 1934, opened up different new dimensions. His work included a comprehensive regression (on data collected from the 1920 Census of Manufactures) for each age–sex group in 38 US cities, considering the following variables: (a) the employment-to-population ratio on real annual earnings in manufacturing industry, (b) the fraction of the city's population who were either foreign-born or black. From this magnum opus, which included a careful examination of time series and cross section data on hours of work and hourly earnings across industries and states, Douglas concluded that the elasticity of hours with respect to wages 'is in all probability somewhere between –0.1 and –0.2'. After *The theory of wages*, there occurred an upsurge in research on labour force participation and hence about the labour decision-making at the market place.[8]

---

[8] Some of the landmark studies in this area include Schoenberg and Douglas (1937), Woytinsky (1940), Durand (1948), Bancroft (1958) and Long (1958). With respect to hours of work, there is the work of Lewis (1957), Bry (1959), Jones (1961) and Finegan (1962). Modern research on labour supply is characterized by a more careful attempt to separate the measurement of income from substitution effects. It dates from Mincer's (1962b) paper on the LFPR of married women and Kosters' (1966) dissertation on the hours worked by men. This literature has already been the subject of a number of very good

Thus, with respect to the decision of a person to make available his/her labour power for any productive activity in the economy, there is a good deal of literature available to us. What emerges from this strand of literature is as follows: (a) labour market transactions are multidimensional (Coase, 1937), and (b) wages play an important distributive and signalling role (Phelps Brown, 1962). And based on rationality, there is a divergence over the realization of employment contracts and sales contracts and wages alone do not lead to a labour market equilibrium (Simon, 1951). There can, as such, not be a universal theory that would guide and explain even a single dimension of such a diverse market structure. The decision to labour, the wages to be paid, the level of work effort to be applied, the range of activities to which the employee may be directed, the duration and content of the work contract and the particular combination of wages and hours worked represents only a subset of the bundle of items involved in the exchange. All these decisions and a myriad of other socio-economic characterizations make the way in which preferences of the labour and opportunities from the market come together to determine outcomes in the labour market.

Labour Market Structure— The Developing World Case

Primarily the labour market in the developing world is informal devoid of a regulatory framework and structured around self-employment and individual workers (Hart, 1973). A typical informal labour market operates at a low level of organization, with little or no division between labour and capital as factors of production and on a small scale. Labour relations—where they exist—are based mostly on casual employment, kinship or personal and social relations rather than contractual arrangements with formal guarantees. The informal sector forms part of

---

surveys: Heckman, Killingsworth and MaCurdy (1981), Keeley (2013) and Killingsworth (1983).

the household sector as household enterprises or, equivalently, unincorporated enterprises owned by households (System of National Accounts, 1993). Given the nature and size of the Indian informal labour market, the present section reviews some of the important literature on informal markets.

Informal economy has been understood and deliberated upon in a multidimensional setting. It is irregular (P. R. Ferman & L. A. Ferman, 1973), subterranean (Gutmann, 1977), underground (Houston, 1987; Simson & White, 1982), black (Dilnot & Morris, 1981) and a shadow economy (Cassel & Cichy, 1986; Frey, Weck, & Pommerehene 1982). The popular media uses terms such as invisible, hidden, submerged, irregular, nonofficial, unrecorded or clandestine (United Stated Department of Labor, 1992). The common thread is that these activities are not recorded or are imperfectly reflected in official national accounting systems with most workers in low-paid employment under unregulated and poor working conditions. The multifaceted nature of the term *informality*[9] has subjected the definition of this concept to competing views, endless debates and frequent transformations in recent decades. There is no clarity in literature about the distinctive features of the informal sector. Informal activity is defined as all economic activities in unregistered enterprises that contribute to gross national product (GNP; Schneider & Enste, 2000). Informality has been understood in accordance to various defining features of an activity. The location of the activity (e.g., home-based, street-based) or the level of organization has been taken as a feature of an informal economy. Informal workers are those who do not benefit from social security like health insurance and are not protected by labour regulation, namely hiring and firing regulation, minimum wage etc. (ILO, 1972).

The ILO definition of informality encompasses many of the elements highlighted earlier and has been cited frequently

[9] Refer to the ILO and WTO study for a more in-depth discussion of the evolution of the definition and measurement of informality (Awad, 2009; Stewart & Sanchez Badin, 2006).

throughout the literature. According to this definition, the informal economy[10] and the activities therein

> are the way of doing things, characterized by (a) ease of entry, (b) reliance on indigenous resources (c) family ownership of enterprises, (d) small scale of operations, (e) labour-intensive and adapted technology, (f) skills acquired outside the formal sector system and (g) unregulated and competitive markets.

The informal sector is characterized by small-scale, labour-intensive, largely unregulated and unregistered, low-technology manufacturing or provision of services (ILO, 1972; Hoekman & Kostecki, 2009). According to this understanding, the informal economy includes (a) informal employment in informal enterprises (including employers, employees, own account operators and unpaid family workers) and (b) informal employment in formal enterprises[11] (including domestic workers, casual or day labourers, temporary or part-time workers, industrial outworkers and unregistered or undeclared workers).

In general phraseology, all unregistered commercial enterprises and all non-commercial enterprises that have no formal structure in terms of organization and operation form a part of the informal sector. Certain criteria, of late, have been laid down[12] to identify the informal sector enterprises; noteworthy among them are as follows: it employs certain number of persons; it operates on an 'illegal' basis—contrary to the

---

[10] The term 'informal sector' has been used in previous definitions, and it refers to employment in informal enterprises. The most recent definition of informality, which includes informal workers in both informal and formal enterprises, is referred to as 'informal employment' or the 'informal economy'.

[11] Firms are classified as informal according to their size and registration status. As in case of India, the informal economy covers enterprises with fewer than five workers, entrepreneurs, self-employed, unpaid family workers and domestic workers (Unni & Rani, 2008).

[12] For an excellent understanding of the various criteria for identification of informal sector across the world and in India, see Naik (2009) and Sethuraman (1976).

government regulations; members of the household of the head of the enterprise work in it; it does not observe fixed hours/days of operation; it does not depend on formal financial institutions for its credit needs; its output is normally distributed directly to the final consumer; almost all those working in it have fewer than six years of schooling and for certain activities it operates in semi-permanent or temporary premises. The generally agreed definition across disciplinary and ideological boundaries is 'informal economy refers to income generating activities that operate outside the regulatory framework of the state' (Castells & Portes, 1989; De Soto, 1989; Feige, 1990; Harding & Jenkins, 1989). The informal sector consists of small-scale units engaged in the production and distribution of goods and services with primary objective of generating employment and income to their participants notwithstanding the constraints on capital, both physical and human, and know-how. On the basis of the activity status, the informal sector has been described as the non-factory sector, which includes those employed in small establishments, the self-employed, the casual labour and homeworkers. It is characterized by ill-defined employer–employee relationship, acute incidence of underemployment, scattered nature of workplace and low wages (Chandra & Pratap, 2001). The informal sector consists of the own account enterprise (OAE) or an establishment where nine or less number of workers work. The enterprise operates at low level of organization, with little or no division between labour and capital as factors of production and on a small scale. Labour relations, where they exist, are based mostly on casual employment, kinship, or personal or social relation rather than contractual arrangement with formal guarantees (Upadhyay, 2007).

About employment, informal economy encompasses a range of different kinds of workers. With the simplifying approach of taking a dualistic view to segment employment (into formal and informal employment), there is a need for more refined distinctions. In this direction, Fields, Leary and López-Calva (1998) draw the distinction between two different forms of informal employment: (a) free entry, low-wage employment that is less desirable than formal sector employment and (b) limited entry, high-wage employment that is more desirable than formal sector employment. The second category refers to workers with enough human and financial capital to leave the formal sector and set up a small freelance business (e.g., as a repairman or a small manufacturer). Another classification of employment commonly referred to in the literature is a model developed by the Women in Informal Employment: Globalizing and Organizing (WIEGO).[13] Similar to Field's approach, the WIEGO framework recognizes heterogeneity within the informal economy. Accordingly, informal employment is broken down across a spectrum according to the type and degree of (a) economic risk (of losing job and/or earnings) and (b) authority (over establishment and other workers; Chen, 2007).

Religious Affiliation and Labour Markets

There is no dearth of literature dealing with the particular questions of religious affiliation and economic outcomes. At the level of individuals and households, economic behaviour and outcomes do correlate with religion. Religious affiliation has started to come into the realm of economic analysis[14] with some stark differences arising among communities which can be ascribed to the teachings and dictates of their respective religions. It is, for example, well established that American Jews on an average earn significantly higher wages and income than non-Jews, a difference largely attributable to their high levels of education (Chiswick, 1983a, 1983b). 'Religion' or religious affiliation has not received the deserved rigorous academic thoughtfulness as an explanatory variable for understanding labour market outcomes, as colour, caste, sex and ethnicity have. Across the contemporary nation states, religion and

---

[13] Located at the Harvard University, WIEGO is a global network focused on securing livelihoods for the working poor, especially women, in the informal economy.

[14] For an excellent understanding of the subject, see Iannaccone (1998).

affiliation thereto has not been believed to have an impact on economic outcomes in general and labour market outcomes in particular. Credence to this argument is provided by the fact that the degree of religiosity is not found to influence consumer's attitudes concerning capitalism, socialism, income redistribution, private property, free trade and government regulation (Mangeloja, 2005). Vastness of every religious tradition and revered literature appear to have enough obscurity to rationalize any number of economic loci. However, it is still maintained by good number of scholars that Christianity has had a positive impact on economic development (Chiswick, 1983a; Greif, 1994). Comparisons have been drawn with the Islamic view and the economic and intellectual development in Islamic countries for most of the last millennium (Kuran 1995, 1997a). Explanations for the same have, it seems, garnered support from the alleged static world view of Islam, especially Protestantism is found to be positively correlated with growth and development (Grier, 1997). However, empirical evidence only rejects the specific channel proposed by Weber[15] (Guiso, Paola, & Luigi, 2003). Studies conducted in this direction conclude that not a more general link between the Protestant ethic and the development of a capitalist attitude is provided by available evidence (Dejong, 2011).

Interestingly as part of his effort to lay the foundations of the modern science of economics, Adam Smith (1776, pp. 740–766) laid the foundation for the economic analysis of religion. Smith argued that self-interest motivates clergy just as it does to secular producers; that market forces constrain churches just as they constrain secular firms and that the benefits of competition, the burdens of monopoly and the hazards of government regulation are as real for religion as for any other sector of the economy. For nearly 200 years, Smith's statements constituted

---

[15] Weber (1930) argued that Protestantism made a previously unseen emphasis on individual responsibility, personal diligence and approved risk-taking and financial self-improvement leading to an era of unprecedented growth and development.

'almost everything that economists, quasi economists have said on [the] subject' of religion (Boulding, 1970). But since the 1970s, and especially in the past few decades, economists and sociologists have returned to Smith's insights. This return has resulted into a thrust on analysing religious behaviour as an instance of rational choice, rather than an exception to it; they have analysed religious behaviour at the individual, group and market level (Iannaccone, 1998).

Most of these studies have been guided by the principle of investigating into the relationship between religiosity and social being. There is a dearth of well-founded research into the relationship between religious affiliation and labour market outcomes. Scholarly engagement in this area tends to relate the general economic behaviour, especially consumption and investment decisions to the religious belief. Labour market participation and adjustments alongside the decisions to truck have broadly been discussed within the realm of investment in human capital wherein religious adherence has been found to have a positive impact. For instance, Chiswick (1983a) argues that US Jews have on an average significantly higher wages and income as compared to the Christian population, largely due to their high levels of education. Brenner and Kiefer (1981) argue that in response to long continuing persecution, Jews emphasize the value of education, as it is portable and non-appropriable versus land or physical capital. Chiswick (1985) notes that Jews acquire high levels of education because of their high rate of return on schooling. Similar exhibits are provided by treading on to explicate the relationship between religious affiliation and health. Epidemiological studies have reported statistically significant religious effects on health and hence on human capital accumulation. Members of strict religious groups are reported to suffer lesser health hazards such as cancer, stroke, hypertension and heart disease and enjoy longer lives. This is ascribed to a strict adherence to several health-related everyday restrictions. Broader correlations between health and religiosity have many causes, including a negative link between faith and stress, or a positive link between church involvement and social support (Levin, 1994). What emerges from these studies when linked to the human capital theory does explain the wage differential, but not necessarily as a function of religious belief or affiliation. There is an effort to establish an indirect link between religious affiliation and labour market behaviour. Notwithstanding the scant references, a clear research platform in this direction is missing at all levels—local, country as well as at the cross-country level. This has led to a vacuum in literature as far as analysing, investigating, understanding and breaking through the cobweb of the mysterious determinants of labour market outcomes of the likes of religion and religious affiliations. Gockel (1969) is perhaps the earliest attempts to examine the relationship between religious denomination and earnings. The major demonstration of the study was that Catholics in the USA have an advantage vis-à-vis Protestants in terms of earning. This result was refuted by Tomes (1984) who did not find any impact of affiliation with the Catholic Church on earnings *per se*, even though Catholics did have a higher marginal return on college education relative to Protestants. In case of Canada, however, Protestants were reported to have experienced higher returns on education (especially, college education) than the Catholics. Jews in Canada were seen to have significantly higher returns on earning than Christians of all denominations (Meng & Sentence, 1984; Tomes, 1983, 1984[16]). The Jewish advantage over people of other religious denominations has also been recorded in the case of the USA. Confirming the results of earlier studies, Steen (1996) found that the relative impact of affiliation to Judaism, Catholicism and the Protestant church(es) on earnings of labourers in the USA, as reported in the studies of Gockel (1969), Chiswick (1983) and Tomes (1984), continues to hold. However, this entire strand of the literature has the serious shortcoming of not been able to segregate the religious affiliation of individuals/groups and the respective components of their human capital. Although it might be the case that

---

[16] Tomes (1985) showed that, ceteris paribus, Jews in Canada earned 12.7 per cent more than the Protestants who, in turn, earned 5.1 per cent more than people of all other religious denominations.

affiliation with a given religion may be associated with inferior human capital, its relationship with religious affiliation has not yet been established. None of the studies takes a holistic view of the socio-economic context of the religious affiliations and economic outcomes in general and the labour market outcomes.

Muslims in Indian Labour Market

India is a country characterized as one of the most diverse nation states of the contemporary era, both in terms of flora and fauna as well as its people. The only country in the recent history that got divided on religious lines still offers home to people belonging to almost all faiths. With Hinduism being followed by 79.5 per cent of the total population, Muslims in terms of the headcount ratio occupy the second place with a population share of 14.2 per cent, given the difference in population numbers form the largest minority. Spread across all the states,[17] Indian Muslims share a history of glory and gory.[18] They have had a transition to and a steep fall from reigning the echelons of power to the most destitute communities in the Indian subcontinent. Rooted in the past, the deprivation of Indian Muslims has come to the limelight of late, only with the commission of the celebrated SCR. This report has become an exceptional document as far as the religion-based analysis of education and economic outcomes of the Indian population are concerned. Barring this report, one does not find much empirical work done in explaining the position of Muslims in Indian

[17] Muslims are a numerical majority in J&K and Lakshadweep. They are a sizable portion of the population in Assam, West Bengal and Kerala. There is a moderate presence of Muslims in Uttar Pradesh, Bihar and Jharkhand. Muslims are at least one-tenth of the population of Karnataka, Uttaranchal, Delhi and Maharashtra.

[18] With the fall of the Mughal Empire and the advent of British followed by the mutiny of 1857, the role, power and prestige of Muslims and also their proximity to the corridors of power diminished and became non-existent in the late 1860s. These developments and the later division of the Indian nation in 1947 have crippled the march of Indian Muslims to a prosperous future.

labour market. However, an effort has been made in this section to summarize some of the available literature in this direction.

In India, most of the studies in the area of socioeconomics deal with caste. The caste structure has been a defining feature of Indian socioeconomics. With an overwhelming Hindu population wherein the primary unit in the society is neither the individual nor the household but the caste and hence, the rights and privileges (or the lack of them) of an individual are because of the latter's membership to a particular caste (Ambedkar, 1987b). Caste as a system of social and economic governance is determined by certain customary rules and norms, which are unique and distinct (Akerlof, 1976, 1980; Ambedkar, 1936, 1987a, 1987b, 1987c; Lal, 1988; Scoville, 1991). Consequently, the caste structure in India has inevitably attracted a good deal of academic attention in the post-independence era (Borooah, 2005; Kijima, 2006). However, the impact of religion on economic outcomes of the population in general and their labour market outcomes in particular has not attracted much of the economists gaze. Noland (2005) used state-level data from India to argue that state-level income during the 1981–1996 period was significantly affected by the proportion of people belonging to Buddhists, Jains and other religions. His paper does not address the microissues related to disparities in earnings, consumption, etc., across the different religious groups. The only two papers till date that use microdata on India to examine inter-religion differences are by Borooah and Iyer (2005) on school enrolment rates across religious groups and by Borooah, Dubey and Iyer (2006) on categories of employment status across different caste/religion groups. Borooah and Iyer (2005) find evidence of a narrowing gap between the enrolment rates of Hindus and Muslims at schools, especially for children with illiterate parents. The marginal impact of religion on enrolment rates is influenced by the size of the community in which the children reside. Borooah, Dubey and Iyer (2006), using a single round of employment survey data (NSSO, 2011) of India, find that the probability of being a regular salaried employee is significantly lower for Muslim labourers than for UC-Hindus.

There is some literature mostly in the form of reports, commentaries, periodicals and research papers which unanimously point towards Muslim exclusion in the labour markets in India. Latest data on development outcomes (Government of India, 2011a; NSSO, 2011) do not show any significant improvements in the conditions of Muslims even after the follow-up to the SCR. Drawing from varied sources, the employment outcomes among Muslims as also their performance on related variables like health, education and poverty are dismal.

A substantial proportion of Muslims—18 per cent male, and 15.4 per cent female—have attained only primary education. Meanwhile at higher, upper primary and above levels, Muslim proportion is significantly lower than that among all other groups including SCs (Fazal, 2013a). Less than half of the Muslim girls in age for primary and upper primary level school were enrolled (Government of India, 2011a). Among all religious communities, Muslims had the lowest net attendance ratio (NAR) at all levels of education, in both rural and urban India. In fact, in rural India, low NAR among STs was comparable with that of the Muslims at the secondary and higher secondary levels. In urban India, NAR for Muslims was even lower than that for SCs and STs at all levels except at the higher secondary level, where they were similar. Data also reveal that it is at upper primary level (mostly in rural areas, but also urban) that the NAR for Muslims shows the biggest drop.

Discrimination in education access and participation therein can vividly be reflected in the employment outcomes because perceptions about discrimination interact with endowments, opportunities, supply side conditions and attitudes giving rise to different patterns of participation in employment and education. This is clear in case of Indian Muslims from the fact that Muslims in India are predominantly self-employed or what in literature of late has been referred as *own account workers*. However, the literature from India views own account workers mostly as disguised wage workers, working in the informal sector, rather than better off entrepreneurs (Breman, 1996; Papola, 1981; Sainath, 1996). For instance, in his study of Rural Gujarat, Breman (1996) focuses on dependent relationships between owners of small own account ventures and larger employers or agents. Similarly, a study in Surat showed that in the diamond industry, smaller firms had dependent relations with traders, suppliers and buyers. 'Shram Shakti', the report of the National Commission on Self-Employed Women and Women in the Informal Sector, provided the earliest and most graphic description of self-employed women and women in the informal sector. The report presents a picture of the non-farm self-employed as small producers and home-based workers, who either supply their produce to middlemen through informal contractual arrangements and retailing establishments or have their own small vending businesses. Most of these studies rely on anthropological fieldwork or descriptive data tabulated from small surveys. These studies within the limitation of narrower scope confirm the viewpoint that the self-employed in India are but small producers in close relationship with the larger economy.

Overall, the extent of Muslim exclusion is all-round and deep-seated. Fazal and Kumar (2013) contend that '...the all India pattern that emerges is of a community steeped in poverty, having low educational attainment, bereft of land and other immovable assets, and largely dependent on self-employment in low income activities'.

Evidence points to discrimination in public provision of services to Muslims as well as play of market discrimination (in relation to employment), both formal and informal structures perpetuate this exclusion (M. Hasan & Z. Hasan, 2013). There is a rich body of evidence pointing to the discrimination against Muslims in job market even more than Dalits, in the private sector, and particularly in the public sector (Basant & Shariff, 2010; Gayer & Jaffrelot, 2012; Thorat, Mahamallik, & Venkatesan, 2007).

Borooah (2010) after defining the risks in labour market outcomes in terms of employment risk ratio[19] and group risk

---

[19] Measures the odds of a person being in regular employment to being in non-regular employment, *given* that the person belongs to a particular group.

ratio[20] argues that participation in regular employment across different social groups is determined by the relative advantage of groups in terms of 'attributes' (e.g., educational attainment) and 'access' (e.g., reservation for specific groups). With the application of the concepts of risk to data for four subgroups in India: forward caste (FC) Hindus, Hindus from the Other Backward Classes, Muslims and Dalits (collectively the SCs and STs) revealed that, on both measures of risk, FC Hindus did best in the Indian labour market. A decomposition of the effects suggested that their superior labour market attributes were partly due to the relatively large number of FC Hindus who were graduates; partly also due to their better access to jobs offering regular employment.

As compared to FC Hindus, Muslims, who, unlike Dalits, are not protected by job reservation, suffered from considerable access disadvantage even after taking into account the handicap of their low education levels. Compared to FC Hindus, the access disadvantage of Muslims was considerably higher than that of the Hindu OBC. The authors conclude with the assertion that:

> if the object of jobs reservation is to correct for discriminatory bias in the jobs market, and if reservation is to be extended beyond Dalits, then Muslims have a more compelling case than the Hindu OBC!

Bhaumik and Chakrabarty (2010), extending the labour market discussion to earnings, explore the determinants of the differences in inter-caste and inter-religion earnings in India during the 1987–1999 period. The data show that while earnings differences between UCs and SC/ST declined between 1987 and 1999, earning differences between Muslims and non-Muslims have increased to the detriment of the former. Interestingly, they also find that more than 'discrimination', 'education

---

[20] Comparing the regular employment chances of two persons, one belonging to one group and the other to another group.

endowment' differences play a bigger role in increasing earnings gaps across groups. Unni (2010), using the NSSO data empirically, explores the labour market imperfections in terms of gender and increasing informality. The estimates also suggest that the Muslim presence in regular jobs is lower than that of other groups, even after accounted for educational and other imbalances. Das (2008) explores another perspective of discrimination in the labour market. She explores the hypothesis derived from the US labour market literature that ethnic minorities tend to respond to discrimination in the formal labour market by building self-employed ventures in the form of ethnic/minority enclaves. The underlying assumption therefore is that exclusion, discrimination or disadvantage in formal jobs may result in minorities setting up enclaves based on non-farm self-employment. And empirically, her results show that while minority enclave hypothesis does not work for Dalits, it does for the Muslims, as the latter tend to choose self-employment in non-farm sector over other activities—regular, casual, self-employment in agriculture—just to stay out of the wage labour force.

Worker population ratio (WPR)—the proportion of an economy's working age population that is employed—is a useful measure of the proportion of population that is actively contributing to the production of goods and services in the economy. Among major religious groups, HDR found WPR being comparable among Hindus, Christians and Sikhs, but much lower in the case of Muslims (Brad Shuck, Rocco & Albornoz, 2011). For example, rural WFPR for Muslim women was only 25 per cent, compared to 70 per cent for Hindu women (Government of India, 2011a).

A variety of factors has been identified to explain the observed relative deprivation among Muslims in India. As Basant (2012) argues, these include differentials in endowments across social groups; actual or perceived discrimination; behaviour patterns or attitudes and supply of educational and employment opportunities. Thus, poor Muslims are further burdened: they suffer problems faced by the poor generally—poor assets, poor capabilities and active discrimination by state and social forces, wanting to maintain the status quo. On top of this, poor Muslims face the additional disabilities specific to belonging to the Muslim community (Basant, 2012).

Conclusion

Research works as reviewed earlier highlight various facets of labour market paradigms. Historical developments and breakthroughs in analysis have been deliberated upon. Ranging from the earliest of microeconomic theories of maximizing behaviour as an explanation of labour market participation forms the central idea of the first section. The theory of utility maximization for the consumers and profit maximization still holds good sway in elucidations for labour market functioning. However, the classical and neoclassical explanations of competitive markets and mobility of the factors of production seem to be losing ground. Even after the development of human capital theory followed by the emergence of the SLM theory, there still does not exist any unanimity at the scholastic level with respect to a universal labour theory. Among different classifications and structures of the labour market, the dominance is indeed garnered by the informal/unorganized market structures. Scholarly works pertaining to the religion dimension of labour market present a mixed picture. Socio-religious status in general and religious affiliation in particular is indicated to be explanatory factors as far as labour market outcomes are concerned. From Marx (1859) to Weber (1958) through Iannaccone (1998) to Fazal (2013a), theorists have attempted to explore its different dimensions. Again, unanimity is elusive. As a case study of the same line of thought, Muslims of India and studies pertaining to them echo some explanations for the linkages between socio-religious affiliation and labour market outcomes, more so in case of such outcomes as participation and employment. However, as the later developments in the subject matter of labour economics of the likes of human capital theory and the SLM theory assert, labour markets are complex as are the exhibited phenomenon. Categorical relationships between religious identity and labour market outcomes cannot be drawn so simplistically. Assertions of the SCR with regard to deprivation of Muslims on various dimensions of sociocultural existence are a starting point in this direction. More importantly, these findings of SCR have got to be looked into a historical context. How far can it be argued that Muslims' lagging performance may be attributed to institutional differences that can be traced back to the British colonial period? How far can the alleged 'conservatism and insularity' of Islam be held responsible for deprivation (if any) of Muslims in general and Indian Muslims in particular?

There are strong advocates and accounts of *demoralization* of the Muslim community, especially after the fall of the Mughal Empire. Emergence of animosity of the attitude of British colonizers against the Muslims and in favour of the Hindus exuberated around this period. How far are all these developments an explanation of the present status of Indian Muslims? These questions are dealt in detail in the next chapter.

2

The Muslim Question
Re-examining History, Politics and Employment Structures

> No study has so potent an influence in forming a nation's mind, a nation's character as a critical and careful study of its past history. And it is by such study alone that an unreasoning and superstitious worship of the past is replaced by a legitimate and manly admiration.
>
> —R. C. Dutt (1893)

This chapter is an attempt to place the emergence of Muslim community and their participation in the labour market in a historical context. The origin of Islam/Muslims in Indian subcontinent dates back to 600 AD. A substantial evidence in this regard could be cited by referring to the world's second oldest mosque Cheraman Juma Masjid and India's first, built around 629 AD in Kodungallur in the state of Kerala (Elliot, 2006). In this chapter, I will be revisiting the relevant history (as it corresponds to Muslims in India) afresh. I will try to explore the earliest Muslim settlements and document the timeline of the rise and fall of the Muslim rule within the framework of politico-economic analysis.[1] The Indian Muslim has a past, so rich and prosperous, that it still forms the cornerstone of socio-economic and cultural fabric of India. However, of late, the narrative of Muslim prosperity with its vibrant cultural and social contributions has gone into oblivion. What has been debated in the literature purely reflects the other stories grounded in misery, economic deprivation and political isolation.[2] What explains this transition of an entire religious community from the seats of power to a state of perpetual economic distress and how far are the statements about religion-based deprivation of Indian Muslims true? Moreover, the questions like: does the available data suggest religion-based economic deprivation of Indian Muslims and is there a mechanism available in the literature that could help explain these propositions on empirical lines are some questions which we have attempted to address in this chapter.

Whatever scant data are available, there indeed are pointers towards a relative and collective deprivation of Muslims in the arena of socio-economic outcomes in general and in economic activity in particular (Ali & Sikand, 2006; Hasan & Menon, 2004; Shariff, 1999; Shariff & Azam, 2004; Reddy, 2003). As Hardy (1972) maintains, *Muslims* in India before 1857 was a diverse community, as opposed to what they were under the direct British rule. How did this transition take place will be explicated in the following sections.

[1] We are trying to understand the Muslim settlement in India and their economic activities, especially employment within the broader premise of the political power relations, first under the Mughals, followed by the British and later in Independent India. There is a clear transfer of authority/hegemony first from the Mughals (Muslims) to the British (Christians) and then to the Indians (chiefly Hindus). Therefore, tracing the economic developments within the premise of these oscillating power relations becomes important, hence the reference to *politico-economic*.

[2] Indian Muslim's suboptimal access to institutions of economic well-being had been a subject of public debate for long. However, with the publication of the SCR in 2006, a rejuvenated debate on the same in the policy circles and academic arenas got new life.

The *Muslim question* as is now being referred to (Norton, 2013) has become an important area of study both within the realm of political philosophy as well as social sciences. In the Indian context, and within the ambit of economic prosperity, Muslims as a community emerged as a class deprived and impoverished at the time of independence (Khalidi, 2006). During the British rule, the question of Muslim under-representation in economic activity has attracted varied explanations. At the forefront lies the claim of an inherent conservatism and insularity deeply rooted in Islam (Hunter, 1876). This *attitudinal claim* (Mondal, 1992) has for long been presented as an explanation for Muslim backwardness in education and invisibility in employment (Kuran, 1995, 1997a). The second explanation lies in the demoralization and self-imposed isolation of the Indian Muslims after the debility of the Mughal Empire, starting with the death of Aurangzeb. This *demoralization thesis* (Khan, 1989) tends to explain the inability of Muslims to assert their position in the company affairs at par with what they were in the immediate past under the Mughals. Biased hiring policies of the British towards Muslims, especially after the revolt of 1857, are a matter of record. This *British bias* (Ahmad, 1993; Khalidi, 2006) as discussed further relegated the Indian Muslims to the lowest of the low both in the labour market as well as in the sociopolitical space. However, any of the three approaches, in isolation, does not explain the issue of slithering Muslim representation in economic and political institutions in the pre-/post-independent India. In this backdrop, this chapter will explain the positioning of Indian Muslims in the medieval economy period and extend the analysis to contemporary times. Impact of colonialism and of the subsequent partition of the subcontinent on the economic positioning of the Muslims will be discussed.

The Plan

This chapter has been divided into six sections. The second section delineates upon the Indian socio-economic fabric in general and that of the Muslims in particular at the advent of the British. This is followed by a discussion on early Muslim settlements and demography in the third section. The fourth section on the *colonial economy and Muslim employment* deals with the changing employment scenarios considering political ups and downs that led to the mutiny of 1857. The fifth section deals with the impact of the 1857 events on Muslim employment and traces the same up to the era of Independence. The sixth section focuses upon partition of the subcontinent and how the events that unfolded during the mid-1940s in particular affected the employment position of Muslims. Post-independence employment scenarios are also dealt with in this section. The seventh section concludes.

Indian Muslims at the Advent of British Rule

The grandeur of the Red Fort in Delhi and the majesty of Taj Mahal in Agra is but a representative of the rich legacy which contemporary Indian Muslims visualize to have belonged to. The contemporary Muslim in India may remotely be related to any of the remarkable pinnacles that his/her ancestors had scaled, but he/she in one way or the other has a sense of belonging to this legacy. The 1857 mutiny has been argued by many as the first detrimental blow to the Muslim glory. Lord Dufferin (1826–1902), the Viceroy of India, in 1881, referred to Indian Muslims as a nation of 50 million cherishing their remembrance of the days when, enthroned at Delhi, they reigned supreme from the Himalayas to Cape Comorin (Lord Dufferin, 1888). These good olden days were lost. By 1888 itself, Muslims in India presented a completely different picture. Cohesion of the community was lost. They had scattered unevenly all over the Indian subcontinent with multiplicity creeping in, in the guise of sectarian beliefs, dietary habits and language. Although most of them were still under Muslim rule but some, as in the empire of Vijayanagar or in the coastal towns of the south, were under non-Muslim rule. This transformation in the power relations, especially after the downslide of the great Mughal Empire, made the Medieval Muslims not to think or act as a nation. Affiliation to a ruling class or a sense of belonging to it had gradually eroded to the extent that had no parallel even when compared to the position of non-Muslim subjects under the domination of Mughal, Afghan and Turks. The Bengali Muslim cultivator or the Gujarati Muslim weaver was less engaged in a common enterprise of ruling India than members of the British working classes in the 19th century, for at least the latter were welcome as soldiers of the ruling power (Hardy, 1972). A nation of glory that it was, in the 18th century, relegated to a community unified at best by few common rituals and by the beliefs and aspirations of a majority—not the totality—of its scholars. This had coincided with the beginning of the British rule in India.

Indian Muslims as they stood at the advent of the British rule were remarkably distinct on all socio-economic and cultural criteria about their immediate past. How did such a turnaround happen? What was the socio-economic condition of Indian Muslims before they began to be affected by the British rule? What role and aspirations did Muslims in India harbour in the pre-British period? Answers to these questions are inevitable in order to understand the current situation of Indian Muslims. An attempt to regard has been made in the sections to follow to explicate these issues in some detail.

Muslim Settlement and Demography

The dawn of Islamic civilization over the subcontinent had reached its zenith shortly after the death of Prophet Muhammad (peace be upon him) in 632 AD, Arab Muslims touched the shores of India as traders (Elliot, 2006). The Muslim conquest in the Indian subcontinent mainly took place from the 12th century onwards (Asimov & Bosworth, 1998). With territorial consolidation only in Sind and in western Punjab, Muslims were still only one-fifth of British India's population largely concentrated in Sindh, and in three out of four people were Muslims (Hardy, 1972). Lowest concentration of Muslims was in the central provinces and Madras, wherein they formed 2.5 per cent and 5 per cent of the total population, respectively. Ranging from a little less than half of the population in Punjab, they were about a half in Bengal proper excluding Bihar and Orissa. Muslims formed more than 10 per cent of the population in the North-Western Provinces and Awadh.

Distribution and size of the Muslim population in Punjab were predominantly shaped by political developments. Following the establishment of military headquarters at Lahore in 1020s by Mahmud of Ghazni, areas of Punjab as Far East as Thanesar remained under Ghaznavid hegemony until it was taken over by the Ghurids in 1186. Emanating from varied civilizations, of the likes of Turk, Afghan, Iranian and even Arab garrisons, administrators and scholars settled in the region. These were later joined in the 13th century by Muslim emigres who migrated because of Mongol invasions of central Asia. Large migrations, especially of Afghans following Amir Timur's campaigns in the contemporary Afghanistan, also got directed towards the plains of western Punjab. These migrations were concurrently added upon by nomadic movements from the hills which resulted in imparting this territory, the character of an area of consolidated Muslim settlement. In the central and eastern Punjab as in the Ganges–Jamuna heartland of Muslim power, Muslims formed a higher proportion of the urban population and a lower proportion of the rural population. Thus, not surprisingly, Punjab exhibited a stronghold of Muslim power during the latter part of Akbar's reign (1556–1605) and in Jahangir's reign (1605–1627). Lahore became the working capital of the empire. The Indo-Gangetic Plain (the Doab) was exposed to Muslims following the Turkish conquest invasion in 1192. Nearly after seven centuries, in 1881, as the decadal census revealed, Muslim population in these plains had swelled to 11 per cent. In the north-western plains, at the same time, Muslims were 13 per cent of the population.

At the beginning of the 13th century, a Muslim *sultanate*[3] was headquartered at Lakhnauti (Gaur) in the district of

---

[3] *Sultanate* is a country ruled by a sultan (a Muslim sovereign). The word sultan has actually come from Arabic meaning power, authority

Malda in Bengal. With the Mughal conquest of Bengal, Dacca became the capital in 1612. The Nawabs of Bengal governed from Murshidabad in the 18th century. However, with regards to the proportion of Muslims in Bengal, the British censuses presented a paradoxical situation.[4] As per the 1881 census in Bengal, Dacca district had more than half its population Muslim. The proportion of Muslims in the districts of Malda and Murshidabad was appreciably less. Gujrat is perhaps one of the earliest contemporary Indian states to have come in contact with the Muslim world. Arabs, as merchants, had settled and moved to the capital 'Patan' much before the conquest of Alauddin Khilji in 1299. Down in the Deccan, the khaliji invasions (1307 and 1312) had paved the way for Muslim imprints, which got reaffirmed during the reign of Muhammad bin Tughluq (1325–1351) and the historic move of the establishment of Daulatabad as second capital for Delhi sultanate. These developments led to a situation in which Turkish, Afghan and Persian soldiers and officials had settled in the Deccan in such sufficient numbers that they in 1347 were in a position to create for themselves the independent Bahmani sultanate. This sultanate was to be a major attraction for Muslim immigrants with professional military and administrative skills, as well as a large number of slaves, the property of Muslim traders, from Iran, the Arab lands and east Africa. By the time (middle of the 18th century), the East India Company attained power supremacy in India, if not as a political force, Islam had surely pressed upon the people of the Indian subcontinent as a way of life and belief.

---

and ruler ship. It as such emerges that a sultanate is a country/land ruled with authority by a sovereign, who more often than not happened to be Muslim.

[4] Muslim populations were believed to be concentrated in the vicinity of the seats of power. However, in case of Bengal, the proportion of Muslims in Malda and Murshidabad were appreciably less. On the contrary, the districts that served as 'rice swamps but had no strategic or political significance' such as Bogra, Rajshahi, Noakhali, Pubna, Bakarganj, Tippera and Mymensingh, had a Muslim population (mostly poor cultivators) forming two-thirds to more than three quarters of the population.

Colonial Economy and Muslim Employment

In the pre-colonial times, no clear demarcation on religious lines could be drawn with respect to economic activity of the 'masses'. Muslims as well as non-Muslims were engaged in *husbandry* and with the provision of varied economic goods and services for others. Except for those who were closer to the echelons of power, say the soldiers, counsels and courtiers of the rulers, there existed an occupational split between the Muslim ruling class and the other Muslims and non-Muslims, which continued from the late 18th century up to the gradual takeover by the British.

Spatial analysis of economic activity of Muslims reveals that around the Indo-Gangetic Plain, they were primarily agriculturalists, artisans or members of the service occupations which grew around courts, as, for example, musicians, bards, perfume sellers and prostitutes. On the class and descend-based classification of Muslims, cultivators as the Malkanas, the Khanzadas and the Lalkhanas (Rajput-descended) and such skilled artisans as weavers, cloth printers, dyers and cotton carders, in the aggregate outnumbered those who, by calling themselves Saiyids, Pathans, Mughals and Shaikhs, claimed foreign descent and thereby ruling status.[5] In Punjab, wherein fewer Muslims claimed foreign descent (only 21 per 1,000), Muslims were predominantly agriculturists. As per the Census 1881, of every 1,000 Punjabi Muslims, 574 were engaged in agriculture, 274 as artisans, 36 as menials and 7 in some form of commerce (Ibbetson, 1881). The situation in Bengal (which included Bihar, Orissa and Chota Nagpur) was no different either. With fewer people claiming foreign origin, 628 per 1,000 were agriculturists—with 31 engaged in textile production and 73 as labourers. Muslims in Gujrat and Bombay presidency—with longer exposure to Muslims (Arab traders)—were predominantly in trade and services. In the Deccan, Muslim existence

---

[5] A calculation in the 1931 census report for the then united provinces put the number of Muslims there claiming foreign descent at 411 per 1,000.

flowed from their ancestry. Their ancestors were a predominant army of armourers, elephant drivers and horse doctors in the *sultanates* of Ahmadnagar and Bijapur. Here again, artisanship and agriculture formed the majority of employment avenues. After a century of Maratha rule in the Deccan, most of the Muslims were engaged in small trade, artisanship and agriculture. Cultivators, traders and boatmen of mainly Tamil origin existed in eastern parts of Madras presidency. In the west, in Malabar, the principal Muslim community, the Mappillas (Moplahs), were fishermen, sailors and coolies along the coast, but inland, in the later 19th century, constituted a rapidly growing community of very poor tenant cultivators.

Tracing the early history of Muslim settlement, demographic and economic activity reveals some interesting insights. First and foremost is the fact that the Muslim population flourished in the vicinity of the *Darbars* (court) and the seats of rule. However, over a period of time they did disperse across the subcontinent. This led Muslims to be identified as a community widely dispersed, much the greater part of which was in fact of native Indian descent and which in most rural areas and in many towns was indistinguishable in occupation from surrounding non-Muslims. At the advent of the British rule, Muslims had a sizeable presence across the subcontinent: ranging from 15 per cent of the total population in the western Burdwan division of Bengal to (67%) in the eastern Bengal divisions of Rajshahi, Dacca and Chittagong. As for Punjab, 33 per cent of the population in the eastern districts and 75 per cent in the western districts were Muslims. In the north-western frontier, Muslims were almost 100 per cent. Deep down in the South, in the western coastal districts of Malabar, Muslims were about 25 per cent of the total population in contrast to about 4 per cent in the eastern districts of the Carnatic. Notably, Muslims were in some areas principally town dwellers and in others principally country dwellers. About 75 per cent of the town dwelling population in the North-Western Provinces was Muslim. However, in Bengal, not more than 3 or 4 per cent of Muslims lived in towns. While Muslims made three quarters or more of the population in western Punjab, less than half of the town dwellers were Muslims. In Bombay, 20 per cent of the urban population was Muslim.

Agriculture, artisanship, trade and commerce, and armoury were the chief occupations of the Indian Muslims at the advent of British rule. However, the occupational structure did vary from region to region, depending upon the regional specificities, for example, in the fertile Indo-Gangetic Plain and in Bengal, Muslims were predominantly agriculturists. In contrast to that, Muslims in Gujrat and Bombay Presidency—because the flourishing of coastal trade and its exposure to Arab world from the earliest times—were predominantly engaged in trade and services.

Muslims, Colonialism and the Partition

> The Musalman chiefs, who are numerous, are very angry at being without employment under Government, or hope of rising in the State or Army, and are continually breaking out into acts of insubordination and violence. [Or again], the country [Rohilkhand] is burdened with a crowd of lazy, profligate self-called suwars[horsemen] who, though many of them are not worth a rupee, conceive it derogatory to their gentility and Patan blood to apply themselves to any honest industry, and obtain for the most part a precarious livelihood by sponging on the industrious tradesmen and farmers, on whom they levy a sort of 'blackmail', or as hangers-on to the few noble and wealthy families yet remaining in the province. Of these men, who have no visible means of maintenance at all and no visible occupation except that of lounging up and down with their swords and shields like the ancient Highlanders, whom in many respects they much resemble, the umber is rated at perhaps, taking all Rohilcund together, not fewer than 100,000; all these men have everything to gain from a change of Government. (Bishop Heber as quoted by Hardy, 1972, p. 35)

Medieval Indian history in general and the empire building during this time, in particular, is the history of Muslims. By 1605, Akbar ruled over the entire North India. Aurangzeb on the other hand by 1690 had traversed as far south as the river Cauvery. Thus, the entire subcontinent, with all its diversity and under various direct and indirect arrangements with the *Delhi Durbar* had recognized the Muslim supremacy. However, following the war of succession after the death of Aurangzeb in 1707 and in the backdrop of the emergence of regional kingdoms of Punjab, Rajputan, Awadh, Bengal and Deccan, the splendour of the Mughal Empire started to dwindle. This degeneration was hastened by the attrition of the Mughal nobility and Nadir shah's raids. As the authority of the Mughal nobility, soldiers, officials and the celebrated intelligentsia dwindled concurrently with the rising authority of the Rajputs, Sikhs and Marathas, their employment choices narrowed down. With the introduction of English, first as the language of governmental and legal business in 1835, and later (1877) as a qualification for the subordinate official career, Muslim monopoly of Persian was lost on the one hand and their averseness to learn English language on the other, which put them at a serious educational disadvantage. Roots of linguistic identification of Hindus and Muslims in India can logically be traced to and around this period. As Christopher R. King (1994) remarks:

> A catalyzing role in the linguistic identification was played by the employment policy of the colonial government. In 1877 the government of Awadh and the North-western Provinces demanded an examination to prove competence in the vernacular as a qualification for government service. The competition was mainly between Hindu Kayasths and Muslims, who favoured using Urdu, on the one hand, and high-caste Hindus (Brahmans, Rajputs, Khatris, and Baniyas) wanting to promote Hindi, on the other.

This shift from Persian to English was going to be difficult, if not impossible, for the Muslim community and put them on a serious disadvantage in terms of educational attainment and hence employment in the public service.[6] This educational disadvantage was to evolve as a serious inhibitor for their employment in the changing power structure. Hindus on the other hand were quick to switch over to English education, as they had done with a switchover to Persian during the Mughal times, to earn a living (Khalidi, 2006).

While all these developments were taking shape, a rebellion broke out against the British. Initially, a caste-based reaction of the Hindu soldiery, the mutiny of 1857, turned out to be of the most disastrous political and socio-economic consequence for the Indian Muslims.[7] The British took the mutiny as a Muslim rebellion largely because of their belief that the Muslims felt dejected under the British Raj. British had actually overtaken the Muslim–Mughal empires and as such any rebellion was perceived to be designed (by Muslims) to reverse the time clock. The available literature also does point out that an overriding role was actually played by the Muslim nobility and soldiery. Consequently, the British took on the Muslims and looked at the entire community with suspicion. Believing that the rebellion was a Muslim conspiracy, they came down more heavily on the Muslims as a community. British mindset and animosity towards the Muslims got established. Muslims were feared to be degraded as a class in revenge by the British (Campbell, 1893, p. 397). The Irish reporter William Howard Russell recorded in 1858 (pp. 73–74):

[6] As Christopher King rightly observes, the economic well-being of these elite groups depended very much on the outcome of this language conflict.

[7] The first sparks of disaffection it was generally agreed, were kindled among the Hindu sepoys who feared an attack upon their caste. But the Muslims then fanned the flames of discontent and placed themselves at the head of the movement, for they saw in these religious grievances the stepping stone to political power. In the British view it was Muslim intrigue and Muslim leadership that converted a sepoy mutiny into a political conspiracy, aimed at the extinction of the British Raj. (Metcalf, 1965, p. 298)

The Mahomedan element in India is that which causes us most trouble and provokes the largest share of our hostility.... Our antagonism to the followers of Mahomed is far stronger than that between us and the worshippers of Shiva and Vishnu. They are unquestionably more dangerous to our rule.

The disbelief in and animosity for Muslims, as it followed the 1857, was to relegate the Muslims to the worst kind of economic distress. With vengeful passions at their height, especially in the period 1858–1860, accounts of the treatment of Muslim pensioners, *jagirdars*[8] and *muafidars*[9] bears testimony to the *British bias* against Muslims. During the weeks when the British military authorities held Delhi at their mercy, they made every citizen who wished to return to the city after expulsion pay a fine. Muslims were required to pay 25 per cent of the value of their real property, while Hindus had to pay only 10 per cent. Confiscation of property and land dealt a death blow to the relative economic position of Muslims and brought in an era of reallocation of the same to the loyalists. In North-Western Provinces, as in elsewhere, confiscation left the Muslim community more damaged in its prestige and pride. Many indeed were killed or impoverished, but some too emerged with their fortunes made (Hardy, 1972). Muslim pension holders were particularly vulnerable to British wrath.[10] The mutiny, however, brought a cancellation or reduction of pension. Many Muslim pensions were forfeited.[11] With the confiscations, there occurred

[8] *Jagir* was a type of feudal land grant in South Asia bestowed by a monarch to a feudal superior, referred to as the *jagirdar* in recognition of his administrative and/or military service.
[9] The loyalist who enjoyed land grants without any rent and tax, in recognition of their loyalty to monarch, were referred to as muafidars.
[10] As reported by Khalidi (2006), citing Percival Spear (1980) Bahadur Shah I (not the last Mughal Emperor Bahadur Shah Zafar) had petitioned British for a stipend increment as long back as 1810.
[11] Although Hardy does maintain that forfeiture of pensions was not necessarily based on religious affiliation but vengeance against British, but keeping in view the suspicion about Muslims and a relatively better entitlements in the pre-colonial period that the British had cultured

a transference in landholding within the Muslim community on the one hand and from Muslims to Hindus on the other. Nobility apart, the lot of the common Muslim was worse, in the post-1857 era and continued with the same fate till Partition. Partly ascribed to the designation of English as the official language (as discussed earlier), the fact remains that Muslims were standing distant from British education and continued to grieve marginalization from official employment. Muslims emerged from 1857 condemned in the eyes of their rulers and with their traditional leaders dead or in exile, they had lost the economic position and social prestige (Hardy, 1972).

On the public employment front, these developments did make a marked difference in the positions on which Muslims were appointed. By 1871, at least in Bengal, Muslims held only 4.4 per cent of gazetted appointments, while Hindus had a share of 32.3 per cent. Majority of the posts were indeed held by British (63.3%) but of the gazetted appointments held by Indians, Hindus, with a population share of 68 per cent, accounted for 88 per cent of the gazette appointments (Khalidi, 2006). A breakdown of population–employment data in terms of different categories of posts (public services, statutory services, executive and judicial services), presence of Muslims in different departments in different provinces reveals that on a population basis, Muslims were under-represented in Bengal, Bombay, Madras and Punjab. As far as the North-Western Province and Oudh are concerned, they were over-represented (Table 2.1).

In the aftermath of the revolt of 1857, the Muslim employment under the British Raj got directly linked to loyalism to it. The chosen few loyalists had bounties to reap, but majority

---

it is not a weak approximation that Muslim forfeitures would have been much larger in number. For example, to quote Hardy, in Bareilly district, however, a consolidated return of forfeitures gives 95 Muslim forfeitures to two Hindus. In other centres of Muslim disaffection, such as Bijnor, Moradabad and Bada'un, Muslim losses of pensions were also great.

TABLE 2.1 Percentage of Muslims Appointed to Public Service in 1871 Compared with Percentage of Muslim Population

Province	Total Population	Muslim Population	Muslim Population (%)	Muslims Appointed in 1871 (%)
Bengal	60,467,724	19,554,203	32	11
Bombay	16,349,206	2,528,344	15	9
Madras	31,282,177	18,722,141	6	1
North-Western Provinces	30,781,204	4,188,751	14	35
Punjab	17,611,498	9,102,488	52	38
Awadh	11,220,232	1,111,290	10	45
Total	167,711,041	38,356,507	23	24

Source: Khalidi (2006).

of the people suffered as far as public employment at all levels was concerned. For example, in magisterial appointments (1861) of the people whom Hardy refers to as *independent gentlemen of property and influence* in the districts of Agra, Meerut, Rohilkhand, Benares, Ajmer, Jhansi and Gorakhpur, only 5 out of 61 were Muslims (North-Western Provinces Government Gazette, 1861, pp. 2087–2089). There were only 14 Muslims out of a total of 48 *talluqdars*[12] in Awadh empowered in 1862–1863 to try civil, revenue or criminal cases as honorary assistant-commissioners (*Parliamentary Paper*, 1865).

In the North-Western Provinces owing to the *suspicion syndrome*, Muslims had lost the overwhelming advantages in official favour which they had enjoyed before 1857. Muslims in 1850–1856 held 72 per cent of judicial positions in the NWFP,

---

[12] It is a term used for Indian landholders in Mughal and British times, responsible for collecting taxes from a district.

TABLE 2.2 *Judicial and Executive Positions in the Uncovenanted Civil Service, 1887*

Province	Muslim Population Share	Post	Share in Employment
Bengal	31.2	Executive	12.9
		Judicial	3.1
Bombay and Sindh	18.3	Executive	7.4
		Judicial	0.8
Madras	6.2	Executive	5.4
		Judicial	1.6
North-Western Provinces and Awadh	13.4	Executive	44
		Judicial	45.9
Punjab	51.3	Executive	41.8
		Judicial	33.6
Assam	26.9	Executive	0.9
		Judicial	0.9
Central Provinces	2.4	Executive and Judicial Combined	16

Source: Hardy (1972) and Khalidi (2006).

which in 1885–1887 had got reduced to 49.5 per cent in the North-Western Provinces and Awadh taken together (Metcalf, 1965). Appointment to executive and judicial positions in the early British Raj reflected a regional bias (Table 2.2).

The areas which were part of the 'suspicion theory' against Muslims for their role in 1857 were neglected. Muslims were to a large extent excluded from public offices in general and public employment in particular. Thus, an interesting phenomenon emerges over here. On the all British India basis, one gets the realization that Muslim representation in public employment was in absolute sync with their population ratio. But at a disaggregated level (as discussed earlier), the existence of a deliberate attempt of exclusion and deprivation in selected areas is vivid. For example, of all the 2,588 judicial and executive positions in the uncovenanted civil service, 514 (20% of total) positions and 1,866 (72%) of total positions were held by Muslims (who were 20% of population) and Hindus (who were 75% of population), respectively.

The marginalization of Indian Muslims continued and reinforced itself across the temporal presence of British in India. As reported by Syed Wazir Hassan, with a population share of 23.5 in 1911, as against the 66.9 per cent share of Hindus, Muslims held 2.6 per cent of all positions carrying a stipend of at least 500 a month. Hindus held 14.5 per cent of such appointments (Khalidi, 2006, pp. 24–27). With the opening of Indian Civil Services (ICS) for Indians, on 12 October 1887, there were 12 Indians in the ICS, all Hindus. By 1913, 9 Muslims as compared to 49 Hindus held ICS positions. From 1887–1913, percentage of Muslims in the ICS was close to their national population share. However, on 1 August 1947, the ICS had strength of 955, of which 103 (10.79%) were Muslims of whom only 12 remained in independent India (Khalidi, 2006, pp. 28–29). Thus, at all levels of employment in Colonial India, Muslims in major provinces were under-represented. However, on an all India basis, their relative employment ratios were almost at par with their population share.

Partition, Independence and Employment — The Muslim Case

It was after 90 years of the revolt of 1857, India got independence in 1947. Muslims, who had suffered the British vengeance disproportionately for their role in 1857 (as discussed earlier), had played a pivotal role in the freedom struggle (Ray, 1983). However, the dawn of the sun over an independent land was shadowed by its partition in the midnight. More disheartening is the fact that this partition was on *the* religious line. Pressed upon by the growing demands for self-rule, in 1920s and 1930s, and in the backdrop of continued civil disobedience movement and the likewise, end of the British rule had become imminent after the Second World War. However, with the victory of the labour party in England, the process was hastened (Whitehead, 2007). Finally, long cherished independence doomed along a religious split in two separate nations. The geographical scenarios created in the subcontinent can be summed up as to have emerged into: *Pakistan (West and East Pakistan, the latter becoming Bangladesh in 1971), a Muslim homeland, and India, with a Hindu majority and significant religious minorities, both independent nations, with the Two-Nation Theory* or the ideology of Pakistan as the basis for the Partition.[13] This indicated that Muslims and Hindus were two separate nations by every definition and, therefore, Muslims should have an autonomous homeland in the Muslim majority areas of British India.[14] This division was flawed. As evidenced by huge migrations of Muslims from India to Pakistan and that of Hindus from Pakistan to India, amidst plunder, bloodshed, loot and arson. The Hindu–Muslim coexistence had become a myth. Communal tensions reached an apex during the Partition years. Outbreak of riots between Hindus and Muslims engulfed India. All over the subcontinent and particularly in the north-western part, hundreds of thousands, and by some estimates millions, of people were massacred (Lapierre & Collins, 1995). Muslims again, as in 1857, were perceived to be responsible for the division of the subcontinent and continue to be shamed for the same. However, emergent literature does assert that Hindus were promoted and Muslims in India were ignored during the earlier part of the 20th century and were gradually reduced to second-class citizens (Mahmood,

---

[13] On the causes and consequences of partition and different opinions regarding the same, refer to, among others, Venkat Dhulipala (2015), Nisid Hajaria (2015), Jeff Hay (2006), Narender Singh Sarila (2005) and D. N. Panigrahi (2004).

[14] Presidential address by poet–philosopher Muhammad Iqbal in 1930 to the Muslim League introducing the two-nation theory in support of a home for the Muslims of South Asia. As summarized by Mallah (2007).

2006).[15] This in part explains the growing demand for a separate homeland for Muslims around the early 1940s. There indeed was a growing discontent among Muslim leadership vis-à-vis post-independence political arrangements. A counterclaim to this set of belief is provided by Khalidi (2006) who while referring to the Muddiman Commission[16] of which M. A. Jinnah was a member asserts that post-1925, there was some sort of adherence to the norm *that all communities should receive due representation in public services.* An informal rule of reservation was followed for some time. However, the same could not be sustained, nor could M. A. Jinnah's demand for a statutory status to the provisions for giving Muslims an adequate share in *all* services of state and in local self-governing bodies be granted (Appadorai, 1934).[17] With many unsettled agendas[18] between the midnight's children,[19] there was an upsurge in riots from 1964 to 1971. The 1965 war escalated Hindu nationalism to the apex. Hindu mistrust of Muslims is evident in the rhetoric

---

[15] '[a] comprehensive analysis of the state of Muslims under British rule is documented by a British author, William Hunter, in his monumental work, Indian Musalman, published in 1871, in which he explains [that in his time]. ... all sorts of employment, high or low, great or small [were] being gradually snatched away from the Mohammedans [Muslims], and given to other races particularly Hindus (Mallah, 2007).'

[16] Established in 1924 with Alexander Muddiman as chairman and representatives of various Indian communities as members this commission was tasked to explore the ways and means of reforms in the employment rules

[17] According to Misra (1986, p. 118), the percentage reserved for Muslims was 13.3.

[18] Of the unsettled questions, the Kashmir issue continues to strain the Indo-Pak relations, in turn, leading to a feeling of mistrust of Indian Muslims for their alleged affinity to Pakistan, given its Muslim character and a shared history.

[19] India and Pakistan, West and East, the latter becoming Bangladesh in 1971, were divided on the midnight of 14 August 1947, hence the term.

claiming that Muslims are Pakistani spies[20] who give signals to Pakistani aircraft (Banerjee, 1990).

This environment of hostility, hatred and mistrust at the time of independence and thereafter was bound to impress upon the socio-economic and political milieu of the newly born democratic state—India. Neither the public offices nor the public authorities could remain insulated from it. Ranging from the office of the home minister[21] to that of the local revenue officials, hostility towards Muslims was rampant and their loyalty towards India questioned. In the central secretariat services in 1965, for example, there were only 6 Muslims in the top two grades out of 681. In the subsequent grade out of a total of 2,000 employees, only 4 were Muslims. Even among the clerks, of 9,900 clerks, only 21 were Muslims (Malhotra & Linden, 1973). In a 1968 survey, it was revealed that only 2 per cent of officials at the highest level were Muslims and they formed less than one half of 1 per cent of the clerks and messengers in the ministries of the central government (Lelyveld, 1968). These representative but indicative statistics provide credence to what Jawaharlal Nehru had noted in early 1953:

> In the services, generally speaking, representation of the minority communities is lessening. In some cases it is very poor indeed........looking through central secretariat figures, as well as some others, I am distressed to find that the position is very disadvantageous to them, chiefly to the Muslims and 'sometimes' to others also. In our defense services there are hardly any Muslims left. In the vast central secretariat of Delhi there are very few Muslims. (Parthasarthi, 1985)

---

[20] Even in 2015, such an attitude towards Muslims has been witnessed as evidenced by news reports and public debates.

[21] Sardar Patel as home minister removed Muslim officials who opted to stay in India according to S. Gopal, as cited in Khalidi (2006). Patel even referred to Maulana Azad's Ministry of Education as 'miniature Pakistan' for the presence of few Muslim officials as per J. N. Sahni, a contemporary journalists.

Thus, plight of Muslims on the public employment front has consistently been worrisome.[22] It was in recognition of this assertion that on 10 May 1980 a high-power panel headed by Gopal Singh was appointed by Indira Gandhi administration to study *economic condition of minorities, SCs and STs*. Given the fact that the revelations of the report sent *shock waves across the corridors of south block*, the entire report was shelved and never brought out in the public domain (Zakaria, 1995). Submitted to the government on 14 June 1983, the report was tabled before the Parliament on 24 August 1990, only after a defeat of the Congress at the centre. Despite the submission to the parliament in 1990, the report is still not commonly available though some selected extracts have been published. Representation of Muslims in the public sector since Gopal Singh's report and even since Independence has remained on an unchanged trajectory. At the dawn of the 21st century, the central government employed 377,666 civilians and categorized the same into four groups. Muslims were a meagre 1.61 per cent, 3 per cent, 4.41 per cent and 5.12 per cent of the Group A, Group B, Group C and Group D employees, respectively (Khalidi, 2006). Thus, even in the liberalized economy set-up, the Indian Muslims could not break the glass ceiling.

Explanations to these scenarios of Muslim employment have been put forth on three broad-based premises as was referred to in the introduction to this chapter. The *attitudinal bias* may for the time being be 'assumed' a universal phenomenon in case of Muslims in general and that of the Indian Muslims in particular. The demoralization thesis surely has got to do some explanation over here. More so, in the aftermath of the partition upon which the Indian Muslims were reduced to a weaker demographic entity at least as far as headcount ratio is concerned. With most of the influential people and people of authority opting for Pakistan,

[22] William Hunter (as referred to earlier), in his monumental work, *Indian Musalmans*, published in 1876, explains [that in his time]...all sorts of employment, high or low, great or small [were] being gradually snatched away from the Mohammedans [Muslims], and given to other races particularly Hindus. Also see Mahmood (2006).

those who were left behind were the *lesser mortals*, without a strong leadership. Muslims in the post-Partition era surely needed a Sir Syed Ahmad Khan of the yesteryears or a Jinnah of the contemporary era, but both were gone. However, explanations for the employment scenarios of Indian Muslims has got shaped and continue to be such, could be valid, but for how long? In a democratic, welfare-seeking, secular republic, howsoever, it has got to such a persistent state of apathy towards the minorities that it cannot be relayed back to the accidents of history. From the foregoing analysis, it as such emerges that the relative deprivation of Indian Muslims in employment in general and public employment and especially in the post-independence era need to be delineated in some detail on empirical grounds backed by reliable data.

It is to in this backdrop that the government of India appointed a Prime Minister's High Level Committee (Justice Sachar Committee) on *social, economic and educational status of the Muslim community in India* in March 2005 with the main objective of assessing the 'Social, Economic and Educational status of Muslims in the states, regions, districts and blocks that they live in, their livelihood activities, their levels of socio-economic development and their asset base and income levels relative to other groups'.[23] The report submitted by the committee on the 17th day of November 2006 made it amply clear that there is a persistent and strongly held perception of discrimination among majority of the Indian Muslim population, not only in the labour market but across all walks of life. Issues of *identity, security and equity* loom large over the Muslim spaces and more so in areas where they are in small numbers.

Credence to such assertions is given by the fact that within the ambit of employment (as the Sachar Committee revealed), Muslim representation in jobs in the government including those in the public sector undertakings compared to other SRCs was considerably low in 2004–2005. In no state of the country, the level of Muslim employment was found to be proportionate to their percentage in the population. At the disaggregated level,

---

[23] https://mha.gov.in/sites/default/files/ar0506-Eng.pdf

situation of government jobs for Muslims was recorded best in Andhra Pradesh where a *fairly close* representation (in proportion to the population) had been achieved. Other states with a better picture of representation were: Karnataka (8.5% job share in a population proportion of 12.2%); Gujarat (5.4% against 9.1%); Tamil Nadu (3.2% against 5.6%). In all other states, percentage of Muslims in government employment was half of their population proportion. The highest percentage figure of government employment for Muslims was recorded in Assam (11.2%) even though it is far less than the state's Muslim population (30.9%). The most glaring cases of Muslims' deprivation in government jobs were found in the states of West Bengal and Kerala where, according to common perception, egalitarianism has been the cherished norm in all walks of life. In West Bengal, where almost 25 per cent population practices the Muslim faith, their share in government jobs was a paltry 4.2 per cent. In Kerala, the Muslim representation in government jobs was 10.4 per cent, a figure that is short of half of their population percentage. In Bihar and UP, the percentages of Muslims in government jobs are found to be less than one-third of their population percentages.

The Committee points out that there is a high share of Muslim workers in self-employment activity, especially in urban areas and in the case of women. The fact should be considered that Muslims in regular jobs in urban areas are much lower in numbers compared to even the SCs/STs. And, surprisingly, the Muslim regular workers get lower daily earnings (salary) in public and private jobs compared to other socio-religious categories, as the Committee points out. The point that needs special notice is that, according to the Committee's findings, Muslim participation in professional and management cadres is quite low. Their participation in security-related activities (e.g., in the police services) is considerably lower than their population share (4% overall). In judiciary, the employment scenario of Muslims was and continues to be alarming both in absolute as well as relative terms. In West Bengal, with a Muslim population of over 25 per cent, Muslims in key positions in the judiciary are only 5 per cent. In Assam, with a Muslim population of

30.9 per cent, this figure is 9.4 per cent. Surprisingly, in Jammu and Kashmir (where the Muslim population is 66.97%), the community's share in the state judiciary is only 48.3 per cent. Andhra Pradesh once again scores over other states in terms of equitable and even more than equitable sharing of jobs: Muslims have a share of 12.4 per cent in the state judiciary against a population share of 9.2 per cent. Findings of SCR are a reminiscent of Muslim deprivation during the post-1857 period.

Conclusion

An attempt to find out the *raison d'etre* for the Muslim backwardness in Independent India brings to the light certain complex issues. Religious identity and belief of a given set of population have temporally been the marker and identifier in the socio-economic and political sphere for the Indian populace in general and Muslims in particular. This identifier has been neutral to the institution of governance. Available accounts and data present indicators to the relative deprivation of Muslims in employment under the British rule, thus lending support to the *demoralization thesis*. The historicity of socio-economic atmosphere has had a profound impact on the present situation of labour market status of Indian Muslims. Fall in Muslim employment during the company rule as well as under the Crown, among other things, lends support to this argument. Independence, it seems, has not turned the clock back. Partition-led Indian Muslims face glass walls in all walks of their socio-economic and political life. It is in a continuum of such historical context that Muslims in India have borne a compounded impact of various circumstances, policies and attitudes in independent India. Findings of SCR at least in the sphere of Muslim employment point towards a continuum of destitution and deprivation in case of Indian Muslims.

Most of the recommendations of SCR were taken up for implementation by the state. It is as such relatable to assess the relative participation ratios of Muslims in the post-Sachar era. That forms the subject matter of the next chapter.

3

Dynamics of Muslim Participation in Indian Labour Market

With independence from the British, India embarked on a path of socialistic approach to economic development. The major focus for wittingly adopting this route for economic growth was to empower majority of the Indians economically and offer them a push to escape the cobweb of poverty in which majority of them were entangled. The colonial legacy of repression and economic destitutions were shared by one and all. However, as flagged in the previous chapters, British had created a situation where Muslims find it difficult to live at peace with the existing power structures in pre-independent India. Due to this political animosity and economic exclusion, Muslims were pushed to extreme poverty and had to face severe economic deprivation which led to their social exclusion in the post-1857 India. The impact of post-1857 exclusion was felt even at the dawn of Independence. For reasons as illustrated in the preceding chapter, the Muslim community in India stood in dire need of affirmative action at the hands of the new government. However, the unfolding events leading to the declaration of independence and the partition of the country in 1947 compounded their miseries. Partition apart from other things brought the religion dimension to the forefront of economic policy and ensuing development interventions. With the partition of the country on communal lines, a myriad of socio-economic issues erupted. India, accommodating Muslims as a religious minority, got caught up with the political strife consequent upon the migration of people across the newly created international borders. The fears of Muslims who could not cross over to the other side of the fence and chose to stay back due to varied reasons cannot be overlooked. It was in this backdrop that Indian Muslims started to become a distinct community, not just that they were domiciled elsewhere, but because of the circumstances that had unfolded at the dawn of Independence. Muslim backwardness and *deprivation* has been taken as a mere perception in post-independent India. Attribution to lack of reliable data in the country on religion with respect to educational and employment statistics has eventually rendered support to this thesis. Even independent researchers have found it difficult to study the problems and planning vis-à-vis education and employment of Muslims. This paucity of credible information and policy insights could be considered one of the reasons for the absence of targeted affirmative action in case of Indian Muslims.

In order to undo the fears and to overcome the anxieties of *Indian Muslims*, the Prime Minister's Office of the Government of India vide notification No. 850/3/C/3/05-Pol commissioned the Sachar Committee on 9 March 2005. The report submitted on 17 November 2006 provided a much-sought empirical insights into the socio-economic and development status of Indian Muslims. This report and its findings were pathbreaking. Given the richness of data sources and analysis as well as its mandate, it has become a foundation for understanding the *Muslim question* on empirical lines. Spread over 12 chapters, the report lucidly brings forth the condition of Indian Muslims with respect to demographic, socio-economic, financial and cultural space. Furthermore, the report offers startling policy insights vis-à-vis Muslim employment and its labour force participation. The report finds the WPR for Muslims to be significantly lower than for all other SRCs in rural areas but only marginally lower in urban areas. This is however attributed to much lower participation in economic activity by women in the community (Sachar Committee, 2006, p. 89). Self-employment activity is found to be the mainstay of employment among Muslims while participation of Muslim workers in salaried jobs (both in the public and the private sectors) is quite low (Sachar Committee, 2006, p. 106). Their employment in regular jobs in urban areas is somewhat limited compared to even the traditionally disadvantaged SCs/STs. Significantly, a large proportion of Muslim workers is engaged in small proprietary enterprises and their participation in formal sector employment is significantly less than the national average. As compared to other SRCs, the participation of Muslim workers in the informal sector enterprises is much higher. For example, as the report calculates, less than 8 per cent of Muslim workers in urban areas are employed in the formal sector as compared to the national average of 21 per cent. The share of Hindu-OBC and SC/ST workers in such jobs in urban areas is as high as 18 per cent and 22 per cent, respectively. The same pattern prevails for both male and female workers and in rural areas. The share of Muslim workers engaged in street vending (especially without any fixed location) is much higher than in other SRCs; more than 12 per cent of Muslim male workers are engaged in street vending as compared to the national average of less than 8 per cent. The percentage of women Muslim workers undertaking work within their own homes is much larger (70%) than for all workers (51%). While the larger engagement in street vending highlights the higher vulnerability of Muslim workers, concentration of Muslim women in home-based work raises issues about spatial mobility and other work-related constraints that women face even today (Government of India, 2006).

Considering the findings of the Sachar Committee, its members also provided a set of recommendations and required interventions in all aspects of socio-economic development of the Muslim community. Most of the recommendations of this

Committee were accepted by the government and a follow-up programme was initiated. Among other things, the SCR placed huge emphasis on the need for improving employment situation and status of the Muslim community. To evaluate the efficacy of the follow-up programme initiated by the government consequent upon the submission of the SCR, the Ministry of Home Affairs (MOHA), Government of India, on 5 August 2013 under order No. 9–2/2013-PP I constituted a committee under the chairmanship of Professor Amitabh Kundu (Kundu Committee, henceforth) with a mandate (among other things) to:

> Evaluate the process of the implementation of decisions of the Government on the recommendations as outlined in the Report of the Prime Minister's High Level Committee on Socio-Economic and Educational Status of the Muslim Community in India (popularly known as Sachar Committee) for institutional reforms and programmatic shifts.

The Committee was also tasked to 'evaluate the outcome indicators (on the basis of latest secondary data) in the areas of focus as identified by Sachar Committee'. Thus, in essence, Kundu Committee was mandated to evaluate the progress made in the follow-up to the recommendations of SCR. One of the major areas of focus of SCR had been to assess the position of Muslim employment, especially in the public and private sector. In the area of employment, Sachar Committee had reported dismal participation of Muslims in the labour market. The SCR observed that Muslims in India are 'relatively more vulnerable in terms of conditions of work as their concentration in informal sector employment is higher and their job conditions (contract length, social-security etc.) even among regular workers are less than those of other SRCs'.

Kundu Committee submitted its report (KCR henceforth) to the Ministry of Minority Affairs on 29 September 2014. However, as reported earlier, the report like the Gopal Singh Commission Report (GSCR) of the 1980s was not made public for quite some time. When accessed (notwithstanding a shabby and carelessly edited report), it was found that KCR in the sphere of employment has observed no change in what SCR had concluded with respect to its mandate, especially in the sphere of employment and work conditions of Muslims. It also came to the same conclusion that 'Muslims are the most deprived minority in the labour market' (KCR, p. 33). However, KCR did not yield much upon the relative positioning of SRCs in the labour market over the two NSSO rounds of 2004–2005 and 2011–2012. No detailed analysis of the labour market participation and employment (for Muslims and other SRCs) over the reference period of the report was discussed. Thus, the inertia of the *Muslim question* was once again made to resonate.

To understand the actual employment of a given socio-religious group within the labour market, one needs to examine the LFPR as well as the WFPR of that group in relation to the reference group. Equally important variables are the relative SERs as well as the relevant URs. For all these rates/ratios, education and age become additional caveat. This chapter details of these important parameters of the Indian labour market. Analysis of labour market participation and explication of the determining factors is also carried out by way of logistic regression.

This chapter is divided into 11 sections. Estimation of and discussion on LFPR and WFPR for different age groups and levels of education form the subject matter of the next six sections. The SER and UR across age and education with a special focus on the socio-religious categories are discussed in the following sections. Results of logistic regression are deliberated upon in a further section.

Labour Force Participation Rate

LFPR is defined as ratio of the labour force to working age population,[1] expressed as a percentage. The labour force is the sum of the number of persons employed and the number of persons unemployed during a particular period, preferably a

[1] Unless mentioned otherwise, the working age population in the current context is the age group of 15–64 years on UPSS.

year.[2] Expanding economic opportunities and increases in the working age population lead to increases in LFPR and WFPR. Increases in school and college enrolments as in case of china (Naughton, 2007) can lead to a fall in these ratios. Increase in young adults attending educational institutions is one of the most important explanations for the decline in LFPR (Planning Commission, 2011). I find evidence for the same in the Indian context. In the Indian context, there has been a decline of 8.1 per cent in the LFPR over the reference period as shown in Table 3.1. However, this decline has varied across SRCs, gender and region. SCs/STs have reported the highest decline of 9.1 per cent and Muslims-General the lowest (2.2%). Women from the Hindu-OBC have retracted by 14.8 per cent from the labour force as against 2.2 per cent by women from the Muslims-General. The decline in the LFPR (for all SRCs and as such for all population) is more in the rural areas than urban.

Women retraction from labour force over the reference period (12.1%) has been three times higher than that of men (4.1%) and this gap between the respective falls across gender are of the same magnitude across all SRCs. These trends appear to be more general and do not speak much about the actual locus of the fall in the LFPR and the possible mechanisms at play with respect to the general decline. To locate the specific age group which may be responsible for this decline, we divided the LFPR across age groups with a class interval of 4. Results for All India as well as SRCs are reported within this framework.

LFPR by Age

Analysis of LFPR is done by dividing the age group 15–64 into 10 subgroups (Tables A.1 and A.2 in the Appendix). This

[2] Resolution concerning statistics of work, employment and labour underutilization, adopted by the 19th International Conference of Labour Statisticians, Geneva, October 2013. Retrieved from http://www.ilo.org/global/statistics and databases/standards-and-guidelines/resolutions-adoptedby international-conferences-of labour statisticians/WCMS_230304/lang en/index.htm

TABLE 3.1 LFPR (2011–2012 and 2004–2005 UPSS)

	Rural								Urban								Total							
	Male		Female		Total		Male		Female		Total		Male		Female		Total		Male		Female		Total		
	R_2	R_1	R_2	R_1	R_2	R_1	R_2	R_1	R_2	R_1	R_2	R_1	R_2	R_1	R_2	R_1	R_2	R_1						
SCs/STs	85.2	90.1	45.4	60.4	65.5	75.4	80.0	82.6	26.4	32.0	54.2	58.5	84.2	88.7	41.7	55.5	63.3	72.4						
Hindus	83.5	88.5	39.0	54.2	61.5	71.4	79.2	81.9	22.4	26.5	51.8	55.6	82.2	86.7	34.2	47.2	58.7	67.3						
Hindu-OBCs	83.2	88.4	38.4	54.7	61.1	71.5	79.7	84.2	23.8	30.2	52.8	58.7	82.3	87.4	34.6	49.4	58.9	68.6						
UC-Hindus	80.8	85.9	29.9	43.8	55.7	65.0	77.9	79.2	19.0	21.0	49.4	51.5	79.5	83.1	25.1	34.5	52.9	59.3						
Muslims	83.8	87.7	24.9	30.0	54.1	58.4	82.7	85.1	16.2	19.0	50.6	53.3	83.4	86.8	21.7	26.3	52.8	56.6						
Muslim-OBCs	82.3	86.3	23.3	32.5	52.1	57.6	83.3	84.3	16.0	21.2	50.2	53.6	82.7	85.5	20.5	28.8	51.4	56.2						
Muslims-General	85.4	88.6	26.1	28.3	55.8	58.9	82.3	85.5	16.4	17.7	51.1	53.4	84.2	87.5	22.5	24.7	54.0	57.0						
Other Minorities	82.0	87.5	42.4	58.2	62.2	72.7	77.6	78.8	27.5	30.7	52.4	55.3	80.4	84.8	37.1	49.9	58.8	67.4						
All Population	83.5	88.4	37.5	51.8	60.7	70.1	79.6	82.1	21.7	25.7	51.6	55.3	82.3	86.6	32.8	44.8	57.9	66.0						

Source: Author's calculations based on NSSO unit-level data.

Note: R_2 refers to 68th (2011–2012) and R_1 refers to the 61st (2004–2005) rounds of NSSO.

classification allows for a better understanding of the changing nature and the politics of labour market participation decline and highlights the points vis-à-vis specific age groups which lead to such a decline. Furthermore, it allows one to understand the transition to labour market across various age groups. This type of approach becomes inevitable in the context of the demographic dividend and the youth bulge which India is experiencing at present. It will allow us to link these demographic developments to the labour market. The first three age groups (15–19, 20–24, 25–29 years) represent major proportion of the population attending educational institutions (Group I henceforth). The next (30–34, 35–39 years) are the most active part of the labour force exhibiting highest reporting rate at the labour market (Group II henceforth). The age groups (40–44, 45–49, 50–54, 55–59, 60–64 years) should again within the socio-economic context of India be an active part of the labour force (Group III henceforth).

As reported earlier, there is a decline of 8.1 per cent in the LFPR across the population over the reference period. Age-based disaggregation of this decline reveals that the decline has mostly been on account of an appreciable fall (15.8%) in LFPR in the age group 15–19 years followed by a 11 per cent fall in the 20–24 years age group. Thus, taken together, Group I accounts for 26.8 per cent fall of the aggregate LFPR. An attempt will be made to discern this drop in LFPR across Group I in relation to education level as well as attendance at educational institutions. It can be argued that an increase in enrolment ratios explains the fall in LFPR.

Group II has exhibited a reduction of 14.6 per cent in the LFPR. This drop is around 48 per cent of the fall exhibited by Group I. In Group III, as we move across age in the ascending order, there is a normalization of the decline in LFPR between 2004–2005 and 2011–2012. Rural–urban comparison reveals an overwhelming decline in the LFPR in rural areas across the age groups. Gender-based comparisons indicate an overwhelming decline in the LFPR (for women) which increases (both in rural and urban areas) as we move across Group II and Group III. The differential in male–female decline in Group I is relatively less wide. However, as we move up the years of age, lesser number of men exit the labour market and generally across time there is a net addition to the labour force. In case of women, there is a never-ending exit from the labour market. Women tend to be relatively more participatory up to 25 years of age. Thus, with age and more so after 25 years of age, women tend to retract from the labour force at extremely high rates, especially in rural areas. This tendency of excessive drop in the LFPR from age Group I, emanating from the rural areas and mainly driven by women, is similar across all the SRCs except Muslims. In case of Muslims (General as well as OBCs) and particularly Muslims-General (men and women), the decline in LFPR emanating from Group I is extremely low as compared to the national average and all other SRCs and in case of women it is lower. To put it the other way, more Muslims (relative to other SRCs) in the age group I continue to report in larger numbers at the labour market. This may actually be a pointer to the fact that Muslims in the age group of 15–24 years are not exhibiting a transition from labour market to educational institutions over the reference period at par with other SRCs. Support to this argument is provided by data on SER as discussed in the eighth section.

In case of females, the same trend is noticeable. Muslim women in Group I find it extremely difficult to move out of the labour force in numbers as the other SRCs are doing. The situation worsens for urban Muslim women. SCs/STs, Hindus, Hindu-OBCs, Hindu-General on the whole exhibited a total decline of 29.1 per cent, 29.5 per cent, 33.2 per cent and 25.4 per cent, respectively, in LFPR in Group I. Decline in LFPR among women in the respective SRCs are 31.3 per cent, 29.1 per cent, 32.1 per cent and 21.0 per cent. Muslims, Muslim-OBCs, Muslims-General have exhibited a decline of 11.6 per cent, 13.3 per cent and 10.9 per cent in the same age group, respectively. In case of women, the decline has been of the order of 4.9 per cent, 11.5 per cent, 1.4 per cent for Muslims, Muslim-OBCs, Muslims-General, respectively. For other minorities, declines in labour force from age Group I has been 27.4 per cent in general and for women it is quite high, that is, 28.4 per cent. Thus, with respect to declines in LFPR in the age group of 15–29 years is the lowest among Muslims. Ramifications of the lower fall in labour force participation of Group I may encompass issues related to human capital and, later, life employability.

LFPR by Education

Education is an important determinant of LFPR. Higher levels of education allow individuals to be more competitive on account of better human capital. It has been argued that higher levels of education generally lead to higher LFPR.[3] Although not captivating the relationship between education level and LFPR, an attempt is made to understand the decline in the LFPR across the educational levels with respect to the SRCs. Comparative perspectives across rural–urban and gender are retained. The decline of 8.1 per cent in the LFPR over the reference period at the national level is disaggregated across educational levels (Tables A.3 and A.4 in the Appendix). Among all levels of education for all relevant population, proportion of population with diploma/certificate courses[4] have, over the reference period, shown a decline of 12.1 per cent followed by a drop of 8.8 per cent across higher secondary level of education as well as among the Not-literate. Fall in the LFPR due to below primary is 6.5 per cent, while decline in the LFPR among PG and above has been the lowest (1.4%), with women (PG and above) in the urban actually showing an increase of 0.5 per cent in the LFPR. Rural–urban comparisons reveal that the decline has been more or less

---

[3] Psacharopoulos and Tzannatos (1991), Bulutay (1996), Tansel (1996) and Kennedy and Hedley (2003) argue that education is the most consistent determinant of LFPR. Kasnakoglu and Dayioglu (1996) argue that educational attainment has large and positive influence over female LFPR.

[4] Noteworthy is the fact that the proportion of such level of education to total literate population is dismally low (around 1%) as such any fluctuation in the participation rate returns very high proportions across the reference periods.

even across the rural–urban spaces, with a 1.5 per cent higher decline in the rural areas. Gender comparisons in the aggregate reveal a three times higher decline in the female LFPR (FLFPR). Male LFPR (MLFPR) over the reference period has come down by 4.3 per cent, mostly contributed by a decline of 10.4 per cent by diploma/certificate courses as against a decline of 12.1 per cent in FLFPR. Here again, the contribution of diploma/certificate courses has been the highest (18.8%). MLFPR across all levels of education has not fallen as strikingly as those of the FLFPR. In fact, if the decline due to diploma/certificate courses is set aside, the decline in MLFPR is less than 3 per cent as against a decline of 11.5 per cent in FLFPR. Differentials between MLFPR and FLFPR are greater up to secondary level of education, get almost similar at secondary and higher secondary level and thereafter the spread again increases with females accounting for larger falls in LFPR. There exist inhibitions to women's transition to higher levels of education. These inhibitions are also at work in case of their enrolment at primary level. Explanations and reasons of the same vary across levels of education. In case of enrolment at primary level, lower emphasis on education of the girl child in India is almost universal. As regard to transition to higher education, marriage, childbearing and housekeeping provide some explanations for lower participation in higher education. Sectoral analysis reveals that the LFPR in rural areas has declined by 9.5 per cent as against a decline of 3.6 per cent in the urban, with females exhibiting excessively higher proportions of decline. Respective male and female declines in the rural areas are 4.9 per cent and 14.3 per cent. In the urban areas, the male/female declines are 4 per cent and 3.6 per cent, respectively. The 12.3 per cent decline in FLFPR in the below primary for females in the rural is marginally less than the decline in their LFPR with graduate level of education (12.7%).

Analysis of LFPR among SRCs across education (at aggregate level) reveals some interesting trends and patterns; mostly consistent with the respective aggregates at the national level. SCs/STs decline in LFPR (9.1%) is comparable to that of Hindus (8.6%), Hindu-OBCs (9.8%) and other minorities. Muslims

(3.8%), Muslim-OBCs (4.9%) Muslims-General (3.0%) exhibit the lowest of the drop in LFPR among all SRCs. This observation from the data is in line with the earlier findings of consistent LFPR among Muslims, generally contributed by men (Sachar Committee, 2006). Among all the SRCs, Muslims-General exhibit the lowest declines in the LFPR both in the rural (3.1%) as well as in the urban (2.3%). Thus, unlike other SRCs, Muslim contribution to the decline in LFPR is the lowest and is not skewed to the urban but almost evenly distributed across the rural–urban spaces. Within the educational categories, highest decline has been contributed by those with diploma/certificate courses (an exhibit of most of the SRCs) and the least by primary education (0.9%). Across all SRCs, this is the lowest fall in case of primary education. FLFPR across education and among the SRCs exhibits notable differences. Against an increase of 6.1 per cent in LFPR among female SC/ST in rural India with educational level of PG and above, Muslim women as well as women of all other SRCs except Muslim-OBCs and UC-Hindus have shown declines. Interestingly, the LFPR of such women among Muslim-OBCs has gone up by 50.8 per cent as against a fall of 58.8 per cent among Muslims-General.[5] Similarly, *rural Muslim* women report a contribution of 30.7 per cent to the rural drop of 5.1 per cent in the LFPR, again the highest for this level of education. To put it in the other way, there is a general tendency among rural Muslim women to report lesser LFPR as the levels of education increase.

Workforce Participation Rate

Among the most basic indicators of a labour market and the economic activity is the WFPR or the WPR, especially when viewed in the context of UR. The former is the proportion of the population that is economically active (usually above 15 years of age so as to discount child labour). WFPR as such

---

[5] Such exorbitant results returned from the data had more to do with the small number of such women among Muslims as a proportion of the total female population.

includes all people who supply labour for the production of goods and services during a specified period. The WFPR actually gives an account of all the people who are there to offer labour in the market. This measure gives a real picture of availability of labour resource in an economy at a particular point of time. The UR rate captures the share of workers in the labour force who could not find a job within the specified reference period. WFPR reports the share of workers in working age population, so it is a better indicator and even a determinant of the UR.

Analysis of data regarding the WPRs across the socio-religious groups in 2004–2005 and 2011–2012 reveals that not much has changed in the intervening years. SRCs are in a general agreement with a secular decline in the WFPR as at the aggregate level (Table 3.2). India witnessed a decline of 7.8 per cent in the overall WFPR (NSSO, 2012). Female WFPR had a decline of 12 per cent and the male WFPR came down by 4.5 per cent. The decline in the aggregate WFPR was more in case of the rural labour market wherein it came down by 9.4 per cent as against the decline of 3.2 per cent in the urban. Again in the rural labour market, participation by women has come down by 14 per cent as against a 5 per cent decline in the participation of men. In contrast to a 1.8 per cent decline in the WFPR of men in the urban areas, female WFPR has gone down by 3.5 per cent.

Explanations for the general decline in the WFPR vary across nations. In the Indian context, the underlying reason for the decline in WPR can be either a higher rate of population growth than the workforce (Chand & Srivastava, 2014) or withdrawal by some from the workforce (Hirway, 2012) or both (Kannan & Raveendran, 2012). Decline in WPR for the male workers, though very small, was due to a comparatively higher rate of growth in the male population as compared to the workforce. However, evidences have shown that past business cycles have been characterized by a negative correlation between UR and the WFPR (Hornstein, 2013) showing thereby that, as the UR declines, the LFPR increases. In the Indian context, a reverse situation of this has been observed across the two time

TABLE 3.2 Workforce Population Ratios 2004–2005 and 2011–2012 (UPSS)

	Rural							Urban							Total (Rural + Urban)						
	Male		Female		Total		Male		Female		Total		Male		Female		Total				
	R_1	R_2	R_1	R_2	R_1	R_2	R_1	R_2	R_1	R_2	R_1	R_2	R_1	R_2	R_1	R_2	R_1	R_2			
SCs/STs	89	83.8	60	44.9	74	64.5	78	77.4	31	25.2	56	52.3	87	82.5	55	41.1	71	62.1			
Hindus	87	82.1	53	38.5	70	60.5	79	76.9	25	21.2	53	50.1	85	80.6	46	33.5	66	57.5			
Hindu-OBCs	87	81.9	54	37.9	71	60.1	82	77.7	28	22.6	56	51.2	86	80.7	48	33.9	67	57.7			
UC-Hindus	84	79.4	43	29.3	63	54.6	76	75.6	19	17.7	49	47.6	81	77.7	33	24.2	57	51.5			
Muslims	86	82.0	29	23.9	57	52.7	82	79.5	18	15.4	51	48.6	85	81.0	25	20.8	55	51.1			
Muslim-OBCs	84	80.6	31	21.9	56	50.6	81	81.1	20	15.3	51	48.8	83	80.8	27	19.4	54	49.9			
Muslims-General	87	83.6	28	25.3	58	54.5	83	78.1	17	15.6	51	48.5	86	81.4	24	21.8	56	52.3			
Other Minorities	85	80.1	56	40.9	70	60.6	75	74.5	27	25.6	52	50.0	82	78.1	47	35.5	65	56.8			
Total Population	87	82.0	51	36.9	69	59.6	79	77.2	24	20.5	53	49.8	85	80.5	44	32.0	64	56.6			

Source: Author's calculations from NSSO data.

Note: R_2 refers to 68th (2011–2012) and R_1 refers to the 61st (2004–2005) rounds of NSSO.

periods. Against a total (rural + urban) decline of 7.4 per cent in the WFPR for the entire population, the WFPR for Muslims has declined by 3.9 per cent. The decline has been highest for Hindu-OBCs (9.3%) followed by SCs/STs (8.9%). Other minorities have exhibited a decline of WFPR of 8.2 per cent. Decline in the workforce participation of Muslim women has been of the magnitude of 4.2 per cent points, just 0.2 per cent higher than their male counterparts (4%), which when compared to the decline in female participation of other SRCs is the lowest. Thus, Muslims (men and women) report the lowest decline in WFPR between 2004–2005 and 2011–2012, among all SRCs. Although overall the participation of Muslim women as a percentage of total working age population continues to be the lowest, this trend of a lower decline in relation to other SRCs is a welcome development. Highest decline in the participation ratio has been exhibited by Hindu-OBC women (14.1%), followed by the SCs/STs (13.9%). The male WFPR has varied over time in the same way, with the highest fall being exhibited by Hindu-OBCs (–5.3%) followed by Muslims-General (–4.6%). In case of women in the category of Muslims-General, the decline has been of 2.2 per cent; however, the overall ratio of decline has been pushed up by 7.6 per cent in the Muslim-OBCs. Thus, in the backdrop of a general decline in labour market participation, Muslims have continued to participate in relatively larger numbers, when compared to their participation in accordance with 2004–2005 data. Among women, those from SC/ST women continue to be the most visible in the labour market but their share has shown a remarkable decline over the reference period. In fact, overall decline in the WFPR of SC/ST women (13.9%) is the second highest after Hindu-OBCs which is marginally high at 14.1 per cent.

Rural–urban comparisons of WFPR do not differ much as far as the decline and its magnitude across the socio-religious groups is concerned. Of the total decline of 9.4 per cent in the WPR in rural India, 14.1 per cent was due to the fall in women participation. Within-group analysis reveals that Muslim women had the least contribution (5%) to this decline and at the other end were SC/ST women who contributed the highest (15.1%). Within the socio-religious groups, women belonging to the Hindu-OBC had the highest fall (16.1%) when compared to the earlier round and Muslims-General (2.7%) had the lowest. Among the male population, all socio-religious groups exhibit identical declines in participation rates (around 5% decline from the WPR in 2004–2005); however, the lowest (decline) again is witnessed in case of Muslims (4%). In urban areas, the WFPR has come down by around 3 per cent across the NSSO rounds for all SRCs. Not much significant variation is observed in the pattern of decline both on the gender as well as socio-religious group-based analysis. However, amid an overall as well as inter-group decline in the WFPR, urban Muslims (OBC) have shown a marginal increase of 0.1 per cent points.

With respect to an overall decline in the participation rates (LFPR and WFPR) over the reference period, many explanations seem to be plausible. Given the transition phase into which Indian economy has been in the post-reform period and an expansion of the industrial as well as the services sector, a transitory fall in the participation rates is inevitable. The transition from pre-industrial agriculture to early industrial and later to industrial economy as it is explained by modernization theorists has a U-shaped effect on labour force participation. Thus, there is a curvilinear rather than a linear relationship between economic development and employment. Diverse opinions are put across to explain the lower participation of women in the labour force. Studies carried out in the West have shown a link existing between the transition of an economy and labour force participation of women. This *modernization thesis* holds that women participation in the labour force can decline during the early transitional stages and then alongside the growth of modern sectors gain momentum. However, in the early stages as the formal labour market grows and agricultural sector jobs decline, more women leave agricultural work. Due to lack of opportunities, they are not often absorbed in other sectors. Therefore, women's employment rates decline. Later, with the growth in the country's occupational structure such as growth in the service and white-collar occupations, women's labour force participation increases again (Anker, Malkas, & Korten, 2003; Oakley 1974). However, critics of the modernization thesis argue religion and culture to be playing critical roles with respect to labour force participation of women (Clark, Ramsbey, & Adler, 1991). They maintain that Islam, because of its ideology of seclusion of women, and Latin America, because of its traditional ideological support for a patriarchal system, inhibit women's entry into the paid labour force (Malhotra, Vanneman, & Kishor, 1995; Obermeyer, 1992). Marshall (1985) and Clark, Rambsey and Adler (1991) especially point to the spurious relationship between development and female employment; when controlling for region, the effect of development is substantially reduced. In the Indian context, however, available evidence does point to lesser visibility of Muslim women in the labour market, partly explained by religious dogma as well as the development pattern at the macrolevel.

WFPR by Age

WFPR, keeping in close with the LFPR over the reference period, has declined by 7.8 per cent (Tables A.5 and A.6 in the Appendix). Group I (15–19 years, 20–24 years and 25–29 years) has accounted for more than one-third of the drop in the WFPR followed by a drop of 15 per cent exhibited by Group II. The trends and patterns in the drop in WFPR are the same as in the case of LFPR, however, with some difference in magnitude. Female WFPR has been continuously falling across all age groups, especially in the rural. The retraction has marginally increased for 25 years of age to 39 years. Interestingly, the fall in WFPR has been the lowest for 60–64 years both, in case of men as well as women. Rural–urban patterns of the drop in WFPR are in close proximity with the drop in LFPR trends (discussed earlier). The decline in the WFPR has been the lowest among Muslims-General (3.3%), one-third of the fall among Hindu-OBCs (9.9%) and almost one-third of the fall among SCs/STs (9.9%). FLFPR has shown the lowest decline in case of Muslims-General (2.2%) with a decline of 1.2 per cent in the urban and 2.3 per cent in the rural. All the three figures quoted in case of Muslims-General are the lowest among the SRCs within the respective categories. Although lower decline may not be a strong indicator to the convergence of Muslim FWFPR and other SRCs, it definitely is a pointer towards it. However, declines in the WFPR in Group I among Muslims (14.7%), Muslim-OBCs (12.3%), Muslims-General (15.7%) are the lowest of all categories, more so in case of the age group of 15–19 years, which from the perspective of educational attendance are the most important. Group I decline in the WFPR among all other SRC are on an average more than double of the decline as returned by Muslims. For example, SCs/STs, Hindus, Hindu-OBCs, UC-Hindus and other minorities report a fall of 37.2 per cent, 28.6 per cent, 31.9 per cent, 29.7 per cent, 23.6 per cent, respectively, in case of Group I. Thus, lesser retraction of Muslims from the workforce in the age groups as aggregated in Group I and more so in case of 15–19 years needs to be looked in some greater detail. Also, decline in the LFPR of females in the aforementioned age groups is much lower than that of the males, and if we tread on to link the trade-off between education and employment, which is clear for the age groups 15–19 and 20–24 years, then Muslims on average are leaving more females out of educational institutions than males by releasing more males in the school going age groups from the labour market, when compared to the release of females. This trend is neither exhibited nor captured by the aggregate decline in WFPR of men and women, either in the rural or in the urban space. Even at the national level, the dispersion in the decline in WFPR among men and women is the least in case of Muslims, but excessively generated by large dispersion between the two in Group I. Thus, the dismal educational outcomes among Indian Muslims continue to exist, more so at the primary and the secondary level.

WFPR by Education

As seen earlier, same patterns emerge with respect to LFPR and WFPR in case of educational attainment. The overall decline in the WFPR is distributed across all the education levels in relation with LFPR and education level (Tables A.7 and A.8 in the Appendix). Larger declines exhibited in case of those who have diploma/certificate courses (9.2%) are accompanied closely by the Not-literate (8.7%).[6] Population with higher secondary education as well as secondary education have exhibited appreciable declines in WFPR over the reference period of 2004–2005 to 2011–2012. The decline is on the lower side (relatively) for primary education and least for PG and above. Across the rural–urban spaces, decline in WFPR in the rural areas (9.3%) has been three times of the decrease in the urban (2.9%). Across all levels of education, the rural–urban declines have larger dispersion, but the gap widens in case of below primary, primary and middle—these are very crucial as far as educational attainment and enrolment ratios are concerned. One conclusion from such observations is that more people (especially in the age group 15–19 and 20–24) are exhibiting lesser labour force participation over time in the rural areas as compared to urban. Gender-based declines exhibit higher differentials in rural areas as against the urban. However, the decline is less in case of the higher levels of education, with WFPR declining by 0.2 per cent for rural women with PG and above as against a decline of 6.5 per cent for rural men. Over the reference period, both men and women in the urban areas (PG and above) have exhibited increases of 1.3 per cent and 3.4 per cent in their respective WFPRs. Explanations to these developments emanate to realization of better returns from higher education within the context of changing economic environment and availability of better jobs, requiring higher qualifications.

Among the SRCs, declines in WFPR are the lowest for Muslims-General (3.3%) and the highest among Hindu-OBCs (9.6%) followed by SCs/STs (9.0%). Hindus and UC-Hindus

---

[6] The decline in WFPR among these categories may be on account of the appreciable increases in the literacy rates over the years; however, the data do not allow to investigate the relationship.

report a decline of 8.3 per cent and 5.9 per cent, respectively. Muslims (3.8%) and Muslim-OBCs (4.2%) exhibit relatively lower declines in WFPR. Across levels of education, the declines exhibit extreme variations. For example, the highest contributor to the decline in WFPR in case of SCs/STs is the diploma/certificate course (9.9%) closely followed by the 'Not-literate' category (9.2%). The decline in the category of below primary, primary and middle (Group A, henceforth) is 16.7 per cent. In case of Hindu-OBCs, higher secondary level of education contributes 11 per cent fall in the WFPR followed by a decline of 9.9 per cent due to the 'Not-literate' category which in turn is higher than the decline due to graduates (8.8%). Group A's contribution to the decline is 20.2 per cent. In case of Muslims, the decline in the WFPR is mainly due to graduates (7.4%), which is also the case with Muslim-OBCs, wherein graduates account for 10.9 per cent of decline in the WFPR. The contribution of Group A in case of Muslims is 6.9 per cent and in case of Muslim-OBCs is slightly lower at 6.5 per cent. Muslims are an interesting exception in terms of the gap in the rural–urban declines in WFPRs across the SRCs. Except for Muslims, the gaps in decline in WFPR across rural–urban are large. For example, the respective rural–urban ratios for SCs/STs (14.9% and 3.4%), Hindus (9.8% and 3.1%), Hindu-OBCs (10.4% and 5.2%) and UC-Hindus (8.8% and 1.4%) exhibit skewedness towards the rural areas. In case of Muslims, the rural–urban declines show more coherence and relation. For example, the respective rural–urban declines for Muslims (4.3% and 2.5%), Muslim-OBCs (5.0 and 2.4%) and Muslims-General (3.3% and 2.9%) are relatively low in magnitude as well as in dispersion. The gender-based differential in rural–urban decline is on the same pattern across all SRCs with female WFPR declining with a higher magnitude than the MLFPR. Across the levels of education, Muslim-OBCs have reported increase in the WPR for PG and above, and the increase in case of women is most striking. Muslim-OBC women in the rural areas with education level of PG and above have exhibited an increase of 75.7 per cent, the highest increase by any educational level among all SRCs. Similarly, rural Muslim-OBC men have reported an increase of

16.9 per cent in the WFPR within the same level of education. On the contrary, women with same level of education in the urban areas have reported a decline of 35.4 per cent in the WPR during the reference period. Muslim women from the General category with same educational level exhibit a decline of 62.3 per cent in WFPR. However, it is noteworthy that the number of Muslim women (both in the General as well as in the OBC category) with such level of education as a proportion of the literate population within Muslims is extremely low as such any increase or decrease in the absolute number inflates or deflates the net rate at a larger scale, as is the case here.

Enrolment in Educational Institutes: SER

Age-based analysis of the labour force and WFPRs returned appreciable declines in case of the 15–19 and 20–24 years' age groups. In the Indian context as elsewhere, this age group comprises of the proportion of population attending educational institutions. A drop in LFPR/WFPR in higher magnitudes over the reference group among these age groups should naturally translate into higher proportions of students in the population. This trend is strikingly present in the Indian case across all SRCs, though with variations (Tables A.9 and A.10 in the Appendix). At the aggregate level, increase in the proportion of students in the 15–19 years, 20–24 years and 25–29 years age groups has been 18.5 per cent, 9.1 per cent and 1 per cent, respectively. Increase in the proportion of females in the student's category is marginally lower than that of the males. However, in case of the age group 15–19 years, females fare marginally better than males as against an unfavourable position in 20–24 years and 25–29 years.[7] Rural–urban comparisons reveal that the increase in the proportion of students in the rural areas has grown by around twice of that of the urban. However, the male–female growth in rural areas has almost been similar in magnitude, with females

---

[7] This phenomenon is a pointer towards higher dropouts among females during transition to higher secondary and graduate education.

registering slightly higher ratios in the age group of 15–19 years as against a lower ratio of almost its half in 20–24 years' age group. At the aggregate in rural areas, increase in the female educational attainment (10.2%) is lower than the male educational attainment (12.0%). This differential is narrower in the urban scenario wherein the respective male female ratios are of the order of 7.7 per cent and 6.6 per cent. Females in the urban space have appreciated their institutional attendance almost at par with males and in case of 25–29 years, their proportional increase to the student ratio is four times of the men as against a crucial negative difference[8] of 2 per cent in the age group of 15–19. For all SRCs, the national level patterns are reinforced across rural–urban spaces and gender. However, the Muslim share to the total increase in the proportion of students (13.7%) has been on the lower side in comparison to all other SRCs. At the aggregate, SCs/STs and Hindus exhibit an increase of about 20 per cent in attendance at educational institutions as against a 23.3 per cent by Hindu-OBCs and 15 per cent by UC-Hindus in the age group of 15–19 years. In case of 20–24 years' age group, Hindus (9.8%), Hindu-OBCs (10.8%), UC-Hindus (13.8%) report very high comparative increases in educational attendance. Other minorities report increase of 14.1 per cent and 11.8 per cent in the age groups of 15–19 years and 20–24 years, respectively. Muslims (13.7% and 5.3%), Muslim-OBCs (13.2% and 5.1%), Muslims-General (15.0% and 6.1%) have exhibited comparatively lesser increases in 15–19 years and 20–24 years student proportions, respectively. Rural–urban differentials are almost of same relative magnitude across all SRCs as proportion of their respective aggregates, except a larger spread (favouring rural areas) in case of UC-Hindus. Gender-based differentials in the increase in educational–institutional attendance are

---

[8] This difference is crucial in the sense that this age group represents the transition from secondary school to higher secondary, within the Indian educational system, wherein women participation is already lesser than the men. There needs to be higher increases for women enrolments across this age group so as to catch up on educational attainment with men.

the least (in rural as well as in urban areas) among Muslims (Muslim-OBCs as well as Muslims-General). For the age group 25–29 years, no significant variations are observed except a proportionally higher increase registered by Hindus (both male and female), and a decline by Muslim-OBCs for females in the rural areas and males in the urban. Females belonging to Muslim-General in the age group 25–29 years report an increase of 4 per cent in educational–institutional attendance across the reference period. This falls in line with our earlier finding of higher retraction of labour force as well as workforce participation of Muslim women in the same age group.

URs by Age and Education[9]

Indian UR (UPSS) for all working age population (15–64 years) was 2.4 per cent in 2004–2005 and has marginally dropped down to 2.2 per cent in 2011–2012 (Tables A.11 and A.12 in the Appendix).[10] Disaggregating the change in unemployment across different levels for the SRCs reveals that unemployment for different SRCs across the same level of education has varied differently. These differences occur across the rural–urban and gender basis. At the aggregate level, the decline of 0.1 per cent has been a result of a decline in the unemployment in the urban areas for both men and women. Employment scenario in the

---

[9] This indicator shows the URs of people according to their education levels. The unemployed are defined as people without work but actively seeking employment and currently available to start work. This indicator measures the percentage of unemployed 15–64-year-olds among 15–64-year-olds in the labour force.

[10] Exact figures for the decline as returned by the data after extraction from respective NSSO rounds are 2.2208 and 2.3644 for 2004–2005 and 2011–2012, respectively, which when subtracted yield a net difference of –0.143585776132605. However, for analysis purposes, the figures were rounded up to one decimal places and as such in practice the actual decline in the UR is actually 0.1 per cent but we retain the 2.4 per cent and 2.2 per cent figures when referring to individual years but report the difference over the reference period as that of –0.1 per cent.

rural areas has remained almost unchanged across the reference period. In the urban areas, decline in unemployment was 0.1 per cent with females recording a decline of 1.7 per cent. This decline in female unemployment is twice the decline exhibited by men (0.8%). Unemployment among rural men has declined by 0.1 per cent and in case of women by 0.2 per cent. Thus, except for urban men, the overall decline in the unemployment over the reference period has been driven by declines in the unemployment of females who have exhibited huge drop in unemployment across higher levels of education. Women in the aggregate have had 4.6 per cent, 7.5 per cent, 4.4 per cent and 5.8 per cent drop in the unemployment levels over secondary, higher secondary, *diploma/certificate* courses and graduate, respectively. The respective shares of decline in UR for men for these levels of education were 1.6 per cent, 0.8 per cent, 1.1 per cent, 0.2 per cent and an increase in unemployment (0.4%) for PG and above (Tables A.13 and A.14 in the Appendix). The decreases in unemployment in case of rural women are more striking, more so for higher secondary, graduate and PG and above levels of education. Rural men with PG and above had the highest of all increases in UR over the reference period. This contrasts with majority of OECD countries who have consistently recorded higher employment rates for higher levels of education. On average across OECD countries, 83 per cent of the population with tertiary education is employed. In Iceland, Norway, Sweden and Switzerland, the average employment rate of tertiary-educated individuals is over 88 per cent. The OECD average falls to about 74 per cent for people with upper secondary and post-secondary non-tertiary education and to just below 56 per cent for those without an upper secondary education (OECD, 2012). For higher levels of education, women have exhibited relatively higher falls in the UR over the men. For the illiterate as well as those with below primary education levels, no significant changes have occurred over the reference period.

Across the SRCs (except Muslims, especially Muslims in the General category) at the aggregate level, no appreciable change in UR (all levels of education taken together) has taken place.

In case of SCs/STs and Hindu-OBCs, Hindus, UC-Hindus and other socio-religious minorities' UR has exhibited declines of 0.1 per cent, 0.5 per cent and 0.9 per cent, respectively. For Muslims and Muslims-General, the UR has gone up by 0.1 per cent and 0.9 per cent, respectively. Across the rural urban space, SCs/STs, Hindu-OBCs, Muslims and Muslims-General have observed increases in the URs of the magnitude of 0.2 per cent, 0.1 per cent, 0.2 per cent and 0.5 per cent, respectively. In the urban area, there is a fall in unemployment across all SRCs except for Muslims-General who exhibit an increase of 1.4 per cent in unemployment for all levels of education. This increase has been driven by large unemployment ratios for higher secondary education (5.1%) and diploma/certificate courses (3.5%). Females as stated earlier show excessive drop in unemployment (at higher levels of education) in both the rural as well as urban areas across all SRCs. This decline in the female UR is more striking in case of Muslims (OBC as well as General) than any other SRC.

In the earlier sections, a broad-based understanding of important labour market ratios has been attempted. It allows for explicating the participation of individuals in the labour market across different socio-economic characteristics. From this analysis, various socio-economic characteristics seem to be effecting the participation of an individual in the labour force. Gender, location, age, educational attainment as well as the socio-religious affiliation seem to be important determinants of labour force participation. However, to ascertain the partial impact of each of these determinants on labour force participation, a logistic regression model is employed in the next section. An attempt is made to identify and account for the effect of various socio-economic variables on labour force participation. Several diagnostic tests are conducted to ensure validity and reliability of the results. The chi-square test which is used to indicate the overall statistical significance of the logistic regression model exhibits a p-value of (Prob > chi2 = 0.00000) implying that the model fits the data reasonably well and provides a better fit than an empty model with no predictors. Similarly, the Pseudo R2 (McFadden's pseudo R-squared) reported in the tables reveal that explanatory variables are meaningful in explaining variations in the response variable. Furthermore, visual inspection of Pearson Standardized Residuals against predicted probabilities displayed no influential observations thus assuming valid and consistent estimates. The results of the same are summarized in the following section.

Determinants of Labour Force Participation: Results from Logistic Model

This section examines factors affecting labour force participation in India. Labour force participation is defined as 'the percentage of the number of employed persons, in any category including self-employed, unpaid family work and causal labour in all sectors of the economy in relation to the total working-age population' (Salazar-Xirinachs et al., 2014). Results of the logit model (Table 3.3) as indicatives of the relationship between the dependent and the explanatory variables are reported. However, to further broaden the understanding, an attempt has been made to understand the magnitude of the impact of a given explanatory variable on the independent variable. For the same, results of the logistic model are also reported (Table A.15 in the Appendix) alongside those of the logit. All estimates from the logistic model are represented by odds ratios.[11] Odds ratios equal to 1 indicate no relationship, 'values greater than 1 show positive relationships and values below 1 display a negative relationship'. By investigating the significance of the exponentiated coefficients, we can immediately establish that all the independent variables identified in the model are statistically significant in determining labour force participation of the individuals.

LFPR is affected by place of residence. Estimates from the logit model reveal that the labour force participation continues to

[11] Odds ratio can be expressed as $p/(1-p)$ where p is the probability of participating in the labour force, which is a function of covariates x.

TABLE 3.3 *Result of Logit Regression for Participation in Employment 2004–2005 and 2011–2012*

			Logit Results			
			NSSO 61st Round		NSSO 68th Round	
Nature of Variable	Broad Category	Variable Name	Coefficient	P > z	Coefficient	P > z
Independent	Individual characteristics	Location	Rural/urban	−0.6596	0.00	−0.4152	0.00
		Sex	Male/female	2.4017	0.00	2.6318	0.00
		Age	Age	0.6294	0.00	0.8868	0.00
		Age squared	Age squared	−0.3836	0.00	−0.4756	0.00
		Education	Primary education	−0.1193	0.00	0.1611	0.00
			Secondary education	−0.6680	0.00	−0.4460	0.00
			Higher secondary/diploma	−0.6953	0.00	−0.6476	0.00
			Graduate & above	0.0834	0.00	0.2812	0.00

Socio-religious status	SCs/STs	0.3579	0.00	0.4237	0.00
	Hindu-OBCs	0.2670	0.00	0.2039	0.00
	Muslim-OBCs	−0.3997	0.00	−0.1857	0.00
	Muslims-General	−0.3707	0.00	−0.0912	0.00
	Other minorities	0.3044	0.00	0.2900	0.00
Household characteristics	Ownership of land	0.1003	0.00	0.0000	0.00
Edu. of household head	Primary education	−0.1777	0.00	−0.1850	0.00
	Secondary education	−0.4808	0.00	−0.3523	0.00
	Higher secondary/diploma	−0.6344	0.00	−0.4149	0.00
	Graduate & above	−0.8257	0.00	−0.7824	0.00

Source: Author's own computation from unit level data of NSSO (61st and 68th rounds).

Note: ** $p < 0.05$.

be higher in the rural areas as compared to the urban. With a significant but negative value, the odds of participation in the urban areas are lower by about 40 per cent in 2004–2005 but have come down to about 34 per cent in 2011–2012. This result is in conformity with the Government of India estimate that the LFPR for rural areas stands at 54.7 per cent which is much greater than that for urban areas, that is, 47.2 per cent (GOI, 2011a).

These results hold true for the entire reference period. Women continue to be less likely to participate in labour force. A negative sign of the coefficient of gender for the logit model confirms this result. Results from the logistic regression give us some approximation of the magnitude of the impact of gender on labour force participation. Labour force participation over the reference period has come down significantly. With an odds ratio of 0.920 for 2004–2005 and a corresponding ratio of 0.635 with negative sign, the probability of women to participate in the labour force has come down by about 29 per cent. This coincides with the findings of the World Bank that women in most countries are less likely than men to participate in the labour force (WHO, UNICEF, UNFPA and The World Bank, 2012). This result is also consistent with the findings obtained by Bjørkhaug and Øyslebø Sørensen (2012), Hatløy et al. (2012), Kebede et al. (2012) and Verick (2014) conducted in developing countries. Similarly, in developed countries, for example, the USA, Japan, Australia and Canada, labour force participation of women is lower than their male counterparts (World Bank, 2014).

Age and age squared were statistically significant across the reference period with expected positive and negative signs. The negative sign of age squared implies that labour force participation increases with age up to a certain point, but then diminishes as individuals get older. Hence, the relationship between age and labour force participation exhibits an inverted U-shape relationship. Furthermore, both age and age squared are found significant in most labour force participation empirical studies.

The levels of education (illiterates, primary, secondary and higher education/diploma) were found to be inversely related to labour force participation in 2004–2005. Education levels of graduation and above on the other hand had a positive impact on labour force participation. In 2011–2012, primary education has had a positive impact on labour force participation indicating that people with primary education in comparison to illiterates are more likely to be participating in the labour force. The relationship of all other levels of educational attainment with labour force participation in 2011–2012 continues to be the same as in 2004–2005. Secondary, higher secondary/ diploma levels of education variables are statistically significant with a negative sign implying that these levels of education are negatively related to labour force participation when compared to that of no education. Primary education contributes to the likelihood of labour force participation in almost the same magnitude in 2004–2005 as well as 2011–2012.

However, secondary education, higher secondary/diploma levels of education variables are statistically significant with a negative sign, indicating that the odds of participation decreased by almost 12 per cent, 49 per cent and 51 per cent, respectively, compared to no education in 2004–2005. Thus, the basic educational attainment is not a prerequisite for entering the labour market in India. Furthermore, secondary education, higher secondary/diploma, graduate and above levels are statistically significant with negative signs. The estimates 0.888 and 0.513 and 0.499 indicate that secondary education, higher secondary/diploma, graduate and above levels have negative effect on labour force participation and decrease the probability of participating by almost 12 per cent, 41 per cent and 51 per cent, respectively, in contrast to individuals without education. Except for secondary education wherein the odds have turned in favour of participation with a positive sign, the impact of education on labour force participation is consistent and has become stronger over the period. Globally, higher education and skill acquisition is linked to favourable labour market outcomes for individuals, including higher labour force participation, higher wages and enhanced job benefits. Also, well-educated individuals are less likely to become unemployed, discouraged or drop out from the labour force. However, in the Indian context, evidence is contrary to this link.

Probability of labour force participation in a multicultural country is also affected by socio-religious status of the individuals. The variable socio-religious status, further classified into relevant socio-religious categories, captures the impact on labour force participation with respect to UC-Hindus. Hindus of the UC, thus, form the reference group in the analysis. Relationship between the socio-religious status of an individual and his participation in the labour force is discussed with reference to UC-Hindus. Socio-religious statuses like SCs/STs Hindu-OBCs and other minorities are positively related to labour force participation. All these SRC statuses are positively related to labour force participation both in 2004–2005 and in 2011–2012. However, the socio-religious status of being a Muslim—both in the General as well as in the OBC category—has a negative relationship with labour force participation of an individual. All SRC statuses, except that of belonging to the Muslim community, has a positive impact on labour force participation in 2011–2012. This result is in conformity with the SCR of 2006.

Thus, what emerges from the logit results is the fact that belonging of an individual to the Muslim community reduces the probability of his participation in the labour force. SCs/STs, Hindu-OBCs and other minorities' status is statistically significant at the 5 per cent level with a positive sign, which highlights that individuals of these socio-religious backgrounds are likely to be employed. Interestingly, belonging to Muslims-General and other minorities decreased the odds of labour force participation by 33 per cent and 31 per cent, respectively, in 2004–2005 but this seems to have slowed down in 2011–2012 to 17 per cent and 8 per cent, respectively, although the relation continues to be negative.

Among the household characteristics, ownership of land has a positive impact on labour force participation. This result holds for both the time periods. Ownership of land by a household increased the probability of participation (of an individual) in the labour force both in 2004–2005 as well as in 2011–2012. Education of the household head and its impact on labour force participation does not vary with the levels of his educational attainment. Across all levels of education, it is observed that individuals with educated heads in the households relate negatively to labour force participation in comparisons to those who have illiterate household heads. Thus, education of the household head is negatively related to the labour force participation of an individual.

Theoretically, the household head as the *breadwinner* of the family is expected to engage in the labour force compared to other household members. With higher levels of education of the household head, odds of labour force participation of the members of the household decrease. This positive link between household head and labour force participation of individuals is in line with the finding of Fadayomi and Olurinola (2014).

Summary and Findings

India has exhibited a decline in the WFPR and LFPR over the reference period. Retraction of women from the labour market has been the major contributing factor to this phenomenon. The major reasons for their retraction seem to emanate from (a) increasing attendance in educational institutions, (b) increased household income, which reduces the need for female labour, (c) changes in measurement methodology related to some types of female employment and (d) insufficient job opportunities for women (Salazar-Xirinachs et al., 2014). The results provided by data indicate that for women, level of education and participation rates have an inverse relationship at least up to secondary education. Socio-economic status of a household may explain this phenomenon. To complement household's income through market work in order to meet minimum subsistence needs may lead women from poorer household out of school and as such increase their participation in the labour market (Dasgupta & Goldar, 2005). With increases in household income, women drop out of the labour force to attend to domestic non-market work. However, the trend is not universal. Women with higher levels of education and affluence have higher participation rates. Literature maintains that 'women benefit from increased investment in their human capital and may be able to obtain jobs with better working conditions and adequate remuneration' (Klasen & Pieters, 2012).

The major exhibits of an analysis of the important labour market ratios (LFPR and WFPR across age and education) reveals a larger retraction of people from the labour market in the age group of 15–19 years. This has had a complementary increase of 18.5 per cent increase in the SER for the age group 15–19 years, although we do not claim to establish a link between the drop in the LFPR and the increase in the SER. However, these declines in LFPR and increases in the student ratio are not evenly distributed across the SRCs. In case of Muslims, the decline in LFPR emanating from age group 15–19 years is extremely low as compared to the national average and all other SRCs and in case of women it is lower. Thus, more Muslims (relative to other SRCs) in the age group 15–19 years continue to report in larger numbers at the labour market and their release from the labour market is relatively inflexible. There does not seem to be any change in this, a crucial aspect of human capital development amid an overall increase in the SER over the reference period. Muslims (13.7% and 5.3%), Muslim-OBCs (13.2% and 5.1%), Muslims-General (15.0% and 6.1%) have exhibited comparatively lesser increases in 15–19 and 20–24 years' student proportions, respectively. This indeed has serious implications on the educational attainment of the Muslims who are already exhibiting lower educational attainment and hence are less visible at higher positions both in the public as well as in the private sector. Even at the front of employment, in case of SCs/STs and Hindu-OBCs, Hindus, UC-Hindus and other minorities' UR has exhibited decline of 0.1 per cent, 0.5 per cent and 0.9 per cent, respectively. For Muslims and Muslims-General, the UR has gone up by 0.1 per cent and 0.9 per cent, respectively.

The logistic regression results as reported here ascertain the Sachar Committee revelations of 2006. Even in 2011–2012, the socio-religious status of being a Muslim—both in the General as well as in the OBC category—has a negative relationship with labour force participation of an individual. All SRC statuses, except that of belonging to the Muslim community, have a positive impact on labour force participation in 2011–2012. Thus, belonging of an individual to the Muslim community reduces the probability of his participation in the labour force. Given the fact that the regression analysis reported here has controlled for all other relevant characteristics of individuals, the negative sign of β_{10} and β_{11} reveal the negative impact of being a Muslim on labour force participation.

Consistent suboptimal employment outcomes as exhibited by Muslims in India and a negative relationship of being a Muslim and the LFPR can be attributed to a variety of factors. Prominent among them are the *attitudinal bias* of the individual and the *discouraged workers effect*. The former refers to an individual's indifference to labour force participation that can emanate from a variety of reasons. Perception of discrimination on the basis of gender, ethnicity, religious affiliation or location are the major causative factors. This in turn can lead to the *discouraged workers effect*. Following which people who perceive discrimination report lower at the labour market. Their employment outcomes worsen. Human capital accumulation can also get negatively impacted, as the perceived returns seem to be low. This pushes these individuals to the lower rung jobs. As reported by Sachar Committee and other related literature, Indian Muslims have a deep rotted perception of being discriminated. Historical accounts as discussed in Chapter 4 do strongly point out to valid reasons for such a perception both in colonial as well as in independent India. To empirically investigate the issue of perception of discrimination and fairness in distribution of employment opportunity in the Indian labour market, we turn to the next chapter. This exercise will allow us to explore some answers to the relationship of being a Muslim and reporting suboptimal employment allocation within the context of opportunity and fairness in the labour market.

4

Examining Employment Opportunities Using the Human Opportunity Index Framework

As discussed in Chapter 3, Indian Muslims are at a relative disadvantaged position vis-a-vis other SRC groups in the Indian labour market. This lacking of Indian Muslims rests on various dimensions. First, their LFPR and WFPR are consistently low. Second, access to and enrolment in educational institutions are also lower. The belonging of an individual to the Muslim community reduces his/her probability of participation in the labour market. Muslims continue to be the most disadvantageous SRC as far as employment is concerned. In the received literature, varied explanations are put forth for this *negative consistency*. Muslims are labelled as 'docile' and 'immune to change' in the varying global scenario: there is 'something' inherent in

Islam that inhibits Muslim participation in the labour market. One of the major arguments given to justify these claims is the occurrence of purdah and relegation of Muslim women to the household chores. Purdah appears to be the most obvious explanation for women's seclusion and their isolation from the labour market.

In isolation, female labour force participation is linked to religious affiliation. However, as argued by Karl Polanyi (1994, p. 162), 'Markets for labour, land and money are easy to distinguish; but it is not so easy to distinguish those parts of a culture the nucleus of which is formed by human beings, their natural surroundings, and productive organizations, respectively'. Explanations for lower labour force participation by women in general and Muslim women in particular are to be understood in the framework as proposed by Polanyi. Labour force participation is multidimensional. Sociocultural, economic and political environment as well as power relations within the society explain labour force participation in general and for women in particular. Undervaluation of women's work is well documented in the received literature. In all socioeconomic settings, women's work is undervalued both in the home as well as outside (Desai & Jain, 1994; Kapadia, 1995; Kemp & Wan Jr., 1986). This gives rise to a gender stratification system in the labour market. Such an arrangement results into women's lower opportunities in the formal labour market. Skill gaps and reproductive responsibilities limit women's access to labour market opportunities. Women tend to be in low paying informal occupations or out of the labour force altogether (Elson, 1999; Ghosh, 1995; Morrison et al., 2007; Sethuraman, 1998). Any attempt to link lesser labour force participation of Muslim women only to their religious affiliation is hence based on perilous foundations.

In this backdrop, this chapter attempts to unsnarl perpetual employment disadvantage of Muslims. Relationship between opportunity/access to employment and labour markets outcomes is investigated. Causative factors of lesser visibility of

Muslims are discussed from the standpoint of opportunity.[1] Circumstances prevalent in the Indian labour market and the characteristic features of the individual(s) who are seeking and are available for work are analysed. The rationale for equating labour market access and opportunities to an individual's circumstances allow an understanding of the labour market dynamics. This approach offers an understanding of the labour market with originality and freshness of the idea and purpose. I construct HOI[2] for Indian labour market and place the SRCs within the emergent framework. Relative position of the Indian Muslims vis-a-vis other SRCs and the total population is analysed.

This approach is motivated by:

- The general perception of discrimination against Muslims in India in all walks of life (Sachar Committee, 2006).[3]

[1] A definition of the concept relevant to our discussion of opportunity is that of Roemer (1998). Roemer spoke of the outcome of interest, say employment, as an 'advantage' and divided the determinants of advantage into two groups: efforts, which are subject to individual choice, and circumstances, which are factors that lie outside the individual's control, namely race, gender, sex, religion, place of birth, etc. Equality of opportunity within a country or society would prevail in a situation in which the distribution of an outcome of interest is independent of circumstances. Equal opportunity levels the playing field, and everybody has, in principle, the potential to achieve the outcomes of their choosing.

[2] It is the coverage rate of a good or service discounted by how equitably it is distributed among groups with different circumstances, such as gender, race and family background and religion. This discount factor is the dissimilarity index.

[3] The SCR refers to various kinds of perceived as well as established cases/instances of discrimination (as reported to it by various stakeholders from within the Muslim community across the Indian states) across many pages of the report. Noteworthy to mention are the assertions made at page numbers: 15, 16, 19, 22 and 24. Variety of discrimination is mentioned to be reported by the members of the community across many Indian states.

- These perceptions could never be either proved or refuted on empirical basis (Sachar Committee, 2006).
- Perception with regards to the discrimination against Muslims is complex, deep and noticeable in all walks of life (Sachar Committee, 2006).
- Discriminatory approach against Muslims has occasioned for them as a perpetual inequality of opportunity in access to and realization of public services in general and enhancement of their capabilities in particular.

This approach marks a departure from earlier studies on inequality of opportunity from two important perspectives: first, *to the best of my knowledge and effort, I could not locate any study discussing employment distributions and individual's accessibility to them within the framework of inequality in access to employment on the basis of circumstances, especially in case of religious affiliation and social status of the treatment group within a countrywide labour market setting.* All the studies reviewed/ searched via different media in the context of opportunity in labour market, although few, are cross-country analysis.[4] Generally constructed on observed income (or its proxies, like consumption), these studies/approaches do not clearly consider employment or jobs for measuring inequality. *Second, in context of India, as also elsewhere, estimating the extent of divergence in access to employment (at disaggregated level)—conditional upon circumstances—in the labour market, by applying the HOI framework has not at all been investigated.* Thus, at least in the Indian case, a new dimension to understand labour market inequalities is added by way of the analysis carried out in this chapter. The central hypothesis is: 'unequal participation rates for differential religious affiliations have got to be understood in context of the differentials (if any) in the access to employment opportunities'.

[4] These include Bourguignon, Ferreira and Menendez (2007); Van de Gaer (1993); Lefranc, Pistolesi and Trannoy (2008) and Ferreira, Gignoux and Aran (2011).

Theoretical Background

Scholars in the field of egalitarianism[5] have determinedly been advocating for a *level playing field*[6] for one and all. With Rawls (1971) work, the idea of egalitarianism took a different direction and came under serious criticism. Rawls introduced the concept of individual responsibility as a qualifier for any notion of equality. This 'Rawalsian intervention' transformed the notion of egalitarianism and its basic tenants took a new course. The effort following Rawls (1971) got directed towards replacing equality of outcomes with equality of opportunities. This was followed by appreciable (both in content and context) socio-philosophical contributions from the left and the right. Amartya Sen (1980) initiated it with oft-quoted three simple but powerfully worded question of *equality of what?* Ronald Dworkin (1981a, 1981b) responded with advocacy of preference of 'equality of resources' over 'equality of welfare', linking the debate back to the Rawlsian system. This was later supplemented by Richard Arneson (1989), who proposed and defended the welfarist tradition of the egalitarian distributive justice but later recanted the same by putting up a framework for what he meant by *equality of opportunity for welfare.* Arneson's response to the Amartya Sen question *equality of what?* is a refined form of the distributive justice plank. Arneson (1999), in the recant of his earlier approach, argues the pursuance of 'equality of opportunity' and 'equal opportunity' with the caveat that it needed to be emphasized. 'What matters fundamentally from the moral standpoint is not the opportunities one gets but the outcomes one's opportunities generate' (Arneson, 1999). Cohen (1989), while defending the Rawlsian framework, argues against an earlier criticism of the same by Robert Nozick (1974) who as per Cohen had misinterpreted the Rawlsian scheme, especially what Cohen refers to as the

---

[5] Egalitarianism in the welfarist tradition of the celebrated social choice theory means equality of welfare or utility. It lays emphasis on equality for all in social, cultural and economic life.

[6] The phrase is due to Roemer (1993).

expensive taste argument.[7] This debate concerning *equality of what?* is still central to the philosophical realm of what should be the aim and focus of equality, and, if at all, equality, as such, is a deemed good objective of individual and society. Arneson's emphasis on equality of opportunity is carried forward with refinements by John Roemer who, besides contributing to the ensuing debate, developed an algorithm for calculating policies aiming at equalizing opportunities for achievement of a given objective in a population (Roemer, 1993, 1998). Roemer (1993), Fleurbaey and Maniquet (1997) and Fleurbaey (1994) argue for *qualified compensations* within the framework of distributive justice. The compensation principle advocated by these scholars advocates for compensating those individuals who lacked access to opportunities as a consequence of certain rigidities prevalent in the social system. Such rigidities are a type of glass ceiling that inhibit the upward socio-economic and political mobility of the underprivileged and marginalized sections of the society. These frameworks addressing different dimensions of the 'transferability' and 'compensation' were updated and summarized in Fleurbaey (2008). Other notable contributions to the debate of equality and equal opportunity are Bossert (1995), Peragine (2004) and Van de gaer (1993). These studies brought in the issue of intergenerational mobility and its impact on opportunities and individual capacities to excel through the human capital channel. Of late, empirical literature is rapidly developing, calculating the extent to which opportunities for the acquisition of various objectives are unequal in various countries (Abras, Hoyos, Narayan, & Tiwari, 2013).

Measurement and quantification were the major focus of the scholarly works on inequality. However, following Rawls and Dworkin, inequality literature has witnessed a change in focus. Renewed emphasis on 'some kinds of inequality being ethically objectionable and the extent to which economists

---

[7] The philosophical literature generated by these pioneers is too large to list here. Book length treatments that should be mentioned are Rakowski (1994) and Hurley (2003).

might be measuring something that is not ethically salient' guided this change. Distinction between morally acceptable and unacceptable inequality is the major contribution of this change. This latter development is perhaps the most important contribution of philosophical egalitarian thought of the last 40 years (Abras, Hoyos, Narayan, & Tiwari 2013). What has percolated from the perspectives of both the social choice theory and the equal opportunity theory is the latter's challenge to the former in terms of establishing that the emphasis on final outcomes is flawed. This conclusion regarding the final outcomes follows, because *final outcomes* such as utility, or even intermediated outcomes, such as income, wealth or education, depend in large part on choices made by individuals themselves. It is only till the individual choices[8] determine the final differences in achievement that the individual can be held responsible. However, following Roemer (1998), identification and decomposition of varied factors contributing to inequality into circumstances and efforts, and their effect on the final outcomes, attracted contributions to the theory (Bourguignon, Ferreira, & Menendez, 2007; Van de gaer, 1993), and measurement techniques (Checchi & Peragine, 2010; Ferreira & Gignoux, 2011), of this phenomenon. The development of measurement techniques in the field of equality of opportunity have put the underlying philosophical debate about equality into latent dormancy, for it has again shifted the attention to quantification of the contributing factors of inequality and their measurement instead. This development of late may perhaps make the answer to the Amartya Sen question much clearer, at least on empirical lines. A shift towards measurement of contributions to inequality would allow identifying the more robust explanatory variables and consequently more attention to be paid towards realization of equality of such explanatory variables. These explanations (as do other realities) might be

---

[8] Sen (1980) was particularly concerned with interpersonal comparability of utility and with the fact that different people may have different maps from the commodity to the utility space. Though important in their own right, those issues are tangential to the discussion at hand.

eluding us due to our ignorance or multiple nuances involved in explication of the same. As argued earlier, Dworkin (1981a), Arneson (1989, 1990), Cohen (1989) and Sen (1984, 1985) are among the pioneering influential authors to have argued against specific *outcomes*—such as incomes—as the appropriate yardstick for evaluating the fairness of a given allocation or social system. Notwithstanding significant differences in nuance,[9] all these authors have conceded that some outcome differences, which are attributable to differences in choices for which individuals can be held responsible, may be ethically acceptable. Thus, the unacceptable inequalities stand identified as those housed in a logically prior space of what Sen called *capabilities* and Roemer had referred to as *circumstances*, upon which the individual has no control and as such cannot be held responsible for. This critical distinction between outcome differences, for which the individual can be held responsible and those for which he/she cannot be, has played a central role in shaping political philosophy for the last half a century. Following Arneson to the extent that opportunities should result into desirable outcomes, I investigate on empirical lines the access to employment opportunities and the resultant outcome of getting employed in the Indian labour market.

Conceptual Framework: Equalizing Opportunity

What follows from the earlier theoretical frameworks is the emergence of the concept of *opportunity* as an alternative to the emphasis upon final *outcome*. This transition of focus has paved the way for formulation of new approaches to realize equality

---

[9] Time and space constraints prevent us from exploring these differences in nuance here. They may well be philosophically important and have been reviewed extensively (see, e.g., Roemer, 1993). The point here is simply that all of these approaches contributed to a shift away from seeking equality in outcomes, and towards assessing social justice with respect to a 'prior' space of enabling conditions faced by individuals, while according an ethically acceptable role to individual responsibility and its consequences.

of opportunity within and across societies (Roemer, 1993). Of late, appreciable progress has been made on the measurement of inequality of opportunity. World development report (World Bank, 2006) commenced the measurement processes by providing the theoretical and policy salience to this concept. The report argued: inequality of opportunity, both within and across nations, resulted in wasted human potential and weakens prospects for overall prosperity. Various approaches to measurement of inequality of opportunity have proliferated in the last 10 years. Broadly, two approaches have been adopted in this direction. The first is generally based on observed income (or its proxies, like consumption).[10] This approach falls within the ambit of traditional statistic approach of economics of quantification of the quantifiable numeric. The second and the latest known is the HOI approach. The HOI was originally formulated by the World Bank and some external researchers to assess country-level progress in making access to basic services such as quality schooling, health care, household and infrastructure amenities equitable.[11]

I adopt the World Bank advocated HOI approach to reveal the labour market opportunities in India for different circumstance groups. This approach ascribes occurrence of inequality to two different sources: (a) differences in circumstances, upon which the individual has no control and cannot be held

---

[10] These include Bourguignon, Ferreira and Menendez (2007); Van de Gaer (1993); Lefranc et al. (2008) and Ferreira, Gignoux and Aran (2011).

[11] In the technical jargon, following Roemer (1998), Römer (2001) and Bourguignon, Ferreira and Menendez (2007) have used either parametric or non-parametric approaches to measurement of inequality of opportunities in a country or region. On the other hand, again following Roemer, Van de gaer (1993), Ooghe and Schokkaert (2007), and Hild and Voorhoeve (2004) have operationalized inequality of opportunities through indirect channel effects. These studies have relied on estimation of the conditional expectations of earnings or consumption from the distribution of average income across several socio-economic categories and performing tests of stochastic dominance.

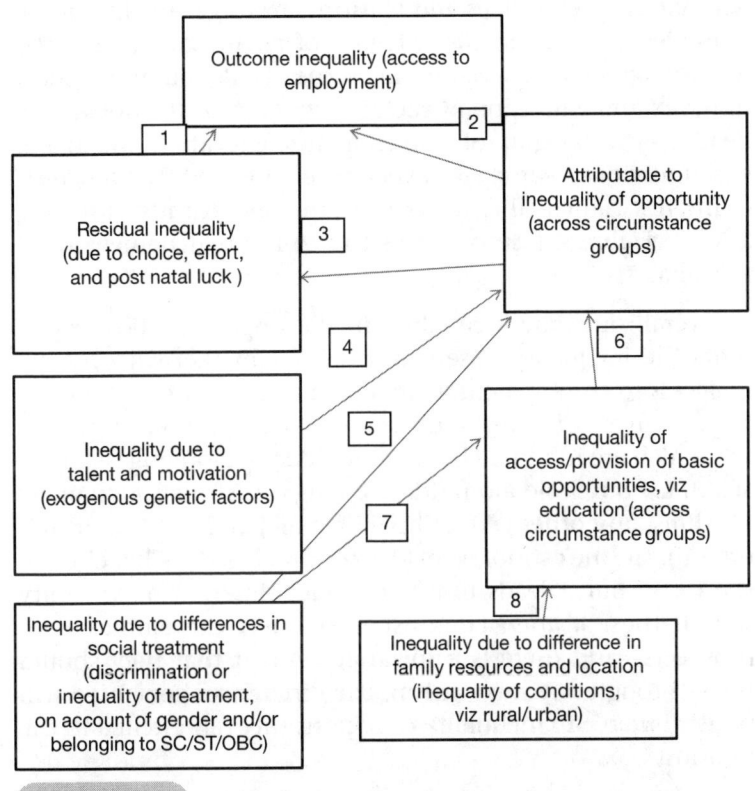

FIGURE 4.1 *Conceptual Framework of HOI Approach*

Source: Adapted from World Bank (2009).

responsible for realization of suboptimal outcomes (unethical inequality) and (b) difference in characteristics, which lie within the ambit of individual effort (the ethical inequality). See graphical illustration below (Figure 4.1) This property of the index allows us to formulate and conceptualize our analysis. Among the representatives of circumstances can be included race, gender, the family and socio-economic group into which an individual was born, the place where he/she was born, as well as any mental or physical characteristics he/she inherited at birth. In the category of characteristics, individual choice behaviour\preferences (education) and age are included. Variables included in the category of circumstances are: the socio-religious status, economic status of the household, location, sex and education of each individual and the household head. In the category of characteristics, education and age of each individual—proxy for experience—are used. The outcome of interest is inequality in access to the opportunity of having a job.[12] Figure 4.1 summarizes the conceptual framework of this analysis.

Overall outcome inequality, in the uppermost box, represents the inequality observed in labour market with respect to access to employment. Outcome inequality arises from two basic sources. *Circumstances* refer to the *a priori* set of properties which are inherited by the individual (belonging to an ST/SC/OBC household alongside the religious affiliation, namely Muslims, any other gender [male/female] and location [rural/urban]). He/she cannot be held accountable for his/her circumstance set but it leads him/her to face different opportunity sets. If these *a priori* circumstances affect the employment prospects—and there is a social agreement that they should not—through any mechanism, the differences generated will be attributable to inequality of opportunity represented in the topmost box.

Within this framework, the difference between the meritocratic approach[13] and the egalitarian view of stochastic independence between distribution of outcomes and circumstances becomes clear (Roemer, 1998). In the former case, any inequality in outcomes would flawlessly relate to differences in effort and choice. In this situation, circumstances might still

---

[12] Detailed description of the variables used and the operationalization procedure are given in the section on variables and data further.

[13] Meritocracy emphasizes final outcomes to be awarded according to skill and effort required for certain position as opposed to the equality of opportunity, with its emphasis on levelling the field before any competition takes place.

condition the outcome as they affect the choice set available to the individual (arrows 1 and 3, closing arrow 2). The egalitarian approach emphasizes the role of both the direct effect of circumstances on outcomes through arrow 2, as well as the indirect effect of circumstances on the set of choices facing the individual that operate through efforts and choice (arrow 3).

For example, in the Indian labour market, let us assume there does not exist any discrimination against any section of the society. However, as in case of Muslims, language barriers, cultural differences, differences in the types of schools attended, medium of instruction within schools result in consistent attainment of lower educational achievements. Some scant literature even relates to the fact that access of Muslim children to basic public services in general and education is lower than other religious communities (Desai & Kulkarni, 2008; Government of India, 2006). Since quality of education received is positively correlated with the expected returns in the labour market (Becker, 1964; Schultz, 1961; Welch, 1970), a rational decision on part of the individual with the aforementioned circumstances is to choose to invest less time in education. Lower earnings are entirely due to differences in education, which in this case has been a resultant of the individual choice. To the *meritocrat*, there does not exist any inequality of opportunity in the labour market for the reference group because education is part of the choice set of the individual, and people would be rewarded precisely in accordance with their educational achievements.

The egalitarian would view this society as opportunity unequal, because outcomes are not independent of circumstances, as emphasized upon earlier. Circumstances (being indigenous) may not affect outcomes directly through the labour market, but they affect them through the educational choices ('efforts' in Roemer's terminology) of the individual. Thus, the distribution of choices finally made is different across the two groups as a result of external impositions. Consequently, there exists a great deal of complementarity between circumstances and characteristics. In this case, even if arrow 2 is shut down, circumstances are affecting outcomes through arrows 1 and 3.

In absence of the linkages mandated by arrow 3, circumstances do not affect the choice set, and also closing down the direct effect through arrow 2 ensures that circumstances have no effect on outcomes. However, in general and in our example this is not the case. Earnings inequality will depend on the educational effort a young individual chooses to make. Is the educational effort independent of circumstances? Improbable! The best (and most empirically well-established) example is the dependence of a person's own schooling (which reflects effort) on parental education (a circumstance from the viewpoint of the child[14]). Available literature (Atkinson, Trinder, & Maynard, 1983; Bowles, 1972; Bowles & Nelson, 1974; Solon, 1992; Zimmerman, 1992) does point to parental income as a good predictor of individual income. Wherever intergenerational income mobility is low, inequality of opportunity is high and family background might have a large influence on economic achievement and welfare. Individuals from different family backgrounds do face very different access to basic services, and, through different channels, family background affects a host of outcomes throughout the lifetime (Behrman & Wolfe, 1984; Heckman & Hotz, 1986).

Apart from visible and quantifiable variables, inequality of opportunity can arise from such characteristics that are exogenous but intrinsic to the person. Observance of genetic endowment of talent and motivation (arrow 4) and their contribution to differences in productivity or achievement can result in a meritocratic environment. Correction of certain genetic disadvantages are reported to have important implications for equalizing opportunities (Jencks & Tach 2006). Roemer (1998) argues genetically inherited traits to be circumstance variables in an education production function.

---

[14] Among many good surveys, see Solon (1999) and Bowles and Gintis (2002).

In the labour market, one might observe differential treatment on the basis of certain circumstances (family background, race or place of origin). Wage differentials between Negros and Whites, men and women are well documented. Differential treatment of equally talented and productive individuals (Lund et al., 2011; Desai et al., 2010; Fazal, 2013a; Thorat & Newman, 2010) in hiring is a case in fact (Elliot, 2001; Papola, 2005).

In all these cases, as shown by arrow 5, inequality is generated by the unequal treatment of equally deserving individuals and, in general, parlance is referred to as discrimination. Inarguably discrimination is undesirable, but the amount of resources that a society should allocate to remove or minimize this inequality is a source of open debate.

Inequality in access to employment can also emanate from differential access to basic opportunities (arrow 6). This access differential can further be ascribed to difference in conditions of groups of a population. Socio-religious and economic groups are a case in example. SCs/STs and women in India are traditionally believed to have been discriminated against (arrow 7). The strong transmission mechanism between circumstances and charactcristics does generate outcome inequality even among equally talented people. Even when acquiring a characteristic, due to discrimination in the process, say even if admission to institutions is fair, but treatment while studying is determined by any circumstances, then experience inequality of outcomes is bound to prevail. Difference in condition also relates to social and economic position of the family (arrow 8). Even if children brought up in poor families are not discriminated against, lack of family resources do not allow them to access services that would allow them to fully utilize their talents. Consequent upon this accumulation of human and physical capital is hampered which eventually has an impact on outcomes like employment. Absence of family resources on the one hand impairs access to basic opportunities and, on the other, does not allow the benefits to be reaped from them.

I operationalize the conceptual framework by drawing from the HOI framework as used in the studies of inequality of opportunity in labour markets in Latin American countries (Barros, Ferreira, Vega, & Saavedra, 2009; Barros, Vega, & Saavedra, 2010). The novelty of this tool lies in the fact that it considers the critical difference between the circumstances and characteristics and their impact on final outcome. At the heart of the analysis lies the coverage rate of a service that goes to shape the prospects of an individual to realize higher human capital and be equipped with the requisite skill set so as to claim the desired outcome within the realm of circumstances. The circumstance-specific coverage rates are then aggregated into a scalar measure that increases with increase in coverage and decreases with the differences in coverage among sections of the population with different circumstances (Barros, Ferreira, Vega, & Saavedra, 2009). This allows us to disaggregate the effect of each of the circumstances on the outcome across groups in isolation of the characteristics. This property of the HOI is important to study, evaluate and establish, if at all 'religious affiliation has any role to play in the realization of a labour market outcome'.

HOI brings together the total number of employment opportunities available to the population and the fairness in distribution of these opportunities across the subsections of the society (Abras, Hoyos, Narayan, & Tiwari, 2013).[15] HOI (H) for an opportunity is the average coverage rate[16] of access ($\bar{C}$) multiplied by a factor [17]$(1 - D)$.

---

[15] Abras, Hoyos, Narayan and Tiwari (2013) attempted to quantify inequality of opportunity in labour market outcomes in Europe and Central Asia using the HOI methodology.

[16] Refers to the total number of opportunities available to the members of a society for attaining a certain outcome.

[17] *(1 − D)* is the equality factor that is equal to one if access to the opportunity is independent of the circumstances, in which HOI is equal to the average coverage rate. *D* can be interpreted as *the share of the total number of opportunities that needs to be reallocated between types to ensure equality of opportunities* (Abras, Hoyos, Narayan, & Tiwari, 2013).

$$H = \bar{C}(1-D) \tag{1}$$

D is the dissimilarity index[18] (henceforth, D-index). With disjoint types,[19] one can compute D as follows:

$$D = \frac{1}{2\bar{C}} \sum_{k=1}^{m} a_k \mid \bar{C} - C_k \mid \tag{2}$$

Here, k denotes a type (group of individuals with a specific set of circumstances); C_k the specific coverage rate of group k; a_k the share of group k in total population and m the numbers of disjoint groups defined by circumstances. D equates to zero when $C = \bar{C}$ for all k types, in which HOI equals the coverage rate. It can be shown that D is equal to the *share* of total opportunities that are misallocated in favour of (against) types that have coverage rates higher (lower) than $\bar{C}$. This also implies that any reallocation of opportunities to—vulnerable groups (those with coverage less than $\bar{C}$) from—non-vulnerable groups (with coverage more than $\bar{C}$) will reduce D and increase HOI. Thus, HOI improves when inequality between types decreases with a fixed number of opportunities in a society, or when the number of opportunities increases and inequality among types stays constant.

In the labour market, participants are characterized by both circumstances as well as characteristics. As such, inequality of opportunity between groups is to be measured. For the same, we estimate the D-index by running a logistic regression model to estimate the relationship between circumstances as well as characteristics of the participants in the labour market. Inequality of opportunity is estimated by decomposing the contribution of the circumstance effect to the D-index. We

[18] Measures the extent of equitable distribution of the opportunities across different groups in a given society.
[19] Disjoint types refer to different groups within a society that are segregated on the basis of difference in circumstances, such as religion, location, gender or social group.

adopt the decomposition proposed by Shorrocks (2013) and adopted by World Bank (2013).

Decomposition of D-index becomes imperative for segregating the contributions of circumstances and characteristics to outcome inequality. This decomposition is based on the Shapley value concept in cooperative games to distribute among the players the surplus produced by a coalition of cooperating players (Hoyos & Narayan, 2011). The straightforward attempt of this approach is to measure how much the estimated D-index would change when a circumstance or characteristic is added to different pre-existing sets of circumstances and characteristics.

The resultant change in outcome inequality would be a reasonable indicator of the contribution of new variable to inequality of opportunities. While implementing this idea, however, one needs to consider the fact that since the variables (circumstances and characteristics) are correlated to each other (as discussed earlier), the change in the inequality measure obtained by adding a variable depends on the initial set or subset of variables to which it is added. Consider a typical D-index, which is given by $D = D(x)$, where x is the vector of circumstances. Moreover, if we have two sets of circumstances A and B, and sets A and B are disjoint, then;

$$D_A = \sum_{S \subseteq N\{A\}} \frac{|S|!(n-|s|-1)!}{n!}[D(S \cup A\}) - D(S)] \quad (3)$$

where N is the set of all circumstances; n variables in total; S is a subset of N (containing s circumstances and/or characteristics) that does not contain A. $D(S)$ is the dissimilarity index estimated with $S.D(S \cup \{A\})$ is the dissimilarity index calculated with the set S and the set of variables A. We can define the contribution of the set of variables A to the dissimilarity index as:

$$M_A = \frac{D_A}{D(N)} \quad (4)$$

where $\sum_{i \in N} M_i = 1$

Thus, the sum of the contributions of all circumstances to D adds up to 100 per cent. Two caveats, among many others, become exceedingly relevant here. First, this approach provides a statistical decomposition of the index and the results do not indicate causality or channels through which unequal access to opportunities is manifested. Second, the estimated contributions of circumstances depend on the choice and definition of opportunities and circumstances (Israeli, 2007; Sastre & Trannoy, 2002).

We estimate the D-index econometrically as follows. Consider any opportunity (being employed on the UPSS in India, defined as a discrete [0–1] variable, with 1 denoting 'Yes' and 0 denoting 'No'). To obtain the conditional probabilities of access to this opportunity (access to employment) for each individual in the NSSO sample on the basis of his/her circumstances and characteristics, a logistic model is estimated, linear in the parameters β, where the event I corresponds to accessing the opportunity and x the set of circumstances and characteristics:

$$\ln\left(\frac{P\{I=1\mid X=(x_1\ldots\ldots,\ldots x_n)\}}{1-P\{I=1\mid X=(x_1\ldots\ldots,\ldots x_n)\}}\right) = \sum_{k=1}^{n} x_k \beta_k \qquad (5)$$

where x_k denotes the row vector of variables representing n circumstances/characteristics and β_k a corresponding column vector of parameters. From the estimation of regression (6), one obtain estimates of the parameters $\{\beta_k\}$, denoted as $\bar{\hat{\beta}}_{k_m}$, where m denotes the sample size.[20] Given the estimated coefficients, one

---

[20] An important caveat to the estimation model is that the list of regressors does not include any interaction terms between the regressors. Given the number of circumstances and characteristics we have in the NSSO sample(s), the large number of observations and the opportunity for which these regressions have to be run, including interactions, would lead to intractable problems in at least some of the cases. If the interactions were included, it would result in a higher D-index (and lower HOI), just as if more circumstances and characteristics were

can obtain for each individual in the sample his/her predicted probability of the opportunity in consideration:

$$\hat{p}_{i,m} = \frac{Exp(xi\,\hat{\beta}_m)}{1+Exp(xi\,\hat{\beta}_m)} \qquad (6)$$

Using the predicted probabilities $\hat{p}$ and sample weights w_i, we can find the predicted overall coverage rate $\hat{\bar{C}}$ and $\hat{D}$, and D-index as:

$$\hat{\bar{C}} = \sum_{i=1}^{m} w_i\,\hat{p}_{i,m} \qquad (7)$$

$$\hat{D} = \frac{1}{2\hat{\bar{C}}} \sum_{i=1}^{m} w_i\,|\hat{p}_{i,m} - \bar{C}| \qquad (8)$$

$$\hat{H} = \hat{C}(1-\hat{D}) \qquad (9)$$

This is alike the approach used in HOI estimation for children's opportunities in past works,[21] with the *crucial difference* that the covariates of the logit now include both circumstances (religion, social status, geographic location and gender) and characteristics (education and age). In other words, our estimated D now considers inequality between groups differentiated by circumstances *as well as* personal characteristics that are not circumstances.

---

added. This in turn implies that the estimated D-index for all SRCs and opportunities is the lower bound of between-group inequality (and the estimated HOI is the upper bound) for a given set of circumstances and characteristics.

[21] As stated earlier, the HOI was originally conceived to account for the opportunities available to children for completing primary education within the limitations of their ecosystems wherein they themselves have no role to affect the outcome. As such, all the major works within the HOI framework address children's opportunity to education.

The decomposition method outlined earlier allows us to estimate the contribution of each covariate to the estimated D-index, as well as the contributions of groups of covariates (e.g., circumstances or non-circumstance characteristics) taken together. The contribution of covariate k to the D-index for an opportunity can be estimated as in (3) and (4) with two differences: (a) $\widehat{D}$ substitutes for D and (b) the set N now includes circumstances and characteristics. As an example, consider the following question: how much does the circumstance gender contribute to the D-index of having a job of a certain desirable type? The Shapley decomposition method would involve measuring the impact of adding gender as a circumstance on the predicted D-index $\widehat{D}$, which involves taking the average of *all* impacts on when gender is added to all possible subsets of the other covariates. This is done by estimating the logistic regression given by (5) for all possible subsets of the covariates excluding gender, and then with gender added to each configuration; obtaining $\widehat{D}$ from all these estimations and using the relationships given by (3) and (4). The contribution of each circumstance to $\widehat{D}$, calculated this way, would add up to 100 per cent.[22]

HOI as an indicator of progress of societies towards ensuring equality of opportunity over time is an important reference to how public policy is practised within a nation. It is to this end that property of additive decomposability of HOI in terms of

---

[22] Instead of treating each circumstance separately, one could also compute Shapley values using the entire set of circumstances as a separate block alongside education and age, and come up with an aggregate contribution of all circumstances, education and age. To get to the contribution of each individual circumstance, one would then implement an additional step and repeat the process limiting the analysis only to circumstances. The absolute contributions obtained from these two methods would most likely be different. The literature does not offer guidance on which is the better method to use. We prefer the method we have used because of its computational simplicity; it is straightforward to apply and also captures the relationship between each circumstance with every characteristic in a flexible manner.

decomposability of changes into scale affect (change in average access rate to employment) and distribution effect (change in the distribution of access to employment across subgroups becomes important. It allows us to track and compare the effort of a society towards opportunity equalization at two different time periods. This can be shown as follows:

Let O_{t_1} and O_{t_2} be the human opportunity indices at time t_1 and time t_2. The average access rates to employment being $\bar{C}t_1$ and $\bar{C}t_2$ and the dissimilarity indices being $\bar{D}t_1$ and $\bar{D}t_2$ at time t_1 and t_2, respectively. Then the change in HOI during time t_1 and t_2 can be decomposed as:

$$O_{t_2} \qquad (10)$$

where O_{t_1} is the scale effect and refers to the change in the overall coverage for the entire population without any changes in inequality and $\bar{C}t_2$ is the distribution effect and refers to the change in distribution of access to opportunity among the circumstance groups. This renders the comparison of HOI values at two different points of time valid and reliable.

Description of Data and the Variables

I use the 61st (2004–2005) and 68th (2011–2012) quinquennial rounds[23] of the employment/unemployment survey data sets of NSSO, India. A quick reference to the variable used is provided in Table 4.1. Access to employment on the UPSS is the outcome variable for it captures the employment status of a person in the year preceding the survey and hence is the most comprehensive of all the available measures. Religion, social status, location, gender of the *ith* individual and education of household head are circumstances affecting the ability of a person to rich his

---

[23] The quinquennial survey on employment and unemployment is one of the most comprehensive surveys conducted regularly by the NSSO in India.

TABLE 4.1 Tabular Construct of the Model for Estimation of Human Opportunity for the Indian Labour Market

Nature of Variable	Broad Category		Operational Explanation
Independent	Circumstance variable	Location	Rural/urban
		Gender	Male/female
		Socio-religious status	SCs/STs
			Hindu-OBCs
			Muslim-OBCs
			Muslims-General
			Other minorities
		Education of household head	Primary education
			Secondary education
			Higher secondary/diploma
			Graduate & above
	Characteristic variable	Age in years (15–64)	Group I (15–24 years)
			Group II (25–39 years)
			Group III (40–64 years)
		Education	Primary education
			Secondary education
			Higher secondary/diploma
			Graduate & above

Source: Author's own.

capabilities and realize from and contribute to human capital. Among the characteristics, education and age are used. HOI for India both at the national as well as disaggregated level after controlling for the socio-religious category status of the population across different levels of age and education is generated.

Results and Discussion

Globally, employment opportunities have been outpaced by the growing labour force. Global employment-to-population ratio—the proportion of the working age population that is employed—have fallen from 62 per cent in 1991 to 60 per cent in 2015 (United Nations, 2015). In 2015, more than 204 million people were unemployed. The employment-to-population ratio in the developing regions of the world has fallen by 3.3 percentage points from 1991 to 2015, while in the developed regions it has declined by 1 percentage point. The largest declines are found in Eastern and Southern Asia, which have experienced drops in the employment-to-population ratio of 6.7 and 4.6 percentage points, respectively. The employment situation has improved slightly in sub-Saharan Africa, but progress in livelihoods has been offset by persistently high underemployment and informal employment, as well as low labour productivity. Youth, especially young women, continue to be disproportionately affected by limited employment opportunities and unemployment. Only 4 in 10 young women and men aged 15–24 are employed in 2015, compared with 5 in 10 in 1991. During this period of 18 years, decline in LFPR for males is substantial for the age groups 10–14 years, 15–19 years, 20–24 years and 60 years or more. For rural females of the age group 10–54 years, decline in LFPR between 1993–1994 and 2011–2012 varied from 10 per cent to 21 per cent and for urban females of the age groups 10–24 years and 30 years or more, it varied from 2 per cent to 7 per cent (ILO, 2012). According to ILO (2018), global UR has stabilized after the rise in 2015. It reports a global unemployment of 5.6 per cent in 2017. The headcount of the unemployed is reported to be in excess of 192 million persons. With expectations of a modest global outlook, a stabilization in unemployment is expected by the end of 2019. Performance of labour markets in developed countries will be driving this stabilization process. In the developed countries, UR is projected to fall by an additional 0.2 percentage points in 2019 to reach 5.3 per cent, a rate below pre-crisis levels. Employment growth in the developing countries continues to be sluggish. It falls short of labour force growth but has nevertheless improved in 2018 compared to 2016.

Employment in India rose markedly by 59.4 million between 1999–2000 and 2004–2005. In the next five years, 2004–2005 to 2009–2010, net employment generated fell severely to only 4.7 million (Mehrotra et al., 2013). Employment growth recovered subsequently, with 10 million new jobs registered between 2009–2010 and 2011–2012. This huge jump in employment ratios as returned by data necessitated a large-scale NSSO survey, only after two years in 2011–2012. The results returned by 2009–2010 data were grossly inconsistent and san explanations. Corrections occasioned upon the NSSO round of 2009–2010 resulted into revision of employment data. Net increase to jobs created over 2004–2005 and 2011–2012 was 14.7 million as against 59.4 million between 1999–2000 and 2004–2005.

In an era of depressed employment generation, distribution of available employment opportunities becomes all the more important from the egalitarian perspective. In the Indian labour market, there is a 9.84 per cent decline in the coverage rate, that is, employment opportunities in the country between 2004–2005 and 2011–2012. It is to be noted that during this period, growth of labour force was higher than employment generation. Group-based distribution of employment reveals that Muslims exhibit lowest coverage rates, higher D-index and lowest HOI (Table 4.2).

Coverage of SCs/STs has declined at a higher rate than the national average. This is partly due to 15 per cent decline in the coverage rate of SCs/STs in the age group of 15–24 years and a subsequent increase in the student enrolment ratio. Retraction of huge female labour force during the reference period also explains the phenomenon of contraction in employment and higher declines in coverage rates for SCs/STs. The D-index has

TABLE 4.2 *HOI in Employment Controlled for SRC Status*

Year	Variable	All India	SCs/STs	Hindu-OBCs	UC-Hindus	Muslim-OBCs	Muslims-General	Other Minorities
2004–2005	Coverage (C)	64.4496	71.2045	67.3201	57.4287	54.1041	55.6078	64.5172
	Dissimilarity (D)	16.9871	12.5776	14.9033	21.8303	25.8193	27.6527	15.6927
	HOI	53.5015	62.2487	57.2871	44.8919	40.1348	40.2308	54.3927
2011–2012	Coverage (C)	56.612	62.181	57.745	51.504	49.899	52.260	56.824
	Dissimilarity (D)	22.229	17.833	21.145	26.731	30.742	28.553	20.079
	HOI	44.027	51.092	45.534	37.736	34.559	37.338	45.414

Source: Author's calculations based on the unit-level data of NSSO 61st and 68th rounds.

shown an increase across all SRCs as well as at the national level. Values of D-index are the highest for Muslims in General category in 2004 and for Muslim-OBCs in 2011–2012. This signifies growing inequality of opportunity within the Muslim-OBCs. Muslim-OBCs do enjoy some reservation in the job market but increasing D-index points towards a need for redistribution of opportunities within this category. On the contrary, SCs/STs enjoy lowest dissimilarity (both in 2004–2005 and 2011–2012). At the country level, a higher D-index points towards the perpetual growing inequity in the labour market and a need for redistribution of job opportunities in pursuit of equal opportunity. HOI has come down by 9.5 per cent for the country—a pointer to declining job opportunities in the economy compounded by growing inequality of opportunity in the labour market. There is a need for employment-oriented investments and further redistribution of the job opportunities created. Muslims both in 2004–2005 as well as in 2011–2012 recorded the lowest HOI. Muslims in the General category were at par with Muslim-OBCs in 2004–2005 but far better in 2011–2012, a pointer towards the perpetual disadvantage of the vulnerable sections within the community. As stated earlier, because of a fall in employment generation over the reference period, there has been a corresponding drop of 9.47 percentage points in the HOI at the aggregate level. But this drop has been minimal (2.89%) in case of Muslims-General and the highest in case of SCs/STs (11.16%). Muslims-General have exhibited a better relative redistribution of the available opportunities testified by the lowest increase in their corresponding D-index. Muslims continue to record higher D-index. The D-index is and has been the lowest for SCs/STs and highest for Muslims-General. Thus, the available employment opportunities (for a given SRC) are better distributed within the SCs/STs and asymmetrically distributed among the Muslims-General category. Muslim-OBCs are keeping close to the Muslims-General at the higher end of the spectrum. There is also need for fair distribution of available employment opportunities among UC-Hindus.

Human Opportunity in Employment for the 15–24 Years Age Group

Employment opportunities across age groups for all SRCs reveal interesting patterns. These are presented in Table 4.3. Of all those in the age group of 15–24 years reporting at the labour market in 2004–2005, 41.40 per cent are covered with a D-index of 20.47 and an HOI of 32.93. Consequent upon lower reporting rate of this age group in 2011–2012, there has been a decline in all the three values at the aggregate level. Coverage rate is the highest for SCs/STs and lowest for UC-Hindus and is in line with the results returned by the data for 2004–2005. However, the dispersion is on the lower side in 2011–2012. As already discussed in the preceding chapters, declines in the participation rates among Muslims have been the lowest and consequently the corresponding declines in their coverage rate are the lowest. However, as has already been argued, lower declines in LFPR and higher coverage rate for the age group of 15–24 years do not match well with the long-term educational development of a society. Better coverage rate of the labour market for 15–24 years of age group for a community that has continuously recorded lower educational attainment is not at all a good option. This means more people who should be reporting at the educational institutions are directed towards and absorbed by the labour market. It is also to be noted from Table 4.3 that highest coverage rate and better HOI are reported by SCs/STs and Muslims. This implies that for these SRCs, individuals in 15–24 years age group are better covered in the labour market. Higher absorptions for this age group, exclusively a phenomenon exhibited by SCs/STs and Muslims, do not do any good for their human capital, if at all human capital is correlated with educational outcomes.

As regard the dissimilarity index, Muslims in 15–24 years' age groups show higher D-index. Thus, distribution of available employment opportunities to Muslims, although relatively lesser, are asymmetrically distributed within the community. The gap between HOI for SCs/STs and Muslims (both OBC and

TABLE 4.3 HOI in Employment for the Age Group 15–24 Years

Year	Variable	Values					
		All India	SCs/STs	Hindu-OBCs	UC-Hindus	Muslim-OBCs	Muslims-General	Other Minorities
2004–2005	Coverage (C)	41.4016	54.6257	49.2311	36.4473	41.2232	42.9459	43.0178
	Dissimilarity (D)	20.4721	15.7022	17.1793	22.1001	27.7548	29.4931	20.6376
	HOI	32.9258	46.0483	40.7736	28.3924	29.7818	30.2798	34.1400
2011–2012	Coverage (C)	33.270	39.557	32.700	24.726	35.354	36.1604	30.824
	Dissimilarity (D)	24.450	21.822	23.215	24.739	29.917	28.385	22.503
	HOI	25.135	30.924	25.108	18.609	24.777	25.896	23.888

Source: Author's calculations based on the unit-level data of NSSO 61st and 68th rounds.

General has widened over the period), though there has not been any marked difference in educational enrolment of the latter. Given that the educational enrolments of these SRCs continue to be almost the same as in 2004–2005 (as reported in Chapter 3), a widening gap in the HOI indicates lesser employment opportunities for Muslims. Logically, it should not have been the case. Given relatively comparable educational achievements over the reference period for a specific age group, HOIs should be converging, which is not the case over here. Hindus (OBC as well as UC) have shown better educational enrolments over the reference period as such their coverage rate as well as the HOI continue to be on the lower side for the specific age group of 15–24 years. So much so that their corresponding declines for coverage rate and HOI have exhibited the highest declines. Differences in coverage rate and HOI in this age group as such are detriment of the disadvantaged groups, where human capital becomes an important determining factor for employment and employability.

Human Opportunity in Employment for the 25–39 Years Age Group

People in the age group of 25–39 years are the most visible in labour market. Educational attainment and other aspects of human capital formation are generally completed at this stage of an individual's life. This age group as such should report the highest of all coverage rates in a flourishing economy across all groups, howsoever defined. Globally, people in this age group exhibit lesser URs than any other age group. With respect to this age group as well as for other groups, the D-index should be lower and the HOI relatively high. Estimates of HOI (Table 4.4) reveal that the coverage rate in 25–39 years' age group in 2004–2005 was 71.22 and the HOI was 59.81 with a dissimilarity index of 16.01. The respective values of these parameters in 2011–2012 are 66.27, 52.18 and 21.26.

TABLE 4.4 HOI in Employment for the Age Group 25–39 Years

Year	Variable	All India	SCs/STs	Hindu-OBCs	UC-Hindus	Muslim-OBCs	Muslims-General	Other Minorities
2004–2005	Coverage (C)	71.2173	77.5295	74.5995	63.9781	61.2932	61.6832	72.1940
	Dissimilarity (D)	16.0110	11.5251	13.5818	21.9451	23.9494	27.4297	13.6355
	HOI	59.8147	68.5942	64.4676	49.9380	46.6139	44.7636	62.3500
2011–2012	Coverage (C)	66.274	72.291	68.250	60.557	57.796	60.795	65.969
	Dissimilarity (D)	21.264	15.630	20.023	26.558	30.132	29.409	19.728
	HOI	52.181	60.991	54.584	44.474	40.380	42.915	52.954

Source: Author's calculations based on the unit-level data of NSSO 61st and 68th rounds.

However, in the period of declining job opportunities across sectors, between 2004–2005 and 2011–2012, the dissimilarity index has increased by 5 per cent and a decline of 7.6 per cent has taken place in the HOI. These values indicate a declining trend in coverage of labour force alongside increasing inequality in opportunity or distribution of available job opportunities across population groups. However, amid declining employment elasticity across the sectors over the reference period and a contraction of employment opportunities, the declines in coverage, HOI in this category, are not scary and simply reflect the macroeconomic scenarios being transmitted to the labour market.

Given the fact that individuals in the age group of 25–39 are the most active in labour market, the overall decline in the coverage has been around 5 per cent. Muslim-OBCs are at the bottom of the pyramid just below Muslims in the General category in 2011–2012. UC-Hindus are in the middle when the coverage rate is arranged in ascending/descending order. Decline in the coverage rate has been the lowest for Muslims in the General category (0.9) and highest for Hindu-OBCs (9.9). SCs/STs and Hindu-OBCs continue to report coverage rates higher than the national average. HOI follows the same pattern. SCs/STs report the highest HOI both in 2004–2005 as well as 2011–2012. D-index in 2011–2012 is the highest for Muslims in the OBC, followed closely by Muslims in the General category and lowest for SCs/STs. Muslims (in General as well as the OBC categories) report highest D-index both in 2004–2005 as well as 2011–2012, indicating, therefore, higher inequities in job opportunities within the group. These results are not surprising given the fact that at all India level, the usual principal status rates of participation in the labour force for the SC, ST and OBC groups during 2012–2013 were 53.7 per cent, 56.7 per cent and 50.8 per cent, respectively, as against 47.5 per cent for the General category, as reported in Chapter 3. The socially disadvantaged groups are found to be better off when compared with the General category on both the parameters of LFPR and UR. LFPR and employment opportunities for Muslims in General category as well as SCs/STs in this age group seem to be positively related. However, these patterns are not observed in case of Muslims in the OBC.

These trends are in sync with other estimations about labour force participation and generation of employment opportunities in the economy over the reference period. There was an increase in employment between 2000 and 2005, and a slowdown of growth of employment during 2005–2012. Between 2005 and 2012, merely 15 million people joined the labour force as against 61 million between 2000 and 2005 (Mehrotra et al., 2013). The slowdown in the pace of growth of labour force is attributed to changes in the demographic profile of the young population, rising enrolments in elementary and secondary schooling due to the efforts of Sarva Shiksha Abhiyan (SSA) and Right to Education, declining child labour, withdrawal of women and their increasing participation in household activities. However, the HOI calculation will not be able to reflect (although it does capture) these changes which are traced back to the structural shifts in the economy at the macrolevel.

Human Opportunity in Employment for the 40–64 Years Age Group

As reported in Chapter 3, individuals in the age group of 40–64 years have exhibited higher LFPR as well as WFPR over the reference period. The coverage rates as well as the opportunity index have been keeping pace with their reporting rates. This age group had slightly better coverage rate as well as the opportunity index than the other two age groups across the reference period. As reported in Table 4.5, dissimilarity index for individuals in the age group of 40–64 years is almost comparable to those in the age group of 25–39 years. The same holds true for all SRCs at both points of time, that is, in 2004–2005 as well as 2011–2012. With declines of 7.21 and 10.29 points in coverage rate and HOI, respectively, the D-index for the age group 40–64 years has increased by 6.44 points at the national

TABLE 4.5 HOI in Employment for the Age Group 40–64 Years

Year	Variable	All India	SCs/STs	Hindu-OBCs	UC-Hindus	Muslim-OBCs	Muslims-General	Other Minorities
2004–2005	Coverage (C)	72.9868	79.4564	75.4059	67.0599	60.6449	62.9375	74.6314
	Dissimilarity (D)	16.1515	11.2317	14.4282	21.1810	26.8976	27.5364	13.6626
	HOI	61.1983	70.5322	64.5261	52.8559	44.3329	45.6068	64.4349
2011–2012	Coverage (C)	65.773	71.140	66.792	61.413	56.835	60.014	67.902
	Dissimilarity (D)	22.592	17.916	21.528	27.160	33.229	29.447	18.798
	HOI	50.913	58.394	52.412	44.733	37.949	42.341	55.138

Source: Author's calculations based on the unit-level data of NSSO 61st and 68th rounds.

level. Declines in coverage rate and the opportunity index are also observed for the 25–39 years' age group. However, there are notable differences in magnitude.

Declining coverage rate as well as employment opportunities in the economy alongside increasing inequalities in the distribution of available opportunities is evident from Table 4.5. The decline in the job opportunities is a result of huge retraction of labour force from the agriculture sector as well as manufacturing. Thirty-six million fewer persons are engaged in agriculture in 2011–2012 compared to the number in 2004–2005—a first in the economic history of India. Manufacturing employment had increased by 11 million or 25 per cent between 1999–2000 and 2004–2005 (from 44 to 55 million), but fell by 3 million to 52 million in the latter half of the decade (Mehrotra et al., 2014). These steep falls in employment opportunities would normally push coverage rates down by large magnitudes. However, the coverage rate was normalized by an expansion of job opportunities in the construction. Employment in construction doubled from its 2004–2005 level of 25 million to 50 million in 2011–2012. Hence, amid huge retraction from the agriculture sector and manufacturing construction work helped to moderate the coverage rates and hence the opportunity index. This structural change at the macroeconomic front is, however, not imbibed symmetrically by the SRCs across age groups. SCs/STs who have been more visible in the construction work continue to report higher coverage rates both in 2004–2005 as well as 2011–2012. Coverage rate as well as opportunity index for SCs/STs is about 10 points higher than that of the national average. Muslims report a coverage rate and HOI that are 10 and 15 points lower than the national level, respectively. Hindu-OBCs report higher coverage as well as HOI than the national average so do the other minorities (Table 4.5). UC-Hindus are in middle of the spectrum. The same is reported for UC-Hindus in the 25–39 year age group. Thus, in 2004, there is evidence of lack of coverage as well as opportunity for Muslims in the Indian labour market. The results of this study provide an answer as well as support to the findings of SCR, who could not establish the reasons for dismal labour market outcomes for Muslims in 2004–2012. This study provides evidence to the fact that there was a lack of opportunity as well as coverage in case of Muslims in 2004, when compared to other SRCs. There has been a sort of normalization of this trend in 2011–2012. With an overall decline of 7.22 points in coverage and 10.28 points in the HOI at the national level, Muslims have recorded the lowest declines among all SRCs. With the coverage rate declining by 8.3 points for SCs/STs and 8.6 points for Hindu-OBCs, Muslims in the General category record a decline of 2.9 points and Muslims in OBC category record a decline of 3.8 points. Same patterns are observed in case of the opportunity index which has declined by 12.13 and 12.11 points, respectively, in case of SCs/STs and Hindu-OBCs. Corresponding declines exhibited by Muslims-General and Muslim-OBCs are 6.38 and 3.26 points. Although the declines in the coverage rate as well as the opportunity index among Muslims are the lowest of all the SRCs, it needs to be noted that Muslims continue to be at the lowest of the SRC pyramid both in terms of coverage as well as in case of opportunity. D-index in case of Muslims is the worst of all SRCs and has deteriorated in case of Muslim-OBCs over the reference period.

HOI and Levels of Educational Attainment

Shultz (1961) and Becker (1962) initiated the literature on human capital and following these pioneering works, education choices in economics have been modelled as important investment decisions. Individuals who opt for education are believed to be making economic sacrifices in order to acquire 'human capital'. This acquired human capital is expected to generate future benefits. Of the major future benefits envisaged by individuals are employability and earnings. Both employability and higher earnings are found to be highly correlated to levels of education across time and space. LFPRs as well as employment opportunities tend to increase as the level of education attained increases. Different levels of educational attainment have differential impacts on both employment outcomes as well as earnings. Adults who had never attended school report the lowest rates of employment/earnings across the board. Individuals with lower levels of educational attainment exhibit higher rates of unemployment. Exceptions to this rule do exist and depend upon the linking patterns between the skills produced by the education system and those needed in the labour market. Any mismatch between the two will affect the impact of level of education and employment opportunities adversely. Generally, adults who never attend school exhibit the lowest rates of employment. Individuals with lower levels of educational attainment have higher rates of unemployment. Graduates as compared to those who did not continue their studies past high school are expected to be employed at higher rates. Employment rates amongst those aged 25–64 increase as the level of education attained increases with an employment rate of 35 per cent for persons with at most primary level education compared with an employment rate of 81 per cent for those with a third-level qualification. URs clearly fall as the level of education attainment increases (Quarterly National Household Survey, 2011).

These trends and patterns are observed across countries. In OECD countries, for example, individuals educated up to the tertiary level report an employment rate of 83 per cent. The average employment rate of tertiary-educated individuals is over 88 per cent in countries like Iceland, Norway, Sweden and Switzerland. However, these ratios come down to 74 per cent for people with upper secondary and post-secondary/non-tertiary education and to just below 56 per cent for those without an upper secondary education (OECD, 2012). A study motivated by the UNESCO to present evidence concerning links between educational attainment and employment outcomes for young adults (aged 25–34 years) in 11 developing countries (which included India) finds that more education does not appear correlated to more success in finding jobs in the labour market. Indeed, with the important exceptions of Argentina and Brazil, both relatively advanced economies, the opposite pattern prevails—unemployment is highest among young adults who are most educated. This is partially the product of the fact that less-educated young people begin their transition to work at an earlier age, and therefore have had a greater length of exposure to the labour market and more time to secure employment. The correlation between education and unemployment may also be driven in part by a disguised income effect. In other words, better educated young adults are more likely to be from wealthier households and therefore better able to afford a spell of unemployment. But the strongly positive link between unemployment and education levels is also suggestive of mismatches between the skills produced by the education system and those needed in the labour market, and of the need for better mechanisms for bringing together skilled job seekers and prospective employers (UNESCO, 2013). In relatively advanced countries, education and employment seem to be positively correlated. However, in the developing countries, this relationship is not observed. Results obtained by the present study, in case of India, also point to such a missing relationship (Tables 4.6 and 4.7).

In the Indian context, employment coverage is excessively favourable to individuals without education and those with educational attainment up to the primary level. Sixty per cent of illiterate and 64 per cent of the people with *up to primary level* education were covered by employment avenues in 2011–2012, as against a coverage rate of 51 per cent and 44 per cent for those with *secondary level* and *higher secondary level* education, respectively. However, individuals with educational attainment of *graduation and above* seem to be fairly covered by employment avenues. Graduates and above report a coverage rate of 61 per cent. The respective HOIs (in 2011–2012) for *illiterates, up to primary level, secondary level, higher secondary level*, and *graduation and above* are 48.85, 49.81, 37.63, 30.50 and 48.34, respectively.

From Tables 4.6 and 4.7, it is vividly clear that irrespective of the SRC status of an individual, there does not exist an employment premium on higher attainment of education at

TABLE 4.6 HOI for Levels of Educational Attainment 2011–2012

Category	Variable	Values across Levels of Education				
		Illiterate	Primary	Secondary	Higher Secondary &/or Diploma	Graduate & Above
Total Population	Coverage (C)	60.4336	64.0855	51.3742	44.1023	61.0205
	Dissimilarity (D)	19.1574	22.2744	26.7525	30.8232	20.7574
	HOI	48.8561	49.8108	37.6303	30.5086	48.3542
SCs/STs	Coverage (C)	66.3009	69.8685	53.2202	45.7161	63.6582
	Dissimilarity (D)	14.9882	17.9132	23.9057	27.7004	19.4486
	HOI	56.3636	57.3528	40.4976	33.0525	51.2776
Hindu-OBCs	Coverage (C)	60.5860	65.9514	53.3706	44.9958	62.2980
	Dissimilarity (D)	18.7298	20.7268	25.4151	31.2163	19.5787
	HOI	49.2384	52.2818	39.8064	30.9498	50.1008
UC-Hindus	Coverage (C)	51.9660	55.4814	49.2321	42.8746	60.0660
	Dissimilarity (D)	21.5620	29.1681	29.8925	33.5086	22.9664
	HOI	40.7611	39.2986	34.5154	28.5079	46.2710

(Continued)

TABLE 4.6 (Continued)

		Values across Levels of Education				
Category	Variable	Illiterate	Primary	Secondary	Higher Secondary &/or Diploma	Graduate & Above
Muslim-OBCs	Coverage (C)	49.4907	55.8064	47.1163	39.5676	56.7336
	Dissimilarity (D)	33.0433	30.1605	30.2082	8.9760	25.0530
	HOI	33.1374	38.9749	32.8834	21.7817	42.5202
Muslims-General	Coverage (C)	54.0104	59.9893	44.6571	42.5478	57.5550
	Dissimilarity (D)	29.5247	26.4701	33.9636	30.6754	24.3115
	HOI	38.0640	44.1101	29.4900	29.4961	43.5625
Other Minorities	Coverage (C)	63.5753	65.7903	52.0305	45.4286	61.3523
	Dissimilarity (D)	16.2541	18.3535	25.2258	28.5971	16.9701
	HOI	53.2417	53.7155	38.9054	32.4373	50.9407

Source: Author's calculations based on the unit-level data of NSSO 68th round.

TABLE 4.7 HOI for Levels of Educational Attainment 2004–2005

Category	Variable	Illiterate	Primary	Secondary	Higher Secondary &/or Diploma	Graduate & Above
				Values across Levels of Education		
Total Population	Coverage (C)	69.1696	69.0901	57.3462	52.9918	64.9325
	Dissimilarity (D)	13.0588	17.8558	22.2855	25.0340	19.1772
	HOI	60.1369	56.7535	44.5663	39.7258	52.4802
SCs/STs	Coverage (C)	75.1197	74.2680	61.8353	52.8996	64.2576
	Dissimilarity (D)	10.3454	14.3821	17.7863	22.4371	19.4205
	HOI	67.3483	63.5867	50.8371	41.0304	51.7784
Hindu-OBCs	Coverage (C)	70.4524	72.8525	60.5825	57.3087	69.8710
	Dissimilarity (D)	11.4806	15.0869	20.1151	22.7052	16.5358
	HOI	62.3640	61.8613	48.3963	44.2966	58.3173
UC-Hindus	Coverage (C)	61.5710	61.6894	53.1046	50.9075	63.2350
	Dissimilarity (D)	14.8915	22.0688	26.2371	27.5063	21.2932
	HOI	52.4021	48.0753	39.1715	36.9048	49.7702

(Continued)

TABLE 4.7 (Continued)

Category	Variable	Illiterate	Primary	Secondary	Higher Secondary &/or Diploma	Graduate & Above
Muslim-OBCs	Coverage (C)	54.9943	58.4513	48.5141	48.0242	64.4408
	Dissimilarity (D)	24.3986	27.6550	29.2788	29.7831	18.9619
	HOI	41.5764	42.2866	34.3097	33.7211	52.2217
Muslims-General	Coverage (C)	55.3498	59.9468	51.9079	45.8438	65.3857
	Dissimilarity (D)	28.3990	28.7847	27.9692	31.5710	19.1974
	HOI	39.6310	42.6913	37.3896	31.3704	52.8334
Other minorities	Coverage (C)	75.5508	71.1392	56.8394	52.2776	62.3393
	Dissimilarity (D)	9.1171	12.9568	20.7089	24.0715	18.2092
	HOI	68.6628	61.9218	45.0686	39.6936	50.9878

Source: Author's calculations based on the unit-level data of NSSO 61st round.

least up to the secondary level. Beyond that, there indeed are better chances of absorption into employment. Employment opportunities increase from no education to primary education, then exhibit a fall, reaching a minimum for those with higher secondary level of education. Thereafter, for individuals with *graduate and above* educational attainment, a relative increase in employment opportunities prevails.

All SRCs exhibit same patterns of coverage and opportunity across levels of education with variations in magnitude. In 2011–2012, Muslims in OBC category have lowest coverage rate as well as opportunity index and SCs/STs exhibit the highest (Table 4.6). SCs/STs are followed by Hindu-OBCs who report better coverage rate and HOI than UC-Hindus at all levels of education. At the national level in 2004–2005, opportunities of employment vis-a-vis levels of education exhibited the same pattern (Table 4.7). Coverage rates were 69 per cent for both illiterates and individuals with primary education followed by those with secondary level of education. Individuals with higher secondary education reported the lowest coverage rates with employment coverage for graduates and above increasing to 65 per cent. Across the SRCs, SCs/STs and other minorities report the highest coverage rates and hence the highest HOI in employment followed by Hindu-OBCs and UC-Hindus. Muslim-OBCs and Muslims-General report almost identical but the lowest coverage rates as well as opportunity index across all levels of education. However, the D-index is worse in case of Muslim-OBCs pointing towards unfavourable distribution of the available opportunities within the Muslims belonging to OBC. Thus, comparing the scenarios of opportunity in employment and the coverage rates across the reference period, not much has changed. The relative position of Muslims both with respect to the national level values as well as across the SRCs has not undergone any change since 2004–2005. Their participation rates and access to employment opportunities have exhibited the same patterns in 2011–2012 as were recorded by Sachar Committee in 2004–2005. The same was further reiterated by the KCR. The present study while analysing the employment situation of the SRCs within the framework of opportunity index finds evidence to continuity in lack of employment opportunities for Muslims even after controlling for characteristic variables like age and education. Across all levels of education and even for the illiterates, the coverage rates as well as the opportunity index in case of Muslims (OBC and General) is the lowest in 2004–2005 and continues to be so in 2011–2012. One of the most alarming observations from the data as presented in Tables 4.6 and 4.7 is the decline in coverage rate and opportunity index of Muslim graduates and those with higher secondary and diploma levels of education both in absolute as well as relative terms. Opportunity index as well as coverage in employment for Muslim graduates and those with higher secondary and diploma was almost identical (although lower than Hindu-OBCs) to all other SRCs in 2004–2005. Surprisingly, there is a steep decline in the coverage rate across these levels of education in employment among the Muslims. Decline in coverage as well as the opportunity index of such magnitude for higher secondary level, and graduates and above is not exhibited by other SRCs. Due to paucity of other studies in this area, the present study is not able to delineate upon the causes of such a decline.

Conclusion

Creation of employment opportunities for available labour force falls within the ambit of social justice and policy prudence. Indian economic policy did not consider expansion of employment opportunities, per se, a priority issue at least till the early 1970s. It was only in mid-1970s that employment generation and expansion of employment opportunities came to the forefront. This was necessitated by growing labour force on the one hand and the failure of the trickle-down effect on the other. Large number of employment generation and poverty alleviation schemes were announced in the 1970s up till the later part of the 1990s. This policy of state-led employment generation effort culminated with the launch of MGNREGA in 2005. As an attempt to provide gainful employment opportunities to the unskilled and the semi-skilled labour force, MGNREGA is the world's largest affirmative action plan. This flagship programme has continuously attracted increased budgetary allocations since inception. For the skilled labour force alongside the public sector, which started to shed some load in the economic affairs, private sector was expected to generate gainful employment opportunities. In the post-reform period, however, the employment elasticities have remained stagnant or have exhibited marginal increases. On the empirical plane, it reflects a discouraged job-seeking behaviour. With falling employment elasticities across sectors, people may be reluctant to report at the labour market. The recent declines in the LFPR might indicate to lesser opportunities in the labour market. In such a scenario, lower UR might be enveloping and wrapping up the joblessness within an economy.

It is evident that employment opportunities have declined in the country, at least over the last couple of years. The traditionally disadvantaged sections of the society, especially on the socio-religious plane, have exhibited higher disparities. In a declining labour opportunity scenario across the economy, Muslims have exhibited relatively higher declines. Not much change is observed in the relative positioning of Muslims in respect of opportunity of employment in the post-Sachar period. Disaggregating the HOI for employment conditional upon educational attainment level as well as age reveals higher relative depravity of Indian Muslims. For all levels of education as identified here, Muslims have the least coverage rate, higher dissimilarity index and lower HOI in the labour market. Over the reference period, not much has changed with respect to their employment avenues. Across all levels of education and even for the 'illiterates', the coverage rates as well as the opportunity index in case of Muslims (OBC and General) is the lowest in 2004–2005 and continues to be so in 2011–2012. On an average, Muslims report a coverage rate and HOI 10 and 15 points, respectively, lower than the national level.

Conclusions and Policy Suggestions

Conclusion

Muslims in India are the largest religious minority. It's the treatment and positioning of such minorities on socio-economic indicators vis-à-vis other groups that determines fairness and distributive justice in a multireligious and multicultural country. Notwithstanding the inclusive character of Indian democracy, there exist wide-ranging disparities between the majority group (Hindus) and minorities (especially Muslims) in independent India. These disparities are more glaring when compared on a pure religious plane. With an overarching disparity in employment as well as education, Indian Muslims have become a distinct entity. They have identified themselves as a disadvantaged group. Studies have documented the negative effects of group-based disparities on socio-economic outcomes. Members of the disadvantaged groups exhibit higher rates of unemployment and experience closed doors to economic opportunities. On the contrary, members of the advantaged groups are privy to more economic security, opportunities to advance and social acceptance. This group-based exclusionary and advantageous/disadvantageous scenarios in socio-economic spheres impacts the perception of their members. The advantageous group perceives a fair world, full of opportunities, allowing realization of individual as well as societal goals of well-being. On the contrary, the world seems unfair, perilous, discriminatory and dangerous to the members of the disadvantaged group. These perceptions of individuals have consequences for their well-being.

The book seeks to deconstruct the *Muslim question* afresh. Given the multidimensional nature of the issues concerning Indian Muslims that include identity, security and equity, it restricts the analysis to their labour market outcomes. Motivation for the same came from variety of developments that have taken place in this area recently. Publication of the SCR in 2006 provided some databased insights into the *perceived discrimination* doctrine about Indian Muslims in various spheres of living. It, however, fell short of establishing any discrimination against the community on the basis of religion in the labour market or elsewhere. The comprehensive report did concede prevalence of a wide-ranging perception of discrimination among the members of Muslim community across Indian states. These perceptions were more glaring in the areas of employment and education. The Committee came up with a series of recommendations and proposed multitude of needed interventions to bring Muslims into the mainstream of economic development and well-being. The central government having accepted all the recommendations of the Committee initiated a multipronged approach to address the identified issues. As a follow-up to the evaluation of success of government interventions post-SCR, the Kundu Committee submitted its report with the observation that in respect of employment, Muslims continue to be the worst performers. It is in this backdrop that this book focused on four broad objectives. The major objective was to empirically investigate the distribution of opportunities of employment across the SRCs. While pursuing this broad objective, it was realized that certain important and related parameters concerning labour market dynamics need to be analysed before one can realistically enquire into the issue of distribution of employment opportunities across a labour market. For example, any attempt to understand the prevailing labour market outcomes of a given socio-religious group, a broad-based understanding of some historical developments that have shaped their present becomes inevitable. Thus, to put the Muslim employment issue into more comprehensive perspective, an attempt was needed to be made to consider the historical data of employment among them. Following that, an assessment of the current labour market ratios such as LFPR, WFPR, the UR as well as the SERs became equally important. Further, an understanding of the current distribution of the labour force and its engagement across activities and industries become inevitable to understand the opportunity of employment at the macrolevel.

It is observed that historical accounts, both Western and indigenous, point to the existence of a strong link between the socio-economic positioning of Muslim masses and political adventures of Muslim leaders. A good deal of literature is available to suggest that in the pre-1857 period, Muslim representation in labour market and public service was decent. Being in the reins of power, as under the Delhi Sultanate, Muslims flourished as a community, although inequalities in standards of life existed both within the community and across communities. However, as Hardy asserts, '*Muslims* in India before 1857 was a different community, as opposed to what they were under the direct British rule'. There was a paradigm shift in employment of Muslims (in public service) as well as in the social structures and British patronage. This shift was guided by the British bias against Muslims for their alleged active involvement in the revolt of 1857. As discussed in this book (Chapter 2), certain institutional changes made by the British, especially after 1857, proved detrimental to the relative positioning of Muslims on the economic plane in general and with respect to employment in particular. With the introduction of English, first as the language of governmental and legal business in 1835, and later (1877) as a qualification for the subordinate official career, Muslim monopoly of Persian was lost on the one hand and their aversion to learning English language on the other put them at a serious educational and consequently employability disadvantage. Loss of official favour enjoyed previously, through confiscation of *jagirs*, left the Muslim elite dispossessed. The same trickled down to the non-elites in the far-off lands. Independence of the Indian subcontinent was preceded by Partition. Division of the country on religious lines compounded the miseries of the Muslim minority in the major land area. Muslims came to be looked down as the *other*. This *othering* of Muslims in independent India compelled them to face glass ceilings in all walks of socio-economic life. Presence of Muslims in echelons of power dwindled. Thus, the major finding from the content analysis of historical information reveals a direct relationship between political power relations and well-being of the adherents of a particular religion. Muslims under Mughal rule were more assertive and participatory in the labour market. However, with transfer of power from Mughals to British, a gradual demoralization of Muslim elites got initiated. Confiscation of properties and introduction of English as an official language put Muslims at a relative disadvantage. According to K. M. Ashraf, under British tutelage, capitalism germinated in India in the Hindu majority areas of Calcutta, Bombay and Madras before 1857. Raja Ram Mohan Roy had initiated his social and education movement among the Hindu middle class. A new middle class emerged among Muslims only after half a century of Roy's social reform movement. It was weak and preferred to grow under British protection. Compared to the educational movements of Calcutta, Bombay and Madras, the Aligarh Movement was dominated by Jagirdars and Nawabs articulating the interest of British rulers. The Hindus in independent India emerged better off on account of these developments in the middle of the 19th century.

Given their depressed educational attainment during the British rule, Muslims in independent India could never find public employment in proportion of their population. Government-appointed commissions in the early 1980s (Gopal Singh report) and mid-2000s (SCR) documented the issues confronting Indian Muslims. Both these reports vividly brought to the light a plethora of literature pointing towards relative deprivation of Muslims in India. There has not been any follow-up to the former report. However, the latter report was followed up with institutional changes and efforts were put forth for redressal of grievances. Mechanisms were put in place to address the issues of security, identity and equity concerning the largest minority. Still, as reported by the post-Sachar Evaluation

Committee, Muslim deprivation in employment continues unabated. Thus, the employment outcomes of Muslims in India continue to be affected by sociopolitical developments and power relations at higher levels.

Behaviour of labour market ratios such as LFPR, WFPR, the UR as well as the SERs reinforces the 'Muslim disadvantage' in the labour markets. There has been a general decline in the LFPR as well as the WFPR in the country over the last decade. Appreciable increases in school and college enrolment rates partly explain the declines in the LFPR and WFPR. Retraction of individuals from agriculture also contributed to the declines in LFPR and WFPR, as did mechanization in agriculture and withdrawal of women and their increasing participation in household activities.

Declines in the LFPR have been relatively lower for Muslims more so in the critical age group of 15–19. This implies more Muslims in the 'school going' age group are trapped in the labour market. With extremely low retraction of individuals in the age group of 15–19, from the labour market, Muslims in the broader age group of 15–24 years are not exhibiting a transition from labour market to educational institutions. Except for Muslims, the gaps in decline in WFPR across rural–urban are large. Among SCs/STs and other socio-religious categories, the declines in WFPR in the rural and urban spaces are almost comparable. However, Muslims in the rural areas are exhibiting higher declines in WFPR than their urban counterparts. One of the important observations from data analysis is the lower decline in female participation among Muslims in comparison to other SRCs. Although Muslim women continue to report lowest levels of WFPR, their retraction from labour market, which is universal in India, is low. This exit of Muslim women at lower rates can lead to some convergence of their participation rate with that of women from other SRCs. Muslims (Muslim-OBCs and Muslims-General) in the age groups of 15–19 years and 20–24 years have exhibited comparatively lesser increases in enrolment at educational institutions. This should be understood with the earlier observation as reported earlier that the labour force retraction among Muslims in the respective age groups has been the lowest. UR in Indian economy has declined by 0.2 per cent over the last decade. However, there has been a marginal increase in unemployment among Muslims (0.1%). Unemployment among Muslims in the General category has gone up by 0.9 per cent. However, for all other SRCs, there have been marginal declines in respective unemployment ratios.

Logistic regression with respect to participation in labour market predicts: belonging of an individual to the Muslim community reduces the probability of his/her participation in the labour force. This prediction is not observed for any other SRC. Negative relationship of LFPR to the socio-religious status of being a Muslim reinforces the suboptimal employment outcomes for them. This builds up the alleged perception of depravity and discrimination among Muslims in India. These intertwined phenomena bring complexity to any empirical study of Muslim labour market outcomes. Methods and methodologies currently available to us are insufficient in explicating such complex and intertwined variables. However, results derived from the logistic regression establish the effect of socio-religious status of an individual upon his/her participation. Hence, labour market participation rates tend to be affected by socio-religious affiliation of an individual.

Now, if labour market participation rates are related to socio-religious affiliation and turn out to be negative for Muslims, does it indicate discrimination? Discrimination is hard to establish. Harder it is to link it to participation rates in a macroeconomic framework. It is even more difficult to brush it aside in context of Indian Muslims. Their historical past and their relative position in the socio-economic milieu of independent India makes the call for discrimination resonate time and again. An empirical investigation of distribution of opportunities of employment across the SRCs partly explains the nuances of alleged discrimination and deprivation of Indian Muslims. The underlying hypothesis over here is that if opportunities of employment are fairly distributed within an egalitarian framework, after controlling for circumstances of individuals then differentials in outcomes cannot be attributed to discrimination, otherwise they can be. Fairer distribution of employment opportunities translates into egalitarian access to them. Thus, in pursuance of the same, the

HOI of the World Bank was operationalized. Nuances of this approach, as discussed in Chapter 4, make it the only available (yet) the most comprehensive frameworks for a study like this. General results returned from the analysis as discussed in Chapter 4 indicate a skewed distribution of and restricted access to employment opportunities for Muslims as well as other historically disadvantaged sections of the society like the SCs/STs. However, in case of SCs/STs, significant improvements in the relevant ratios are observed. This does not happen in case of Muslims. Disaggregating the HOI for employment conditional upon educational attainment level as well as age reveals higher relative depravity of Indian Muslims. For all levels of education, Muslims have the least coverage rate, higher D-index and lower HOI in the labour market. Between SCR, its follow-up and the Kundu Committee's evaluation of progress made on follow-up to the SCR, not much has changed with respect to Muslim's employment and labour market participation. Across all levels of education and even for the illiterates, the coverage rates as well as the opportunity index in case of Muslims (Muslim-OBCs and Muslims-General) is the lowest in 2004–2005 and continues to be so in 2011–2012. On an average, Muslims report a coverage rate and HOI 10 and 15 points, respectively, lower than the national level. Empirical estimation of coverage of employment, the access to available employment opportunities and the disparity across and within the socio-religious categories reflect a Muslim disadvantage in the Indian labour market. Thus, religious affiliation, in general, and that for Indian Muslims, in particular, in isolation, does tend to be a determinant of employment outcomes. With Muslims exhibiting lesser coverage rates, higher D-index and lower opportunity index, it is contended that in the Indian labour market coverage of and access to employment opportunities is affected by socio-religious status of an individual.

On the theoretical frame, there is still a huge scope to develop tools and methodologies to address the issues of equity, fairness and opportunity in labour markets. The book is a modest attempt of applying the human opportunity framework to labour market analysis. But the scope still remains to improve on it. Plugging in the impact of wage rate as an important explanatory factor of labour force participation remains a major handicap of macroeconomic studies of Indian labour market. This is due to the unavailability of reliable wage data covering all sectors, although it is available for agricultural wage as a time series data. The issue of religious identity and belief set of a given population remains an ideological black box, more so in context of the labour market. It has been a marker and identifier in the socio-economic and political sphere of Colonial India. However, as discussed here and contrary to policy opinion, it continues to dominate the public space and has had a tendency to remain neutral to the institution of governance. The issue of women participation and their lower reporting rates, as the study finds, has to be abridged with the definition covering the concept of work. NSSO data used here considers women engaged *only in housework* as those out of labour force. However, the specified housework actually does involve regular participation in activities for producing/acquiring food, fuel, fodder, clothing and other commodities. It is recommended that women engaged in these specified activities for home use should be considered a part of the labour force. This would, in turn, then push the participation rate of women up from the accounting perspective.

In conclusion, I would contend that socio-religious status of an individual continues to dominate his/her life outcomes in general and his/her employment outcome in particular. Religion continues to be an identifier and there exists a significant relationship between the socio-religious status of an individual and his access to employment. In case of Indian Muslims, the consequential impact of historical developments continues to impact their present and it is becoming increasingly difficult for public policy to arrest the same. There indeed have been some positive developments over the reference period regarding the socio-economic positioning of Indian Muslims. This includes, among others, the declining share in self-employment and a slide in LFPR in the age group of 15–19. An increase in SERs alongside an insignificant decline in labour force participation of women is encouraging. However, the more pressing issue of equity and livelihood, which we believe among other things as giving rise to the issue of security, still persists.

Policy Suggestions

In the light of the of the major findings of this work in general and the assertions made in this conclusion in particular, it is suggested that efficient affirmative action is extremely required for Indian Muslims to be pulled out of the socio-economic morass. As discussed in the preceding chapters, the *attitudinal bias* attributed to Muslims for relatively worse employment outcomes has got to be seen in tandem with the *demoralization thesis* at the hands of sociocultural inhibitions and public apathy. True it is that an informed empirical establishment of these phenomenon is almost impossible. However, there is enough evidence to suggest the existence of the same. Psychological studies have dealt with the effects of perceived injustices on life outcomes of an individual as well as of a community. It is, as such, high time for public policy to intervene in a targeted manner to address the same. Identification of issues related to equity and fairness is a non-issue but redressal of the same is not. The justice delivery system in identified cases of deprivation needs to be speeded up. Within the ambit of a democratic welfare state, the state cannot absolve itself of the provision of basic public goods on any pretext, more so in case of population groups whose relative depravity has been established, both by government-appointed committees: academic as well as policy research. Principles of balanced regional development, when invoked in the Indian context, demand a revamped effort to be made in investment in Muslim populated areas. These investments should encompass basic social infrastructure alongside a targeted investment in human capital. Educational investments have got to be sensitive to localized issues. Language and medium of instruction need to be local at least up to the primary level, after which gradual transitions to universal mediums of instruction can be made. These efforts will for sure translate into better life outcomes of the individuals in general and the community in particular, the employment outcomes being one of them. With respect to employment outcomes of Muslims in India, apart from the established observations of them being concentrated in informal labour, generally performing menial jobs with self-employment as the rampant activity status, the present study has added a more disturbing dimension to it. It was observed that the coverage rate of employment, the D-index as well as the opportunity index for employment among Muslims is relatively lower. This indeed is more concerning, keeping in view the other available evidence on the *Muslim question*. It is in this regard that targeted effort by the public authorities by means of specialized employment and skill development programmes becomes inevitable. Coverage of Muslims in the existing employment generation programmes has got to be encouraged and ensured. Further, although unrelated to the issue of coverage, it is recommended that the flagship programme like MGNREGA can further be lifted to impart skill development training for at least 6 hours a week within the premises of the work site. This can go a long way in imparting skill to the unskilled.

Traditionally, Muslim minority communities have been associated with many of the arts and crafts. Also, most of these industries are in the informal sector; a large number of them are either in family or household-based units. Most of them have no or poor access to formal sources of credit, modern technology and formal training and exposure to skill development. As such, they are unable to face challenges which are before them. Keeping in mind the factors, government and non-government efforts in terms of public–private partnership are much needed for the revival of traditional arts and crafts (TACs). An effective implementation of a revival mechanism guided by training Muslim youth in TACs, linking them to the larger market and upgrading their skill may not only arrest the decline in the TACs but would also be helpful in protecting and promoting the livelihoods of a large number of Muslim minority populations who have been heavily dependent on these industries for centuries. Initiatives are needed to revive the demand for TACs in the global market. With a multipronged approach to upgrade the skills of artisans and craftsmen on the one hand and facilitating their output to the extended market on the other hand, such initiatives will go a long way at revival and sustainability of these arts and crafts.

I am conscious of the complexities faced by public policy while pursuing a sensitive issue like religion-based and religion-biased development agenda in a diverse country like India. However, it is reiterated that the basic functions of a democratic welfare state ought to be delivered. Within this line of thought, the role of Muslim community and philanthropists in general and Muslim philanthropists in particular becomes exceedingly critical. Elementary economic models of cooperation suggest the benefits of community participation in economic well-being. Thus, it is recommended that an informed debate about the role of NGOs, civil society and not-for-profit organizations in area-based development and individual-centric investment is the need of the hour. With an institutional mechanism bridging philanthropic activity to delivery system at ground in place, it can be argued that certain positive change will be inevitable.

Importance of self-initiative and agency has no replacement. The ancient Greek proverbial phrase 'God helps those who help themselves' as well as the Quranic revelation 'Indeed Allah will not change the conditions of a population until they change what is in themselves' (Quran 13:11) are a reference to same. Existence or non-existence of policy initiatives makes no difference in absence of individual reception to it. Muslims as individuals and as a community need to believe their capacities and capabilities to revive and to excel in all walks of life. Public initiatives need to be supplemented with individual and community support. Household attitude to economic activity in general and that of the women in particular needs a shift. The same can be achieved by a system of community-based individual-centric localized effort to be carried by local individuals at the lowest possible level.

Policy research and data generation by way of case studies and large-scale household survey with targeted research objectives addressing various dimensions of security, equity and fairness among Indian Muslims are still scant. A big push is required by all the stakeholders in this direction. Established research institutions and universities can play a pivotal role in this direction.

Appendix

TABLE A.1 *LFPR (UPSS) for Various Age Groups 2011–2012*

LFPR (UPSS) for Various Age Groups 2011–2012

Socio-religious Category	Age Group	Rural			Urban			Total		
		Male	Female	Total	Male	Female	Total	Male	Female	Total
SCs/STs	15–19	39.1	20.3	30.5	29.7	8.8	20.6	37.2	18.2	28.6
	20–24	85.1	37.9	61.1	72.7	20.9	46.4	82.3	34.0	57.8
	25–29	97.1	44.8	70.4	95.9	27.1	63.1	96.8	41.1	68.8
	30–34	99.2	51.5	74.1	98.6	29.3	66.2	99.1	47.5	72.6
	35–39	99.3	57.2	77.2	99.3	36.5	67.1	99.3	53.4	75.3
	40–44	98.7	57.2	79.4	99.4	35.3	67.0	98.8	52.8	77.1
	45–49	99.2	58.7	80.5	96.4	37.2	68.7	98.6	54.1	78.0
	50–54	96.7	54.2	75.3	93.4	29.1	62.3	96.1	49.6	72.9
	55–59	91.5	47.7	68.4	84.5	28.8	58.8	90.2	44.8	66.8
	60–64	81.9	40.9	62.1	47.7	19.6	33.2	77.1	37.6	57.8
	Total	85.2	45.4	65.5	80.0	26.4	54.2	84.2	41.7	63.3

(Continued)

TABLE A.1 (Continued)

LFPR (UPSS) for Various Age Groups 2011–2012

Socio-religious Category	Age Group	Rural			Urban			Total		
		Male	Female	Total	Male	Female	Total	Male	Female	Total
Hindus	15–19	32.0	16.2	24.8	21.4	8.0	15.4	29.2	14.1	22.4
	20–24	78.4	30.6	54.5	63.2	20.0	42.3	73.7	27.5	50.8
	25–29	96.4	38.0	66.1	94.8	26.5	60.9	95.9	34.5	64.5
	30–34	99.1	44.4	70.4	99.0	26.8	63.5	99.0	39.2	68.3
	35–39	99.2	50.3	73.6	99.0	29.6	64.5	99.1	44.6	71.0
	40–44	98.8	50.7	75.9	98.7	28.5	64.9	98.8	44.4	72.8
	45–49	98.8	50.9	76.4	97.9	24.8	64.4	98.5	43.2	72.8
	50–54	96.8	46.3	72.4	94.9	22.8	59.5	96.3	39.4	68.7
	55–59	93.5	41.5	67.2	86.7	18.6	53.7	91.6	35.3	63.4
	60–64	83.1	32.0	57.3	48.3	11.5	29.4	74.3	26.6	50.1
	Total	83.5	39.0	61.5	79.2	22.4	51.8	82.2	34.2	58.7
Hindu-OBCs	15–19	30.5	15.2	23.6	22.1	9.5	16.4	28.5	13.9	21.9
	20–24	78.6	28.6	54.4	63.1	21.8	43.2	74.3	26.7	51.2
	25–29	96.7	38.1	65.6	94.8	26.2	60.4	96.1	34.7	64.0

	Age									
	30–34	98.6	43.6	69.7	99.5	29.5	64.8	98.9	39.7	68.2
	35–39	98.9	49.9	73.2	99.2	31.2	65.6	99.0	45.2	71.2
	40–44	99.3	49.4	74.9	98.7	29.1	65.9	99.1	44.3	72.6
	45–49	98.5	50.5	76.3	98.7	24.0	65.2	98.6	43.5	73.4
	50–54	97.6	47.3	73.8	94.9	26.2	61.7	97.0	41.9	70.8
	55–59	94.7	42.8	68.8	85.7	18.9	51.5	92.6	36.9	64.6
	60–64	84.9	31.3	57.3	53.8	15.9	34.9	78.0	28.0	52.5
	Total	83.2	38.4	61.1	79.7	23.8	52.8	82.3	34.6	58.9
UC-Hindus	15–19	22.0	10.5	16.9	14.1	5.4	10.2	18.8	8.4	14.1
	20–24	66.4	23.1	44.2	57.2	17.7	38.6	62.1	20.8	41.7
	25–29	94.0	26.3	60.0	93.9	26.7	60.0	94.0	26.4	60.0
	30–34	99.6	34.8	65.4	98.7	23.1	60.9	99.2	29.5	63.3
	35–39	99.2	39.3	68.7	98.8	24.5	62.0	99.0	32.7	65.6
	40–44	98.3	42.7	72.1	98.4	24.8	63.4	98.3	34.7	68.3
	45–49	98.7	41.5	70.6	98.0	19.6	61.4	98.4	31.9	66.5
	50–54	95.6	34.5	66.8	95.8	17.7	57.1	95.7	26.9	62.5
	55–59	94.3	28.7	61.8	88.4	14.4	53.3	91.7	22.5	58.0
	60–64	78.8	23.0	49.2	43.5	5.4	23.4	63.7	15.4	38.2
	Total	80.8	29.9	55.7	77.9	19.0	49.4	79.5	25.1	52.9

(Continued)

TABLE A.1 (Continued)

LFPR (UPSS) for Various Age Groups 2011–2012

Socio-religious Category	Age Group	Rural			Urban			Total		
		Male	Female	Total	Male	Female	Total	Male	Female	Total
Muslims	15–19	42.1	18.5	30.8	43.5	12.6	29.4	42.6	16.4	30.2
	20–24	82.1	21.2	51.5	80.8	15.6	50.0	81.5	18.9	50.8
	25–29	95.9	24.9	58.3	97.7	15.6	59.4	96.7	21.6	58.8
	30–34	98.9	30.8	61.4	98.5	18.8	56.3	98.7	26.3	59.5
	35–39	99.1	27.8	60.4	98.4	20.5	59.8	98.8	25.1	60.2
	40–44	98.3	28.1	62.7	99.2	19.2	62.4	98.7	25.0	62.6
	45–49	99.3	28.3	67.0	98.2	18.7	60.0	98.9	24.9	64.6
	50–54	95.5	25.2	63.6	93.1	14.1	54.4	94.7	21.2	60.4
	55–59	94.1	22.7	58.6	88.3	12.0	50.1	92.1	19.0	55.7
	60–64	80.2	27.1	53.6	52.0	11.3	30.6	70.0	21.0	45.0
	Total	83.8	24.9	54.1	82.7	16.2	50.6	83.4	21.7	52.8
Muslim-OBCs	15–19	38.2	16.5	28.0	44.8	13.2	29.7	40.6	15.3	28.7
	20–24	84.6	18.5	50.8	80.9	16.1	50.9	83.0	17.5	50.8
	25–29	94.1	21.0	54.3	98.3	16.2	59.1	95.9	19.3	56.2
	30–34	99.4	25.8	60.0	98.4	16.7	54.7	99.0	22.1	57.8
	35–39	98.4	28.6	59.9	99.0	18.7	59.6	98.7	24.9	59.8

	Age									
	40–44	99.9	28.3	62.5	98.6	20.9	63.9	99.4	25.8	63.0
	45–49	98.9	27.6	65.2	98.4	18.3	54.9	98.7	24.1	61.7
	50–54	91.4	27.3	59.5	93.1	16.9	55.3	92.0	23.5	57.9
	55–59	92.4	22.6	57.8	88.5	8.6	47.3	91.1	17.6	54.1
	60–64	79.8	29.8	52.8	57.0	10.7	31.9	70.8	22.2	44.5
	Total	82.3	23.3	52.1	83.3	16.0	50.2	82.7	20.5	51.4
Muslims-General	15–19	46.4	20.1	33.3	43.0	12.1	29.4	45.1	17.4	31.9
	20–24	79.7	22.6	51.6	80.8	14.7	49.1	80.2	19.2	50.5
	25–29	98.0	29.3	62.7	97.0	15.4	60.2	97.6	24.2	61.7
	30–34	98.4	35.6	63.2	98.5	21.1	58.1	98.4	30.6	61.3
	35–39	99.6	26.3	59.8	97.8	22.2	59.8	98.9	24.8	59.8
	40–44	96.9	27.9	62.9	99.8	17.9	61.4	98.0	24.3	62.3
	45–49	99.5	28.4	68.5	98.1	19.2	64.9	99.1	25.4	67.3
	50–54	98.6	21.7	67.0	92.8	10.8	52.4	96.9	17.7	62.3
	55–59	95.6	22.2	58.8	88.1	15.6	53.1	92.9	19.9	56.8
	60–64	80.4	23.2	54.4	45.1	12.3	28.6	68.8	19.1	45.4
	Total	85.4	26.1	55.8	82.3	16.4	51.1	84.2	22.5	54.0

(Continued)

TABLE A.1 (Continued)

LFPR (UPSS) for Various Age Groups 2011–2012

Socio-religious Category	Age Group	Rural			Urban			Total		
		Male	Female	Total	Male	Female	Total	Male	Female	Total
Other Minorities	15–19	32.5	13.1	23.5	16.5	5.6	11.8	27.5	11.0	20.0
	20–24	76.8	36.1	56.6	57.6	29.1	42.5	70.0	33.4	51.4
	25–29	95.3	46.8	70.3	92.3	34.0	63.5	94.1	42.1	67.8
	30–34	98.1	51.5	73.3	98.4	34.5	62.5	98.2	45.5	69.6
	35–39	98.3	57.0	76.3	99.7	33.5	65.7	98.8	48.9	72.6
	40–44	98.8	53.5	77.8	99.3	34.9	68.5	99.0	47.0	74.6
	45–49	97.6	52.8	75.9	97.3	31.7	64.5	97.5	44.5	71.6
	50–54	95.4	49.5	73.4	94.2	26.6	60.9	95.0	40.3	68.5
	55–59	91.6	37.5	62.7	86.1	19.0	50.5	89.7	31.0	58.4
	60–64	70.8	36.1	53.0	57.0	12.4	34.5	66.3	28.7	47.1
	Total	82.0	42.4	62.2	77.6	27.5	52.4	80.4	37.1	58.8

All Population									
15–19	33.3	16.4	25.6	25.6	8.9	18.1	31.1	14.3	23.5
20–24	78.8	29.7	54.2	66.4	19.7	43.8	74.7	26.5	50.9
25–29	96.3	36.9	65.4	95.1	25.3	60.8	95.9	33.2	63.9
30–34	99.0	43.1	69.4	98.9	25.9	62.4	99.0	37.8	67.2
35–39	99.1	48.1	72.3	99.0	28.4	63.8	99.1	42.4	69.8
40–44	98.8	48.2	74.5	98.8	27.6	64.7	98.8	42.1	71.6
45–49	98.8	48.4	75.3	97.9	24.5	63.8	98.5	41.1	71.7
50–54	96.6	44.4	71.5	94.6	21.9	58.9	96.0	37.5	67.7
55–59	93.5	39.4	66.1	86.9	17.7	53.0	91.5	33.3	62.3
60–64	82.2	31.8	56.7	49.4	11.5	29.9	73.4	26.2	49.4
Total	83.5	37.5	60.7	79.6	21.7	51.6	82.3	32.8	57.9

Source: Author's calculations based on unit-level data of NSSO 2011–2012.

TABLE A.2 *LFPR (UPSS) for Various Age Groups: 2004–2005*

Socio-religious Category		Rural			Urban			Total		
		Male	Female	Total	Male	Female	Total	Male	Female	Total
SCs/STs	15–19	59.8	41.7	51.5	46.9	15.1	32.8	57.2	36.6	47.9
	20–24	91.6	51.2	70.6	79.7	27.2	55.3	89.1	47.0	67.6
	25–29	98.2	62.7	80.2	96.0	29.9	65.0	97.8	57.2	77.5
	30–34	98.6	69.5	83.2	97.7	38.8	66.9	98.5	64.4	80.5
	35–39	99.5	72.3	86.0	98.2	45.3	71.4	99.3	67.5	83.5
	40–44	98.7	71.2	85.6	97.2	42.0	72.1	98.5	66.1	83.1
	45–49	98.4	71.5	85.7	97.9	37.0	67.7	98.3	65.2	82.5
	50–54	96.8	64.3	81.5	91.3	38.6	67.3	95.8	59.9	79.0
	55–59	93.4	60.2	76.4	88.0	33.8	62.4	92.5	56.4	74.3
	60–64	84.1	42.5	62.3	44.1	21.6	32.1	78.9	39.7	58.3
	Total	90.1	60.4	75.4	82.6	32.0	58.5	88.7	55.5	72.4
Hindus	15–19	52.4	35.3	44.5	35.6	14.3	26.0	48.1	30.1	39.9
	20–24	89.4	45.6	66.9	75.1	26.3	52.1	85.2	40.5	62.8
	25–29	98.3	55.3	76.3	95.2	27.4	63.0	97.4	48.1	72.6
	30–34	98.9	62.0	79.2	98.7	31.1	65.7	98.9	54.3	75.6
	35–39	99.2	67.0	83.0	98.5	35.5	67.5	99.0	58.8	78.9

40–44	98.6	65.2	82.4	98.3	32.2	67.3	98.5	56.5	78.3
45–49	98.4	64.7	82.5	98.0	27.7	64.9	98.3	54.9	77.9
50–54	96.5	58.4	78.1	94.2	26.1	62.6	95.9	50.2	74.1
55–59	93.4	52.7	73.0	83.2	22.9	54.0	90.9	45.6	68.4
60–64	82.2	38.8	59.7	45.4	14.4	29.8	73.7	33.4	52.9
Total	88.5	54.2	71.4	81.9	26.5	55.6	86.7	47.2	67.3
Hindu-OBCs 15–19	51.9	35.2	44.2	43.6	18.9	32.7	50.0	31.8	41.6
20–24	89.8	44.6	66.4	79.1	28.0	55.2	87.1	41.0	63.7
25–29	98.7	54.8	76.2	96.4	30.3	64.3	98.2	49.1	73.4
30–34	99.1	61.8	78.8	99.0	34.7	68.1	99.0	56.1	76.4
35–39	99.0	68.4	83.4	98.8	38.7	69.3	98.9	61.6	80.1
40–44	98.4	67.2	83.3	98.6	35.8	68.2	98.4	59.9	79.8
45–49	98.4	66.0	83.3	98.2	34.0	69.4	98.3	59.0	80.2
50–54	96.9	59.6	78.7	93.8	32.0	66.4	96.3	54.5	76.2
55–59	93.2	54.4	74.1	85.6	24.9	54.8	91.7	48.4	70.2
60–64	81.8	41.8	61.1	55.0	19.6	36.9	76.8	37.7	56.6
Total	88.4	54.7	71.5	84.2	30.2	58.7	87.4	49.4	68.6

(Continued)

TABLE A.2 *(Continued)*

Socio-religious Category		Rural			Urban			Total		
		Male	Female	Total	Male	Female	Total	Male	Female	Total
UC-Hindus	15–19	41.1	23.3	32.9	19.7	9.3	14.8	32.9	17.9	26.0
	20–24	84.5	38.7	61.9	68.2	23.7	47.0	77.2	32.2	55.4
	25–29	97.6	45.1	70.3	93.6	23.8	60.6	95.8	36.4	66.1
	30–34	99.0	51.0	73.7	98.8	25.8	63.4	98.9	40.5	69.2
	35–39	99.0	56.0	77.3	98.3	28.4	64.2	98.7	44.9	71.9
	40–44	98.7	53.3	76.2	98.8	25.7	64.5	98.7	41.9	71.2
	45–49	98.5	53.1	76.3	97.8	18.9	59.9	98.2	38.8	69.4
	50–54	95.5	47.4	72.2	95.3	18.2	58.4	95.4	34.7	66.1
	55–59	93.2	40.4	67.0	80.3	17.5	50.6	87.9	31.6	60.5
	60–64	80.4	30.2	54.4	38.2	8.0	23.4	64.0	22.1	42.8
	Total	85.9	43.8	65.0	79.2	21.0	51.5	83.1	34.5	59.3
Muslims	15–19	57.7	21.3	40.1	53.0	14.6	34.6	56.0	18.9	38.1
	20–24	88.4	23.1	54.2	86.6	17.9	55.1	87.7	21.3	54.6
	25–29	97.9	31.4	62.8	98.6	16.8	59.4	98.2	26.5	61.6
	30–34	98.9	33.7	63.2	98.9	21.7	61.0	98.9	30.0	62.5
	35–39	98.8	39.5	67.5	97.6	24.1	61.7	98.4	34.6	65.6

	40–44	98.0	36.8	68.0	98.1	24.8	61.6	98.0	32.7	65.9
	45–49	96.7	32.5	66.4	95.2	19.4	59.6	96.2	28.0	64.1
	50–54	94.4	37.0	66.4	93.8	23.7	59.4	94.2	32.5	64.0
	55–59	92.6	26.9	61.0	86.9	12.5	50.1	90.7	21.9	57.3
	60–64	83.4	25.9	53.8	60.4	16.7	38.0	75.6	22.8	48.5
	Total	87.7	30.0	58.4	85.1	19.0	53.3	86.8	26.3	56.6
Muslim-OBCs	15–19	56.1	21.0	38.9	51.6	17.5	35.6	54.5	19.8	37.7
	20–24	90.1	25.3	52.8	88.1	23.0	59.0	89.2	24.5	55.2
	25–29	95.9	30.7	59.4	98.0	18.5	58.2	96.7	26.6	59.0
	30–34	98.5	37.0	65.1	98.8	23.7	61.6	98.6	33.0	64.0
	35–39	98.0	43.0	66.8	97.3	26.9	59.7	97.8	37.9	64.5
	40–44	96.3	46.2	70.0	97.1	24.6	63.1	96.6	39.7	67.8
	45–49	95.1	35.4	66.8	93.2	18.6	56.2	94.5	29.6	63.2
	50–54	93.4	38.5	66.5	90.0	24.8	59.6	92.2	33.8	64.1
	55–59	90.2	28.9	58.2	80.5	15.4	45.9	87.1	24.5	54.2
	60–64	74.8	34.3	50.7	69.7	19.0	41.8	72.9	29.3	47.7
	Total	86.3	32.5	57.6	84.3	21.2	53.6	85.5	28.8	56.2

(Continued)

TABLE A.2 *(Continued)*

Socio-religious Category		Rural			Urban			Total		
		Male	Female	Total	Male	Female	Total	Male	Female	Total
Muslims-General	15–19	58.7	21.7	41.0	53.1	13.4	34.5	56.7	18.8	38.7
	20–24	87.9	21.4	55.3	86.0	15.0	53.4	87.2	19.2	54.6
	25–29	98.9	32.0	65.0	99.0	16.0	60.5	98.9	26.6	63.4
	30–34	99.3	31.7	62.1	99.1	20.0	60.5	99.2	28.1	61.6
	35–39	99.2	36.6	67.8	97.8	22.2	62.8	98.7	32.0	66.1
	40–44	98.8	30.8	66.6	98.7	24.4	60.7	98.8	28.5	64.6
	45–49	97.6	30.0	65.9	96.4	20.7	63.2	97.2	26.9	65.0
	50–54	94.8	36.1	66.2	96.4	23.3	59.0	95.3	31.8	63.9
	55–59	94.2	25.6	63.1	89.3	10.7	50.4	92.6	20.1	58.7
	60–64	88.6	18.5	56.0	54.9	14.9	35.4	77.5	17.2	49.0
	Total	88.6	28.3	58.9	85.5	17.7	53.4	87.5	24.7	57.0
Other Minorities	15–19	49.3	29.3	39.5	25.0	13.9	20.2	41.4	25.0	33.7
	20–24	87.5	55.0	70.4	73.1	28.0	52.1	82.9	47.8	65.0
	25–29	96.5	62.0	79.3	94.9	32.1	65.6	95.9	53.2	75.0

	Age								
	30–34	97.5	66.5	80.9	97.8	43.7	66.6	97.5	59.2	76.5
	35–39	99.0	70.9	84.5	99.1	36.1	68.6	99.1	60.4	79.5
	40–44	98.0	71.7	85.6	98.9	38.8	67.2	98.3	60.3	79.7
	45–49	97.0	67.4	82.3	97.9	33.3	66.9	97.3	57.0	77.5
	50–54	96.1	57.7	77.6	91.7	28.4	61.8	94.7	48.3	72.5
	55–59	90.6	61.7	76.0	77.5	26.2	52.5	86.3	50.5	68.4
	60–64	82.1	47.5	64.2	48.0	13.1	30.2	72.1	37.7	54.4
	Total	87.5	58.2	72.7	78.8	30.7	55.3	84.8	49.9	67.4
All Population	15–19	52.9	33.1	43.7	38.1	14.4	27.3	48.8	28.1	39.3
	20–24	89.1	43.5	65.6	76.9	25.0	52.6	85.4	38.5	61.9
	25–29	98.2	53.0	75.0	95.7	26.1	62.6	97.4	45.8	71.5
	30–34	98.8	59.3	77.6	98.7	30.8	65.1	98.8	51.9	74.2
	35–39	99.1	64.2	81.5	98.4	34.0	66.8	98.9	56.1	77.5
	40–44	98.5	62.7	81.1	98.3	31.7	66.5	98.5	54.1	77.0
	45–49	98.2	61.6	80.9	97.6	26.9	64.3	98.0	52.1	76.3
	50–54	96.3	56.2	76.9	93.9	25.9	62.1	95.6	48.1	72.9
	55–59	93.1	50.9	72.1	83.2	21.8	53.3	90.5	43.5	67.2
	60–64	82.3	38.2	59.4	47.6	14.6	30.9	73.8	32.6	52.5
	Total	88.4	51.8	70.1	82.1	25.7	55.3	86.6	44.8	66.0

Source: Author's calculations based on unit-level data of NSSO 2004–2005.

TABLE A.3 *LFPR (UPSS) for Various Levels of Educational Attainment (2011–2012)*

| Socio-religious Category | Level of Education | LFPR for Various Levels of Education (15–64 Years) ||||||||||
| | | Rural ||| Urban ||| Total |||
		Male	Female	Total	Male	Female	Total	Male	Female	Total
SCs/STs	Not-literate	94.6	53.7	68.6	91.4	32.4	51.3	94.2	51.1	66.6
	Below primary	96.2	45.5	74.0	89.9	31.6	62.9	95.3	43.5	72.4
	Primary	91.5	41.8	70.8	90.0	29.3	61.7	91.2	39.4	69.2
	Middle	78.1	30.4	59.3	79.4	20.3	53.7	78.4	27.9	58.0
	Secondary	65.1	26.2	50.6	68.2	15.1	46.9	66.0	22.7	49.5
	Higher secondary	62.3	22.2	48.4	62.4	14.6	41.8	62.4	19.1	46.1
	Diploma/Certificate	85.3	59.9	79.0	78.8	50.3	71.4	82.0	54.8	75.1
	Graduate	83.9	44.6	73.2	86.7	33.9	66.6	85.3	38.0	69.7
	PG and above	92.1	54.5	85.4	91.1	48.0	72.5	91.6	49.3	77.3
	Total	85.2	45.4	65.5	80.0	26.4	54.2	84.2	41.7	63.2
Hindus	Not-literate	95.2	48.3	64.2	91.2	30.2	49.1	94.7	45.7	62.2
	Below primary	95.4	38.6	68.4	93.4	27.1	59.4	95.1	36.3	66.7
	Primary	91.1	38.8	67.1	91.2	24.4	58.4	91.1	35.3	65.1
	Middle	79.6	29.2	58.9	80.2	17.9	51.5	79.7	25.9	56.9
	Secondary	68.7	23.5	51.8	68.5	12.9	43.5	68.7	19.2	48.8

	Higher secondary	64.2	18.4	47.2	61.9	11.8	38.5	63.3	15.1	43.3
	Diploma/Certificate	83.4	51.1	75.3	74.7	37.7	64.4	78.8	43.6	69.5
	Graduate	84.6	31.6	67.8	85.1	27.0	61.1	84.9	28.3	63.4
	PG and above	91.6	51.3	79.4	93.1	44.1	72.5	92.6	45.6	74.4
	Total	83.5	39.0	61.5	79.2	22.4	51.8	82.2	34.2	58.7
Hindu-OBCs	Not-literate	96.2	45.8	62.5	92.6	31.5	49.8	95.8	43.7	60.8
	Below primary	95.2	39.3	68.8	95.4	30.8	62.3	95.2	37.4	67.5
	Primary	90.1	40.6	67.1	91.7	26.6	60.2	90.5	37.1	65.4
	Middle	80.3	30.3	60.3	80.9	19.2	53.5	80.5	27.3	58.6
	Secondary	68.5	23.7	52.2	69.3	14.3	44.3	68.7	20.2	49.7
	Higher secondary	64.0	18.6	47.3	61.5	11.5	38.5	63.1	15.3	43.7
	Diploma/Certificate	83.5	55.5	75.5	76.9	36.2	65.5	80.2	46.1	70.6
	Graduate	82.7	34.3	67.6	84.0	29.8	62.4	83.4	31.4	64.5
	PG and above	93.1	54.3	80.7	93.1	47.8	76.7	93.1	49.8	78.1
	Total	83.2	38.4	61.1	79.7	23.8	52.8	82.3	34.6	58.9
UC-Hindus	Not-literate	92.4	40.0	54.7	87.1	22.8	42.9	91.1	36.4	52.1
	Below primary	94.1	26.9	55.9	93.9	15.8	48.2	94.0	24.3	54.1
	Primary	92.4	32.1	59.7	90.9	17.4	52.1	91.9	27.8	57.4
	Middle	79.6	27.5	55.8	79.3	15.6	47.0	79.5	22.9	52.6

(Continued)

TABLE A.3 *(Continued)*

LFPR for Various Levels of Education (15–64 Years)

Socio-religious Category	Level of Education	Rural			Urban			Total		
		Male	Female	Total	Male	Female	Total	Male	Female	Total
	Secondary	72.9	22.6	53.0	68.0	10.9	41.1	70.9	16.8	47.6
	Higher secondary	66.0	16.8	46.5	62.5	11.5	37.8	64.3	13.7	41.9
	Diploma/Certificate	81.3	34.1	72.4	71.1	35.3	60.8	75.4	35.0	65.4
	Graduate	87.1	26.2	66.0	85.3	25.1	59.5	85.8	25.4	61.3
	PG and above	90.1	48.3	76.1	93.4	42.0	70.6	92.6	43.0	71.7
	Total	80.8	29.9	55.7	77.9	19.0	49.4	79.5	25.1	52.9
Muslims	Not-literate	96.0	27.9	53.5	91.7	21.0	48.5	94.7	25.9	52.1
	Below primary	93.4	21.6	58.4	91.5	24.6	62.1	92.8	22.5	59.6
	Primary	89.5	28.9	62.0	88.1	15.1	54.3	89.0	23.8	59.2
	Middle	75.5	17.8	51.1	81.1	11.2	50.4	77.8	15.0	50.8
	Secondary	64.9	15.7	45.4	71.2	6.0	42.4	67.8	10.8	44.0
	Higher secondary	56.6	22.5	43.8	67.3	10.1	41.0	62.0	15.2	42.3
	Diploma/Certificate	82.0	55.9	73.3	72.5	31.1	62.5	75.8	42.4	66.6
	Graduate	79.3	31.5	63.9	86.9	20.3	61.3	84.2	23.7	62.1
	PG and above	89.2	62.0	81.6	92.9	52.2	75.2	91.5	54.4	77.1
	Total	83.8	24.9	54.1	82.7	16.2	50.6	83.4	21.7	52.8

Muslim-OBCs	Not-literate	95.6	25.9	51.1	90.9	18.7	47.5	94.0	23.8	50.0
	Below primary	93.6	18.3	57.3	90.9	25.9	59.0	92.7	21.1	57.9
	Primary	85.8	24.1	56.9	89.9	14.2	54.4	87.4	20.3	56.0
	Middle	73.3	18.8	52.4	81.5	11.4	51.2	76.2	15.8	51.9
	Secondary	66.3	16.5	46.3	71.2	7.0	43.7	68.6	11.8	45.1
	Higher secondary	51.1	18.6	36.9	66.4	12.0	40.4	59.0	15.0	38.7
	Diploma/Certificate	79.4	55.6	69.4	85.5	22.6	71.0	83.6	39.6	70.4
	Graduate	77.1	38.4	61.5	87.4	20.2	58.9	84.0	25.9	59.8
	PG and above	97.9	89.1	95.5	92.1	46.3	71.7	94.4	56.6	79.7
	Total	82.3	23.3	52.1	83.3	16.0	50.2	82.7	20.5	51.4
Muslims-General	Not-literate	96.4	29.6	55.9	92.9	24.2	50.1	95.5	28.1	54.4
	Below primary	93.2	23.9	58.8	92.1	22.3	65.8	92.8	23.5	60.8
	Primary	92.5	33.1	65.9	86.7	15.6	54.4	90.5	27.0	61.9
	Middle	78.6	15.4	48.8	81.5	11.0	50.0	79.9	13.5	49.3
	Secondary	64.0	14.7	44.6	71.1	5.0	41.0	67.2	9.8	42.9
	Higher secondary	61.5	26.7	50.7	67.7	8.5	41.5	64.6	15.1	45.6
	Diploma/Certificate	84.8	56.2	78.2	55.1	40.8	51.5	66.6	46.3	61.6
	Graduate	81.0	25.7	65.6	86.3	20.4	62.1	84.3	21.9	63.3
	PG and above	76.0	35.7	63.7	93.2	57.8	78.2	88.2	53.4	74.5
	Total	85.4	26.0	55.8	82.3	16.4	51.1	84.2	22.5	54.0

(Continued)

TABLE A.3 *(Continued)*

Socio-religious Category	Level of Education	LFPR for Various Levels of Education (15–64 Years)								
		Rural			Urban			Total		
		Male	Female	Total	Male	Female	Total	Male	Female	Total
Other Minorities	Not-literate	91.2	50.9	66.6	88.4	28.3	47.9	90.8	46.9	63.6
	Below primary	94.7	52.4	73.8	90.9	31.7	59.1	93.9	47.8	70.7
	Primary	92.5	42.8	66.6	87.7	32.4	57.4	91.4	40.4	64.5
	Middle	76.5	37.4	58.8	75.4	20.4	49.6	76.2	32.4	56.2
	Secondary	72.8	34.7	56.2	71.4	15.3	43.5	72.3	26.4	51.3
	Higher secondary	70.2	25.9	49.8	61.7	16.9	39.7	66.2	21.3	44.9
	Diploma/Certificate	81.8	49.1	70.3	87.1	48.1	70.3	84.5	48.5	70.3
	Graduate	79.7	45.4	64.4	83.2	41.9	63.6	82.1	42.9	63.8
	PG and above	96.9	54.0	70.6	96.2	58.3	79.5	96.3	56.9	77.1
	Total	82.0	42.4	62.2	77.6	27.5	52.4	80.4	37.1	58.8

All Population										
	Not-literate	95.2	45.8	62.9	91.2	27.9	48.9	94.6	42.9	60.7
	Below primary	95.1	36.8	67.3	92.8	26.7	60.0	94.7	34.6	65.8
	Primary	90.9	37.7	66.3	90.3	22.8	57.4	90.8	33.8	64.1
	Middle	79.0	28.4	58.1	80.1	16.9	51.2	79.3	24.8	56.1
	Secondary	68.6	23.5	51.5	69.1	12.2	43.4	68.8	18.8	48.5
	Higher secondary	64.0	19.3	47.1	62.5	12.0	38.8	63.3	15.6	43.3
	Diploma/Certificate	83.2	51.2	74.7	75.5	38.7	64.8	79.1	44.2	69.3
	Graduate	84.0	32.8	67.3	85.1	27.8	61.3	84.7	29.3	63.3
	PG and above	91.7	52.2	79.0	93.3	45.5	73.1	92.8	47.0	74.7
	Total	83.5	37.5	60.7	79.6	21.7	51.6	82.3	32.8	57.9

Source: Author's calculations based on unit-level data of NSSO 2011–2012.

TABLE A.4 LFPR (UPSS) for Various Levels of Educational Attainment (2004–2005)

Socio-religious Category	Level of Education	LFPR for Various Levels of Education 2004-2005 (15-64 Years)								
		Rural			Urban			Total		
		Male	Female	Total	Male	Female	Total	Male	Female	Total
SCs/STs	Not-literate	96.4	66.1	77.9	92.3	40.1	57.7	96.0	63.1	75.7
	Below primary	95.6	56.0	80.3	93.9	30.2	68.9	95.3	51.8	78.5
	Primary	90.4	49.9	75.8	91.3	29.4	64.9	90.6	45.1	73.5
	Middle	81.4	44.4	69.1	80.6	21.1	57.5	81.3	38.0	66.3
	Secondary	73.1	35.0	61.2	71.8	20.2	52.7	72.7	29.6	58.4
	Higher secondary	73.5	37.6	62.5	54.9	19.2	41.2	67.3	30.0	54.7
	Diploma/Certificate	90.4	61.4	80.6	85.1	51.9	72.2	88.0	56.6	76.7
	Graduate	89.5	45.8	79.5	81.7	33.3	63.5	86.1	38.2	71.7
	PG and above	96.2	48.5	83.3	87.0	59.0	78.1	92.0	53.9	80.8
	Total	90.1	60.4	75.4	82.6	32.0	58.5	88.7	55.5	72.4
Hindus	Not-literate	95.5	62.1	73.9	90.9	36.7	54.3	95.0	58.8	71.5
	Below primary	95.2	52.1	76.8	92.8	28.8	61.8	94.8	47.2	73.9
	Primary	91.3	47.6	73.2	90.9	26.9	60.5	91.2	42.0	70.1
	Middle	82.2	39.7	66.5	81.3	18.2	53.3	81.9	32.5	62.6
	Secondary	76.0	33.6	61.4	73.0	14.7	48.2	74.9	25.2	56.2

Group	Education										
	Higher secondary	75.2	29.6	60.7	64.3	15.0	43.8	70.5	21.7	52.7
	Diploma/Certificate	90.1	69.1	84.3	88.6	57.0	79.8	89.3	62.0	81.7
	Graduate	91.4	42.9	79.7	85.9	32.1	64.5	88.1	34.7	69.8
	PG and above	95.9	54.1	85.2	92.2	42.0	71.3	93.5	44.6	75.5
	Total	88.5	54.2	71.4	81.9	26.5	55.6	86.7	47.2	67.3
Hindu-OBCs	Not-literate	95.1	61.1	72.7	91.6	39.1	56.2	94.7	58.4	70.7
	Below primary	95.1	54.9	78.1	94.2	34.2	64.6	95.0	50.6	75.6
	Primary	91.5	50.4	74.7	93.2	32.3	65.4	91.9	45.7	72.5
	Middle	82.2	40.8	67.3	84.6	20.7	56.6	82.8	34.6	64.5
	Secondary	76.5	34.4	62.5	74.1	16.9	50.4	75.8	27.7	58.5
	Higher secondary	76.8	30.6	62.3	66.6	16.3	46.8	73.1	24.2	56.3
	Diploma/Certificate	90.6	70.4	84.8	88.3	69.7	84.3	89.4	70.1	84.5
	Graduate	90.3	49.6	81.8	85.2	41.8	70.2	87.8	44.4	75.6
	PG and above	97.6	64.4	90.2	94.6	48.9	78.3	96.1	53.9	83.5
	Total	88.4	54.7	71.5	84.2	30.2	58.7	87.4	49.4	68.6
UC-Hindus	Not-literate	93.5	53.9	65.7	85.6	26.7	44.4	92.0	49.0	61.8
	Below primary	94.3	44.1	67.6	88.9	21.3	51.0	93.0	38.3	63.5
	Primary	92.1	42.9	67.2	86.1	19.5	49.9	90.4	35.6	62.0
	Middle	82.7	35.1	62.2	77.3	14.6	47.0	80.8	27.0	56.6

(Continued)

TABLE A.4 (Continued)

LFPR for Various Levels of Education 2004–2005 (15–64 Years)

Socio-religious Category	Level of Education	Rural Male	Rural Female	Rural Total	Urban Male	Urban Female	Urban Total	Total Male	Total Female	Total Total
	Secondary	77.7	32.5	60.3	72.3	12.3	45.0	75.2	21.9	53.0
	Higher secondary	74.7	26.2	58.0	65.3	13.8	42.6	69.7	18.3	49.0
	Diploma/Certificate	89.7	74.8	86.3	89.6	51.7	78.0	89.6	57.6	80.6
	Graduate	93.0	38.7	77.9	86.6	29.4	62.7	88.5	31.2	66.7
	PG and above	94.4	46.6	80.2	92.0	40.4	69.1	92.6	41.4	71.5
	Total	85.9	43.8	64.9	79.2	21.0	51.5	83.1	34.5	59.3
Muslims	Not-literate	94.8	34.0	57.5	90.5	22.9	49.7	93.7	31.2	55.5
	Below primary	92.5	23.1	62.0	93.2	18.5	60.4	92.8	21.7	61.5
	Primary	88.9	23.1	60.6	91.5	15.0	59.0	89.8	20.3	60.1
	Middle	79.9	22.7	57.6	80.5	14.5	52.1	80.2	19.1	55.3
	Secondary	70.2	21.8	53.0	76.0	7.7	47.1	73.0	13.9	50.0
	Higher secondary	64.1	23.1	50.4	66.1	12.2	42.5	65.1	16.2	45.9
	Diploma/Certificate	86.3	59.9	76.0	88.9	59.3	78.4	88.0	59.5	77.6
	Graduate	82.8	62.2	78.9	86.8	30.9	66.6	85.3	37.2	70.5
	PG and above	99.3	65.7	93.4	96.5	61.8	84.5	97.2	62.2	86.2
	Total	87.7	30.0	58.4	85.1	19.0	53.3	86.8	26.3	56.6

Muslim-OBCs	Not-literate	93.6	37.3	57.7	88.4	24.5	49.1	92.1	33.9	55.4
	Below primary	88.3	21.5	59.2	93.4	21.2	63.5	90.0	21.4	60.6
	Primary	85.5	23.0	58.8	89.7	16.1	59.5	87.3	20.2	59.1
	Middle	80.6	23.5	57.3	79.8	15.3	52.3	80.3	20.3	55.4
	Secondary	68.0	23.4	48.9	74.0	11.7	47.2	70.8	17.9	48.1
	Higher secondary	69.5	24.5	50.1	64.9	23.4	50.5	67.1	24.1	50.3
	Diploma/Certificate	83.9	63.7	74.9	92.5	66.8	83.0	88.2	65.0	78.6
	Graduate	80.0	79.3	79.9	81.0	37.6	66.6	80.6	51.0	72.0
	PG and above	98.2	38.3	85.9	96.9	82.1	93.9	97.4	63.8	90.6
	Total	86.3	32.5	57.6	84.3	21.2	53.6	85.5	28.9	56.2
Muslims-General	Not-literate	95.5	31.7	57.4	92.1	21.6	50.1	94.7	29.3	55.7
	Below primary	94.9	24.1	63.5	93.2	17.0	58.3	94.4	22.1	62.0
	Primary	90.6	23.2	61.5	92.8	14.3	58.8	91.3	20.4	60.7
	Middle	79.6	21.9	58.0	80.9	13.6	52.0	80.1	17.9	55.3
	Secondary	71.2	19.3	55.2	76.2	5.7	46.9	73.7	11.0	50.7
	Higher secondary	62.0	21.8	51.1	66.7	10.8	42.6	64.6	14.0	46.0
	Diploma/Certificate	92.9	39.9	79.7	88.7	54.7	76.9	89.5	52.7	77.4
	Graduate	84.0	48.0	77.7	88.4	31.4	67.9	86.9	34.1	70.8
	PG and above	100.0	94.5	99.2	96.5	60.1	83.1	97.1	62.3	85.3
	Total	88.6	28.3	58.9	85.5	17.7	53.4	87.5	24.7	57.0

(Continued)

TABLE A.4 (Continued)

| Socio-religious Category | Level of Education | LFPR for Various Levels of Education 2004–2005 (15–64 Years) ||||||||||
| | | Rural ||| Urban ||| Total |||
		Male	Female	Total	Male	Female	Total	Male	Female	Total
Other Minorities	Not-literate	94.8	67.7	78.5	84.9	40.3	55.0	93.8	64.3	75.8
	Below primary	95.6	61.1	78.0	86.1	35.4	63.8	93.5	56.7	75.3
	Primary	90.5	59.3	75.2	80.5	28.7	53.5	88.3	51.8	70.2
	Middle	81.0	46.6	66.2	78.2	22.5	51.5	80.2	38.8	61.8
	Secondary	80.7	43.6	65.0	69.1	21.7	46.2	76.5	34.4	57.7
	Higher secondary	76.0	41.3	59.3	65.7	21.9	45.4	70.6	31.6	52.2
	Diploma/Certificate	92.4	71.7	83.0	91.7	63.2	80.6	92.1	68.3	82.0
	Graduate	89.2	59.1	76.6	88.7	38.1	66.2	88.8	43.5	69.0
	PG and above	95.8	61.2	77.6	91.3	53.1	74.8	92.1	55.0	75.4
	Total	87.6	58.2	72.7	78.8	30.7	55.3	84.8	49.9	67.4

		All							Population		
Not-literate	95.4	59.0	72.1	90.6	33.7	53.2	94.7	55.4	69.4
Below primary	94.9	49.1	75.1	92.6	27.2	61.6	94.5	44.3	72.3
Primary	91.0	45.4	71.8	90.5	25.0	59.9	90.9	39.7	68.7
Middle	81.9	38.5	65.6	81.0	17.9	53.0	81.7	31.4	61.8
Secondary	76.0	33.7	61.1	73.0	14.6	47.9	74.9	25.0	55.8
Higher secondary	74.6	30.4	59.9	64.6	15.4	43.8	70.1	22.3	52.1
Diploma/Certificate	90.3	69.1	83.6	88.9	58.0	79.7	89.5	63.0	81.5
Graduate	90.7	45.5	79.5	86.2	32.6	64.8	87.9	35.7	69.7
PG and above	96.0	55.2	85.0	92.4	44.1	72.4	93.6	46.5	76.1
Total	88.3	51.8	70.1	82.1	25.7	55.3	86.6	44.8	66.0

Source: Author's calculations based on unit-level data of NSSO 2004–2005.

TABLE A.5 *WFPR (UPSS) for Different Age Groups 2011–2012*

WFPR by Age Group 2011–2012

Socio-religious Category	Age Group	Rural			Urban			Total		
		Male	Female	Total	Male	Female	Total	Male	Female	Total
SCs/STs	15–19	35.6	19.4	28.2	26.4	7.4	18.1	33.8	17.2	26.2
	20–24	80.8	36.5	58.3	66.2	17.5	41.4	77.5	32.2	54.5
	25–29	95.4	43.7	69.0	92.0	25.3	60.2	94.6	39.9	67.1
	30–34	98.3	51.3	73.6	96.0	28.0	64.2	97.8	47.1	71.7
	35–39	99.3	57.1	77.1	98.6	36.4	66.8	99.1	53.4	75.2
	40–44	98.6	57.2	79.4	98.7	35.2	66.7	98.7	52.7	77.0
	45–49	99.2	58.7	80.5	96.0	36.7	68.2	98.5	54.0	77.9
	50–54	96.7	54.2	75.3	93.2	29.1	62.2	96.0	49.6	72.8
	55–59	91.4	47.7	68.4	84.5	28.8	58.7	90.1	44.8	66.8
	60–64	81.8	40.9	62.0	47.7	19.6	33.2	77.0	37.6	57.8
	Total	83.8	44.9	64.5	77.4	25.2	52.3	82.5	41.1	62.1
Hindus	15–19	29.3	15.7	23.1	18.7	7.1	13.5	26.5	13.4	20.6
	20–24	73.7	28.9	51.3	57.0	16.0	37.2	68.5	25.1	47.0
	25–29	94.3	37.0	64.6	89.9	24.2	57.3	92.9	33.1	62.3
	30–34	98.2	44.0	69.7	97.4	25.6	62.1	97.9	38.6	67.4

	Age	C1	C2	C3	C4	C5	C6	C7	C8
	35–39	99.0	50.2	73.5	98.6	29.4	64.2	98.9	44.4	70.8
	40–44	98.8	50.6	75.8	98.4	28.4	64.7	98.7	44.3	72.6
	45–49	98.8	50.8	76.4	97.6	24.7	64.2	98.4	43.1	72.7
	50–54	96.8	46.3	72.4	94.3	22.8	59.2	96.1	39.4	68.6
	55–59	93.5	41.3	67.1	86.6	18.6	53.6	91.5	35.2	63.3
	60–64	83.1	32.0	57.2	48.3	11.5	29.4	74.2	26.6	50.0
	Total	82.1	38.5	60.5	76.9	21.2	50.1	80.6	33.5	57.5
Hindu-OBCs	15–19	28.0	14.8	22.1	19.3	8.7	14.6	25.9	13.4	20.3
	20–24	73.9	26.9	51.1	57.0	18.0	38.2	69.2	24.4	47.5
	25–29	94.6	37.1	64.0	90.5	23.9	57.2	93.3	33.3	62.0
	30–34	97.8	43.2	69.1	98.6	28.3	63.7	98.1	39.0	67.5
	35–39	98.6	49.7	73.0	98.8	30.9	65.3	98.7	45.0	70.9
	40–44	99.2	49.3	74.8	98.6	29.1	65.8	99.1	44.2	72.5
	45–49	98.5	50.4	76.3	98.6	23.9	65.1	98.5	43.5	73.3
	50–54	97.6	47.3	73.8	94.8	26.2	61.7	96.9	41.9	70.8
	55–59	94.7	42.4	68.6	85.6	18.9	51.4	92.6	36.6	64.5
	60–64	84.8	31.3	57.3	53.7	15.9	34.9	77.9	28.0	52.4
	Total	81.9	37.9	60.1	77.7	22.6	51.2	80.7	33.9	57.7

(Continued)

TABLE A.5 (Continued)

WFPR by Age Group 2011–2012

Socio-religious Category	Age Group	Rural			Urban			Total		
		Male	Female	Total	Male	Female	Total	Male	Female	Total
UC-Hindus	15–19	20.1	10.1	15.6	11.9	4.7	8.7	16.8	7.9	12.8
	20–24	61.0	20.4	40.3	50.7	13.1	33.0	56.2	17.3	37.0
	25–29	91.3	25.0	58.0	87.6	23.8	55.4	89.6	24.5	56.9
	30–34	98.5	34.2	64.5	96.7	21.9	59.4	97.6	28.6	62.1
	35–39	99.0	39.3	68.6	98.5	24.2	61.6	98.8	32.5	65.4
	40–44	98.1	42.5	72.0	98.1	24.6	63.1	98.1	34.5	68.1
	45–49	98.7	41.5	70.6	97.6	19.6	61.2	98.2	31.9	66.3
	50–54	95.6	34.5	66.8	94.6	17.7	56.5	95.1	26.9	62.3
	55–59	94.3	28.7	61.7	88.2	14.4	53.2	91.6	22.5	58.0
	60–64	78.8	23.0	49.2	43.5	5.4	23.4	63.6	15.4	38.1
	Total	79.4	29.3	54.6	75.6	17.7	47.6	77.7	24.2	51.5
Muslims	15–19	37.7	16.2	27.3	37.8	11.4	25.7	37.8	14.4	26.7
	20–24	77.7	19.4	48.4	71.9	13.7	44.4	75.1	17.1	46.7
	25–29	94.0	23.2	56.5	94.9	14.6	57.5	94.4	20.1	56.9
	30–34	98.2	30.3	60.8	97.5	18.2	55.6	97.9	25.8	58.8

	35–39	98.7	27.5	60.0	98.1	20.4	59.6	98.5	24.8	59.8
	40–44	98.2	28.1	62.6	99.1	19.1	62.3	98.6	25.0	62.5
	45–49	99.3	28.0	66.9	98.1	18.7	59.9	98.9	24.7	64.5
	50–54	95.5	25.2	63.6	92.7	14.0	54.1	94.5	21.1	60.3
	55–59	94.1	22.7	58.6	88.3	12.0	50.1	92.1	19.0	55.7
	60–64	80.2	27.1	53.6	51.5	11.3	30.4	69.8	21.0	45.0
	Total	82.0	23.9	52.7	79.5	15.4	48.6	81.0	20.8	51.1
Muslim-OBCs	15–19	34.2	13.3	24.4	41.8	12.2	27.7	37.0	12.9	25.7
	20–24	81.0	16.2	47.8	74.0	14.3	46.4	77.9	15.5	47.2
	25–29	92.8	19.0	52.7	96.3	15.5	57.7	94.3	17.8	54.6
	30–34	98.6	24.9	59.1	97.7	16.0	54.0	98.2	21.3	57.0
	35–39	97.6	27.8	59.1	98.7	18.7	59.5	98.1	24.4	59.3
	40–44	99.6	28.3	62.3	98.5	20.8	63.8	99.2	25.7	62.9
	45–49	98.9	27.6	65.2	98.4	18.3	54.9	98.7	24.1	61.7
	50–54	91.4	27.3	59.5	93.0	16.9	55.3	92.0	23.5	57.9
	55–59	92.4	22.6	57.8	88.5	8.6	47.3	91.1	17.6	54.1
	60–64	79.8	29.8	52.8	56.2	10.7	31.6	70.4	22.2	44.4
	Total	80.6	21.9	50.6	81.1	15.3	48.8	80.8	19.4	49.9

(Continued)

TABLE A.5 (Continued)

WFPR by Age Group 2011-2012

Socio-religious Category	Age Group	Rural			Urban			Total		
		Male	Female	Total	Male	Female	Total	Male	Female	Total
Muslims-General	15–19	42.3	18.5	30.4	34.9	10.5	24.1	39.3	15.8	28.1
	20–24	74.5	21.4	48.3	69.8	12.8	42.4	72.4	17.7	45.8
	25–29	95.6	27.8	60.7	93.5	14.0	57.6	94.7	22.8	59.5
	30–34	97.9	35.5	62.9	97.2	20.7	57.3	97.6	30.4	60.9
	35–39	99.6	26.3	59.8	97.4	22.1	59.5	98.7	24.7	59.7
	40–44	96.9	27.9	62.9	99.7	17.9	61.4	98.0	24.3	62.3
	45–49	99.5	27.8	68.2	97.8	19.2	64.7	99.0	24.9	67.0
	50–54	98.6	21.6	67.0	91.9	10.8	52.0	96.7	17.7	62.1
	55–59	95.6	22.2	58.8	88.1	15.6	53.1	92.9	19.9	56.8
	60–64	80.4	23.2	54.4	45.1	12.3	28.6	68.8	19.1	45.4
	Total	83.6	25.3	54.5	78.1	15.6	48.5	81.4	21.8	52.3
Other Minorities	15–19	27.9	12.0	20.5	13.8	2.9	9.1	23.5	9.4	17.1
	20–24	72.8	31.3	52.2	45.9	22.9	33.7	63.3	28.1	45.3
	25–29	91.5	44.2	67.1	88.1	30.4	59.6	90.2	39.1	64.3

Age									
30–34	97.1	49.3	71.7	94.5	33.4	60.2	96.3	43.7	67.7
35–39	97.7	56.3	75.7	99.2	32.1	64.8	98.2	48.0	71.9
40–44	98.7	53.5	77.8	99.0	34.9	68.4	98.8	47.0	74.5
45–49	97.6	52.8	75.9	97.1	31.6	64.4	97.4	44.5	71.5
50–54	95.4	49.5	73.4	93.7	26.6	60.6	94.8	40.3	68.3
55–59	91.6	37.5	62.7	86.1	19.0	50.5	89.6	31.0	58.3
60–64	70.8	36.1	53.0	57.0	12.4	34.5	66.3	28.7	47.1
Total	80.1	40.9	60.6	74.5	25.6	50.0	78.1	35.5	56.8
All Population									
15–19	30.3	15.6	23.6	22.3	7.8	15.8	28.1	13.4	21.4
20–24	74.2	27.8	51.0	59.4	16.0	38.4	69.2	24.1	46.9
25–29	94.2	35.7	63.7	90.6	23.1	57.5	93.0	31.7	61.7
30–34	98.1	42.6	68.8	97.3	24.8	61.0	97.8	37.1	66.3
35–39	98.9	48.0	72.1	98.6	28.1	63.5	98.8	42.2	69.5
40–44	98.7	48.2	74.5	98.5	27.5	64.6	98.7	42.0	71.5
45–49	98.8	48.4	75.3	97.6	24.4	63.6	98.4	41.0	71.6
50–54	96.6	44.4	71.5	94.1	21.9	58.6	95.8	37.5	67.6
55–59	93.5	39.3	66.0	86.8	17.7	52.9	91.5	33.2	62.2
60–64	82.2	31.8	56.7	49.4	11.5	29.9	73.3	26.2	49.3
Total	82.0	36.9	59.6	77.2	20.5	49.8	80.5	32.0	56.6

Source: Author's calculations based on unit-level data of NSSO 2011–2012.

TABLE A.6 WFPR (UPSS) for Different Age Groups 2004–2005

WPR for Different Age Groups 2004–2005

Socio-religious Category	Age Group	Rural			Urban			Total		
		Male	Female	Total	Male	Female	Total	Male	Female	Total
SCs/STs	15–19	56.5	40.8	49.4	39.1	13.6	27.8	53.0	35.6	45.1
	20–24	87.9	49.3	67.8	69.8	23.6	48.3	84.0	44.8	64.0
	25–29	97.1	61.8	79.2	91.1	26.3	60.7	95.9	55.8	75.9
	30–34	98.0	69.1	82.7	94.4	37.9	64.9	97.4	63.8	79.7
	35–39	99.4	72.1	85.9	97.6	44.8	70.8	99.1	67.3	83.3
	40–44	98.7	71.2	85.5	97.0	41.9	71.9	98.4	66.1	83.1
	45–49	98.2	71.3	85.5	97.7	37.0	67.6	98.2	65.1	82.4
	50–54	96.8	64.3	81.5	90.7	38.5	67.0	95.7	59.9	79.0
	55–59	93.2	60.2	76.3	87.9	33.8	62.4	92.3	56.4	74.2
	60–64	84.1	42.3	62.3	44.1	21.6	32.1	78.9	39.5	58.2
	Total	88.8	59.8	74.4	78.4	30.6	55.6	86.9	54.7	71.1
Hindus	15–19	49.5	34.3	42.5	31.1	12.7	22.9	44.8	28.9	37.6
	20–24	85.3	43.5	63.8	66.7	21.5	45.5	79.8	37.8	58.7
	25–29	96.7	53.7	74.7	90.5	24.1	58.9	95.0	46.1	70.4
	30–34	98.3	61.2	78.5	96.7	29.4	63.8	97.9	53.3	74.6

	35–39	99.0	66.6	82.7	97.7	34.2	66.4	98.6	58.2	78.4
	40–44	98.5	65.0	82.2	97.9	31.6	66.8	98.3	56.2	78.0
	45–49	98.3	64.6	82.4	97.3	27.4	64.4	98.1	54.8	77.6
	50–54	96.5	58.3	78.1	93.3	26.0	62.1	95.7	50.1	73.9
	55–59	93.3	52.6	73.0	82.9	22.9	53.8	90.7	45.5	68.3
	60–64	82.2	38.7	59.6	45.3	14.4	29.7	73.6	33.3	52.8
	Total	87.1	53.4	70.3	78.8	24.7	53.1	84.9	46.1	65.8
Hindu-OBCs	15–19	49.2	34.2	42.3	39.3	17.2	29.6	46.9	30.6	39.5
	20–24	86.0	42.6	63.6	71.9	23.3	49.1	82.4	38.4	60.2
	25–29	97.4	52.8	74.6	93.1	27.0	61.0	96.3	46.9	71.3
	30–34	98.6	60.9	78.1	97.4	32.9	66.4	98.3	55.0	75.4
	35–39	98.8	68.1	83.2	98.3	36.8	68.0	98.7	61.0	79.7
	40–44	98.3	67.0	83.1	98.3	34.9	67.6	98.3	59.6	79.5
	45–49	98.3	65.9	83.3	97.6	33.7	68.9	98.1	58.8	80.0
	50–54	96.9	59.5	78.6	93.6	31.9	66.2	96.2	54.4	76.1
	55–59	93.2	54.3	74.0	85.1	24.9	54.6	91.6	48.4	70.2
	60–64	81.6	41.7	61.0	54.9	19.5	36.9	76.6	37.6	56.5
	Total	87.2	53.8	70.5	81.6	28.2	56.4	85.8	48.3	67.3

(Continued)

TABLE A.6 *(Continued)*

WPR for Different Age Groups 2004–2005

Socio-religious Category	Age Group	Rural			Urban			Total		
		Male	Female	Total	Male	Female	Total	Male	Female	Total
UC-Hindus	15–19	38.0	22.0	30.6	17.2	7.7	12.8	30.1	16.5	23.8
	20–24	79.1	35.5	57.6	59.4	18.3	39.8	70.3	28.1	49.8
	25–29	94.7	43.3	68.0	87.6	20.5	55.8	91.5	34.1	62.8
	30–34	98.0	49.8	72.6	97.1	23.7	61.5	97.6	39.0	67.8
	35–39	98.6	55.0	76.5	97.3	27.2	63.1	98.1	43.8	71.0
	40–44	98.4	52.9	75.9	98.2	25.1	63.9	98.3	41.4	70.8
	45–49	98.3	53.0	76.2	96.7	18.6	59.2	97.6	38.6	69.0
	50–54	95.5	47.2	72.1	93.9	18.1	57.6	94.8	34.5	65.7
	55–59	93.2	40.3	66.9	80.0	17.5	50.5	87.8	31.5	60.4
	60–64	80.4	30.2	54.4	38.2	8.0	23.4	64.0	22.1	42.8
	Total	84.2	42.6	63.5	76.2	19.2	49.0	80.8	33.1	57.4
Muslims	15–19	53.9	19.6	37.3	47.9	13.2	31.4	51.8	17.3	35.2
	20–24	84.6	20.3	51.0	79.1	14.2	49.4	82.4	18.2	50.4
	25–29	96.5	29.5	61.2	94.6	15.0	56.4	95.8	24.7	59.5
	30–34	97.5	32.8	62.1	98.0	20.7	60.0	97.7	29.1	61.4

35–39	98.6	39.5	67.4	97.2	24.1	61.4	98.1	34.6	65.4
40–44	97.6	36.6	67.7	97.8	24.8	61.5	97.7	32.6	65.6
45–49	96.4	32.5	66.3	95.2	19.4	59.5	96.0	28.0	64.0
50–54	94.3	37.0	66.3	93.4	23.7	59.2	94.0	32.5	64.0
55–59	92.5	26.9	61.0	86.9	12.5	50.1	90.6	21.9	57.2
60–64	83.3	25.9	53.7	60.3	16.7	38.0	75.5	22.8	48.4
Total	86.0	28.9	56.9	82.1	17.7	51.1	84.6	25.1	54.9
Muslim-OBCs									
15–19	51.8	19.2	35.8	47.9	15.3	32.6	50.4	17.8	34.7
20–24	84.9	20.1	47.5	78.2	19.5	51.9	81.9	19.9	49.2
25–29	94.3	26.7	56.5	94.6	15.4	54.9	94.4	22.9	55.9
30–34	96.6	35.4	63.4	97.3	22.1	60.0	96.9	31.4	62.3
35–39	97.5	42.9	66.6	97.1	26.8	59.6	97.4	37.9	64.3
40–44	95.5	46.2	69.7	97.1	24.6	63.1	96.1	39.7	67.5
45–49	95.0	35.4	66.7	93.0	18.6	56.2	94.3	29.6	63.2
50–54	93.4	38.5	66.5	90.0	24.8	59.6	92.2	33.8	64.1
55–59	90.2	28.9	58.2	80.4	15.4	45.9	87.0	24.5	54.2
60–64	74.8	34.3	50.7	69.7	19.0	41.8	72.9	29.3	47.7
Total	84.1	30.7	55.6	81.1	19.7	51.2	83.0	27.1	54.1

(Continued)

TABLE A.6 *(Continued)*

WPR for Different Age Groups 2004–2005

Socio-religious Category	Age Group	Rural			Urban			Total		
		Male	Female	Total	Male	Female	Total	Male	Female	Total
Muslims-General	15–19	55.3	20.0	38.4	47.2	12.5	30.9	52.4	17.4	35.8
	20–24	84.7	20.4	53.1	80.3	11.4	48.6	83.0	17.2	51.4
	25–29	97.5	31.5	64.1	94.6	15.0	57.7	96.4	25.9	61.8
	30–34	98.7	31.3	61.7	98.4	19.5	59.9	98.6	27.7	61.1
	35–39	99.1	36.6	67.7	97.3	22.2	62.5	98.5	32.0	65.9
	40–44	98.6	30.5	66.4	98.2	24.4	60.5	98.5	28.3	64.3
	45–49	97.3	30.0	65.7	96.4	20.7	63.2	97.0	26.9	64.9
	50–54	94.8	36.1	66.1	95.7	23.3	58.7	95.1	31.8	63.7
	55–59	94.0	25.6	63.0	89.3	10.7	50.4	92.4	20.1	58.6
	60–64	88.4	18.5	55.9	54.9	14.9	35.4	77.3	17.2	48.9
	Total	87.1	27.6	57.8	82.6	16.8	51.4	85.5	24.0	55.6
Other Minorities	15–19	43.2	26.4	35.0	20.0	12.1	16.6	35.7	22.4	29.4
	20–24	80.7	47.8	63.4	59.3	18.4	40.3	73.9	39.9	56.6
	25–29	94.0	57.8	75.9	87.6	25.9	58.8	91.9	48.4	70.6
	30–34	96.3	64.8	79.4	96.5	39.2	63.5	96.3	56.6	74.6

	Age									
	35–39	98.8	70.1	84.0	99.0	33.8	67.4	98.9	59.2	78.8
	40–44	97.6	71.0	85.1	98.6	38.1	66.6	97.9	59.5	79.1
	45–49	97.0	67.3	82.2	94.8	33.2	65.3	96.3	56.9	76.9
	50–54	96.1	57.2	77.4	90.5	28.4	61.1	94.3	48.0	72.1
	55–59	90.5	61.7	76.0	77.1	26.2	52.2	86.1	50.5	68.3
	60–64	81.4	47.5	63.9	48.0	12.4	29.9	71.6	37.5	54.0
All	Total	85.1	55.7	70.3	74.5	27.4	51.6	81.8	47.2	64.5
Population	15–19	49.7	31.9	41.5	33.5	12.8	24.1	45.3	26.8	36.8
	20–24	84.9	41.0	62.3	68.4	20.1	45.8	79.8	35.4	57.5
	25–29	96.6	51.3	73.3	90.9	22.9	58.6	94.9	43.7	69.1
	30–34	98.1	58.4	76.9	96.9	29.0	63.3	97.8	50.8	73.1
	35–39	98.9	63.9	81.2	97.7	32.8	65.8	98.6	55.6	77.0
	40–44	98.3	62.5	80.9	98.0	31.2	66.1	98.2	53.8	76.7
	45–49	98.1	61.5	80.8	96.8	26.7	63.8	97.7	51.9	76.1
	50–54	96.3	56.1	76.9	93.1	25.8	61.6	95.4	48.0	72.7
	55–59	93.0	50.9	72.0	82.9	21.8	53.2	90.4	43.5	67.1
	60–64	82.2	38.1	59.3	47.6	14.6	30.9	73.7	32.5	52.5
	Total	86.9	50.8	68.9	79.0	23.8	52.7	84.7	43.6	64.4

Source: Author's calculations based on unit-level data of NSSO 2004–2005.

TABLE A.7 *WFPR by General Level of Education (15–64 Years) 2011–2012*

Socio-religious Category	Level of Education	2011–2012 WFPR by General Education Level (15–64 Years)								
		Rural			Urban			Total		
		Male	Female	Total	Male	Female	Total	Male	Female	Total
SCs/STs	Not-literate	94.1	53.6	68.4	90.7	32.2	50.9	93.8	51.0	66.4
	Below primary	95.7	45.4	73.7	88.0	31.1	61.7	94.7	43.3	72.0
	Primary	89.6	41.7	69.7	87.7	29.0	60.3	89.3	39.3	68.0
	Middle	76.5	29.8	58.1	77.0	19.7	52.1	76.6	27.3	56.7
	Secondary	63.6	23.7	48.8	65.8	14.3	45.2	64.3	20.7	47.7
	Higher secondary	59.3	19.9	45.7	60.1	12.9	39.8	59.6	17.0	43.6
	Diploma/Certificate	76.2	49.4	69.5	72.5	43.9	65.1	74.3	46.5	67.2
	Graduate	76.1	35.9	65.1	81.4	26.2	60.4	78.7	29.9	62.6
	PG and above	78.1	42.3	71.7	85.4	39.9	65.8	82.0	40.4	68.0
	Total	83.7	44.9	64.5	77.4	25.2	52.3	82.5	41.1	62.1
Hindus	Not-literate	94.8	48.3	64.1	90.4	30.1	48.8	94.2	45.7	62.0
	Below primary	94.9	38.6	68.2	91.7	26.6	58.3	94.4	36.2	66.3
	Primary	89.9	38.7	66.4	90.0	24.1	57.6	89.9	35.1	64.3
	Middle	78.2	28.8	57.9	78.7	17.5	50.4	78.3	25.4	55.9
	Secondary	67.5	22.2	50.6	67.1	12.3	42.4	67.4	18.2	47.7

	Higher secondary	62.3	17.0	45.5	59.5	10.8	36.7	61.1	13.9	41.6
	Diploma/Certificate	76.2	41.4	67.5	71.5	33.7	61.0	73.7	37.1	64.0
	Graduate	78.8	26.2	62.0	80.9	23.3	57.1	80.1	24.2	58.8
	PG and above	83.8	41.9	71.1	88.9	38.9	67.9	87.3	39.5	68.8
	Total	82.1	38.5	60.5	76.9	21.2	50.1	80.6	33.5	57.5
Hindu-OBCs	Not-literate	95.8	45.7	62.3	91.9	31.5	49.6	95.3	43.7	60.6
	Below primary	94.8	39.2	68.6	94.2	30.2	61.4	94.7	37.3	67.2
	Primary	89.3	40.4	66.6	91.1	26.5	59.9	89.7	36.9	64.9
	Middle	78.8	29.6	59.1	79.8	18.9	52.8	79.1	26.7	57.5
	Secondary	67.2	22.7	51.0	68.2	13.3	43.3	67.5	19.3	48.6
	Higher secondary	62.4	17.5	45.9	58.9	10.4	36.6	61.1	14.2	42.1
	Diploma/Certificate	74.3	43.4	65.4	73.5	31.4	61.7	73.9	37.5	63.6
	Graduate	76.6	29.7	62.0	79.3	25.1	57.7	78.1	26.7	59.5
	PG and above	85.3	43.2	71.8	88.2	41.3	71.2	87.2	41.9	71.4
	Total	81.9	37.9	60.1	77.7	22.6	51.2	80.7	33.9	57.7
UC-Hindus	Not-literate	92.2	40.0	54.6	86.2	22.6	42.5	90.8	36.3	52.0
	Below primary	93.0	26.9	55.4	91.4	15.4	46.9	92.6	24.2	53.5
	Primary	91.4	32.0	59.2	89.8	16.5	51.1	90.9	27.5	56.8
	Middle	78.8	27.3	55.4	77.5	15.1	45.9	78.4	22.6	51.9

(Continued)

TABLE A.7 (Continued)

2011–2012 WFPR by General Education Level (15–64 Years)

Socio-religious Category	Level of Education	Rural Male	Rural Female	Rural Total	Urban Male	Urban Female	Urban Total	Total Male	Total Female	Total Total
	Secondary	72.1	21.8	52.2	66.8	10.6	40.2	69.8	16.2	46.7
	Higher secondary	64.3	15.5	45.0	60.2	10.7	36.2	62.3	12.7	40.3
	Diploma/Certificate	78.0	31.1	69.2	69.1	33.1	58.8	72.9	32.5	62.9
	Graduate	82.0	21.0	60.9	81.5	22.5	56.2	81.7	22.1	57.5
	PG and above	84.6	40.4	69.8	89.9	37.7	66.7	88.6	38.1	67.4
	Total	79.4	29.3	54.6	75.6	17.7	47.6	77.7	24.2	51.5
Muslims	Not-literate	95.2	27.5	53.0	91.0	20.8	48.1	94.0	25.6	51.6
	Below primary	91.4	21.2	57.1	87.7	24.6	60.0	90.1	22.2	58.0
	Primary	88.1	28.6	61.1	85.8	14.7	53.0	87.3	23.5	58.1
	Middle	73.5	15.8	49.0	78.7	10.2	48.6	75.5	13.4	48.8
	Secondary	61.9	14.2	43.0	68.8	5.4	40.8	65.1	9.8	41.9
	Higher secondary	54.2	18.0	40.6	61.4	8.9	37.2	57.9	12.6	38.8
	Diploma/Certificate	80.7	40.5	67.3	66.6	31.0	58.0	71.4	35.3	61.5
	Graduate	73.8	20.0	56.5	77.2	16.2	53.7	76.0	17.3	54.6
	PG and above	83.2	53.4	74.9	86.6	47.1	69.4	85.4	48.5	71.1
	Total	82.0	23.9	52.7	79.5	15.4	48.6	81.0	20.8	51.1

Muslim-OBCs	Not-literate	94.7	25.4	50.5	90.4	18.6	47.3	93.3	23.4	49.5
	Below primary	92.0	18.3	56.5	89.9	25.9	58.5	91.3	21.1	57.2
	Primary	84.8	23.8	56.3	86.9	13.6	52.5	85.6	19.9	54.8
	Middle	71.4	15.7	50.0	80.0	11.3	50.3	74.5	13.9	50.1
	secondary	62.8	13.8	43.2	68.8	6.0	41.9	65.6	9.9	42.6
	Higher secondary	48.7	13.8	33.4	64.4	10.7	38.7	56.7	12.1	36.2
	Diploma/Certificate	77.7	33.5	59.2	81.9	22.6	68.2	80.6	28.2	64.9
	Graduate	74.5	27.6	55.6	77.1	14.7	50.6	76.2	18.7	52.2
	PG and above	94.0	76.5	89.1	88.1	38.2	65.8	90.5	47.4	73.7
	Total	80.6	21.9	50.6	81.1	15.3	48.8	80.8	19.4	49.9
Muslims-General	Not-literate	95.9	29.4	55.6	91.9	23.7	49.5	94.9	27.9	54.0
	Below primary	90.6	23.1	57.2	85.5	22.3	61.7	89.0	22.9	58.5
	Primary	91.4	32.8	65.2	85.1	15.6	53.5	89.2	26.7	61.1
	Middle	76.2	14.3	47.0	78.3	9.2	47.4	77.1	12.1	47.2
	Secondary	61.2	14.4	42.8	68.8	4.9	39.7	64.6	9.5	41.3
	Higher secondary	59.1	22.5	47.7	58.3	7.3	35.7	58.7	12.8	41.1
	Diploma/Certificate	83.8	56.2	77.5	46.0	40.8	44.7	60.7	46.3	57.2
	Graduate	73.8	13.4	57.0	76.7	17.2	54.9	75.6	16.1	55.6
	PG and above	69.5	30.8	57.7	85.0	55.0	72.3	80.4	50.2	68.5
	Total	83.6	25.3	54.5	78.1	15.6	48.5	81.4	21.8	52.3

(Continued)

TABLE A.7 *(Continued)*

2011–2012 WFPR by General Education Level (15–64 Years)

Socio-religious Category	Level of Education	Rural Male	Rural Female	Rural Total	Urban Male	Urban Female	Urban Total	Total Male	Total Female	Total Total
Other Minorities	Not-literate	91.2	50.9	66.6	88.4	28.3	47.9	90.8	46.9	63.6
	Below primary	94.0	52.4	73.5	90.9	31.6	59.1	93.4	47.7	70.4
	Primary	90.5	42.3	65.5	85.8	32.2	56.4	89.5	39.9	63.4
	Middle	74.2	36.5	57.2	71.5	20.2	47.4	73.5	31.7	54.4
	Secondary	72.2	32.7	55.0	70.7	12.5	41.8	71.6	24.1	49.8
	Higher secondary	66.3	23.3	46.5	58.2	15.6	37.3	62.4	19.4	42.0
	Diploma/Certificate	74.4	40.9	62.5	78.0	42.7	62.8	76.2	42.0	62.7
	Graduate	74.0	36.4	57.2	78.1	37.8	58.9	76.8	37.4	58.4
	PG and above	87.9	37.7	57.1	93.5	53.3	75.8	92.4	48.1	70.9
	Total	80.1	41.0	60.6	74.5	25.6	50.0	78.1	35.5	56.8

All Population	Not-literate	94.7	45.7	62.7	90.5	27.8	48.6	94.1	42.8	60.4
	Below primary	94.4	36.7	66.9	90.6	26.3	58.7	93.7	34.5	65.2
	Primary	89.6	37.5	65.6	88.8	22.4	56.5	89.4	33.5	63.3
	Middle	77.5	27.7	56.9	78.4	16.3	50.0	77.7	24.2	54.9
	Secondary	67.3	22.2	50.2	67.6	11.4	42.2	67.4	17.7	47.2
	Higher secondary	61.9	17.6	45.2	59.6	11.0	36.8	60.9	14.2	41.4
	Diploma/Certificate	76.3	41.3	67.0	71.6	34.8	60.9	73.8	37.6	63.7
	Graduate	78.2	26.7	61.4	80.4	24.1	57.0	79.6	24.8	58.5
	PG and above	83.9	41.9	70.4	89.1	40.3	68.5	87.5	40.7	69.0
	Total	82.0	36.9	59.6	77.2	20.5	49.8	80.5	32.0	56.6

Source: Author's calculations based on unit-level data of NSSO 2011–2012.

TABLE A.8 *WFPR (UPSS) by General Level of Education (15–64 Years) 2004–2005*

WFPR by Level of Education (15–64 Years)

Socio-religious Category	Level of Education	Rural			Urban			Total		
		Male	Female	Total	Male	Female	Total	Male	Female	Total
SCs/STs	Not-literate	96.0	66.0	77.6	91.0	39.9	57.1	95.5	63.0	75.4
	Below primary	95.0	55.6	79.8	90.1	29.4	66.3	94.2	51.3	77.6
	Primary	89.3	49.2	74.8	87.8	28.5	62.5	89.0	44.4	72.3
	Middle	79.9	43.0	67.6	74.9	19.5	53.4	78.7	36.6	64.1
	Secondary	70.1	32.1	58.2	67.6	17.7	49.1	69.3	26.8	55.2
	Higher secondary	68.2	30.3	56.5	51.8	16.2	38.1	62.7	24.5	49.8
	Diploma/Certificate	84.8	51.7	73.6	71.0	46.9	61.7	78.5	49.3	68.0
	Graduate	80.3	33.2	69.6	73.5	24.5	55.1	77.4	27.9	62.5
	PG and above	88.7	37.1	74.8	78.1	44.7	67.4	83.9	41.0	71.3
	Total	88.8	59.8	74.4	78.4	30.6	55.6	86.9	54.7	71.1
Hindus	Not-literate	95.1	61.9	73.7	90.0	36.5	53.9	94.5	58.6	71.2
	Below primary	94.4	51.5	76.0	90.5	27.9	60.2	93.7	46.5	73.0
	Primary	90.3	47.1	72.4	89.0	26.1	59.1	90.0	41.4	69.2
	Middle	81.1	38.5	65.3	78.0	16.7	50.8	80.2	31.3	61.1

	Secondary	73.8	30.6	58.9	69.9	12.9	45.6	72.4	22.7	53.7
	Higher secondary	71.8	25.7	57.1	61.7	12.9	41.5	67.4	18.8	49.7
	Diploma/Certificate	83.7	54.6	75.7	82.1	48.0	72.6	82.7	50.8	73.9
	Graduate	85.8	30.4	72.5	80.9	26.6	59.4	82.9	27.5	63.9
	PG and above	90.8	42.0	78.3	88.1	35.2	66.0	89.1	36.6	69.8
	Total	87.1	53.4	70.3	78.8	24.7	53.1	84.9	46.1	65.8
Hindu-OBCs	Not-literate	94.7	61.0	72.5	91.2	38.8	55.8	94.3	58.3	70.5
	Below primary	94.2	54.3	77.3	93.1	32.6	63.3	94.0	49.8	74.7
	Primary	90.5	50.1	74.0	91.9	31.9	64.5	90.8	45.3	71.7
	Middle	81.4	39.6	66.4	82.3	19.4	54.8	81.6	33.4	63.3
	Secondary	74.4	31.3	60.1	71.2	14.2	47.5	73.4	24.7	55.9
	Higher secondary	73.7	26.4	58.9	64.4	12.8	44.2	70.3	20.4	53.1
	Diploma/Certificate	84.0	53.1	75.0	80.9	57.1	75.8	82.4	54.8	75.4
	Graduate	85.9	31.5	74.6	78.2	31.7	62.1	82.2	31.6	67.9
	PG and above	92.8	46.4	82.6	91.0	39.8	72.7	91.9	42.0	77.1
	Total	87.2	53.8	70.5	81.6	28.3	56.4	85.8	48.3	67.3
UC-Hindus	Not-literate	93.1	53.7	65.5	84.6	26.7	44.1	91.5	48.8	61.6
	Below primary	93.3	43.1	66.6	87.1	21.2	50.2	91.9	37.5	62.6
	Primary	91.5	42.4	66.7	84.7	18.3	48.6	89.6	34.8	61.2

(Continued)

TABLE A.8 (Continued)

WFPR by Level of Education (15–64 Years)

Socio-religious Category	Level of Education	Rural Male	Rural Female	Rural Total	Urban Male	Urban Female	Urban Total	Total Male	Total Female	Total Total
	Middle	81.3	34.4	61.2	74.2	13.3	44.7	78.9	26.0	55.1
	Secondary	75.5	29.7	57.9	69.5	11.2	43.0	72.8	20.0	50.7
	Higher secondary	72.1	23.4	55.3	62.6	12.4	40.4	67.0	16.4	46.7
	Diploma/Certificate	82.4	62.1	77.7	84.9	43.8	72.4	84.1	48.5	74.1
	Graduate	87.7	30.2	71.7	82.8	25.6	58.9	84.3	26.5	62.2
	PG and above	89.9	38.8	74.7	88.3	34.3	64.3	88.7	35.1	66.7
	Total	84.2	42.6	63.5	76.2	19.2	49.0	80.8	33.1	57.4
Muslims	Not-literate	94.4	33.7	57.2	89.4	22.9	49.2	93.1	31.0	55.2
	Below primary	91.1	22.9	61.1	92.5	18.3	59.9	91.5	21.5	60.7
	Primary	87.0	22.5	59.2	89.0	14.5	57.3	87.7	19.7	58.6
	Middle	77.2	20.1	54.9	76.8	13.5	49.5	77.0	17.2	52.6
	Secondary	66.4	17.6	49.1	72.7	5.6	44.3	69.4	10.9	46.6
	Higher secondary	61.6	11.9	45.0	60.5	9.1	38.0	61.0	10.1	41.0
	Diploma/Certificate	78.5	34.8	61.4	81.7	52.1	71.3	80.6	45.5	67.8

	Graduate	76.1	34.8	68.2	80.5	21.1	59.0	78.8	23.8	62.0
	PG and above	83.2	47.1	76.9	86.1	51.8	74.3	85.5	51.3	74.8
	Total	86.0	28.9	57.0	82.1	17.8	51.1	84.6	25.2	54.9
Muslim-OBCs	Not-literate	93.3	37.1	57.5	86.6	24.5	48.4	91.4	33.7	55.0
	Below primary	87.0	21.2	58.3	92.1	20.7	62.5	88.7	21.0	59.7
	Primary	83.2	22.5	57.3	87.6	16.1	58.2	85.1	19.8	57.7
	Middle	76.1	18.2	52.5	76.1	12.6	49.0	76.1	16.0	51.2
	Secondary	64.0	16.8	43.8	67.8	5.9	41.2	65.8	11.7	42.6
	Higher secondary	66.9	9.9	42.3	58.9	14.0	43.2	62.8	11.7	42.8
	Diploma/Certificate	75.9	34.5	57.4	90.5	52.3	76.3	83.1	41.9	66.2
	Graduate	74.1	43.0	67.0	74.8	31.5	60.4	74.5	35.2	63.1
	PG and above	77.0	0.8	61.4	79.8	73.6	78.6	78.7	43.2	71.6
	Total	84.1	30.7	55.6	81.1	19.7	51.2	83.0	27.1	54.1
Muslim-General	Not-literate	95.1	31.3	57.1	91.5	21.5	49.9	94.3	29.0	55.4
	Below primary	93.3	24.0	62.6	92.8	17.0	58.1	93.2	22.0	61.3
	Primary	88.8	22.5	60.2	90.1	13.4	56.9	89.2	19.6	59.2
	Middle	78.0	21.7	57.0	77.3	13.4	49.9	77.7	17.7	53.8
	Secondary	67.4	17.2	51.9	74.2	5.4	45.6	70.7	10.0	48.5

(Continued)

TABLE A.8 (Continued)

WFPR by Level of Education (15–64 Years)

Socio-religious Category	Level of Education	Rural			Urban			Total		
		Male	Female	Total	Male	Female	Total	Male	Female	Total
	Higher secondary	59.5	14.0	47.1	61.3	9.2	38.9	60.5	10.6	42.1
	Diploma/Certificate	85.1	36.6	73.0	78.7	52.0	69.4	80.0	49.9	70.1
	Graduate	78.9	24.1	69.3	81.6	20.5	59.7	80.7	21.1	62.5
	PG and above	87.2	93.1	88.1	87.4	49.9	73.6	87.4	52.6	75.7
	Total	87.1	27.7	57.8	82.6	16.8	51.5	85.5	24.0	55.6
Other Minorities	Not-literate	94.2	67.7	78.2	84.0	40.3	54.7	93.2	64.3	75.6
	Below primary	94.7	60.7	77.4	85.9	35.3	63.6	92.8	56.3	74.7
	Primary	89.9	58.4	74.5	79.4	27.6	52.3	87.6	50.9	69.3
	Middle	78.9	44.8	64.2	73.9	20.3	48.2	77.5	36.9	59.4
	Secondary	76.4	38.9	60.6	65.5	18.6	42.8	72.5	30.3	53.7
	Higher secondary	69.5	29.0	50.1	63.6	17.6	42.3	66.5	23.3	46.1
	Diploma/Certificate	82.3	54.3	69.6	80.6	52.7	69.7	81.5	53.6	69.6
	Graduate	79.8	47.5	66.3	79.8	32.3	58.7	79.8	36.2	60.8
	PG and above	89.4	41.5	64.2	86.7	44.2	68.4	87.2	43.6	67.5
	Total	85.1	55.7	70.3	74.5	27.4	51.6	81.8	47.2	64.5

All Population									
Not-literate	95.0	58.9	71.9	89.6	33.5	52.7	94.3	55.2	69.2
Below primary	94.0	48.6	74.3	90.7	26.5	60.3	93.4	43.7	71.4
Primary	89.9	44.9	71.0	88.5	24.2	58.4	89.6	39.1	67.7
Middle	80.6	37.2	64.3	77.5	16.5	50.5	79.7	30.1	60.1
Secondary	73.5	30.5	58.3	69.9	12.6	45.3	72.1	22.4	53.0
Higher secondary	71.1	25.2	55.9	61.8	13.0	41.2	66.9	18.6	48.8
Diploma/Certificate	83.2	53.1	73.8	81.9	49.0	72.2	82.5	50.9	72.9
Graduate	84.9	32.4	71.9	80.8	26.9	59.3	82.4	28.2	63.5
PG and above	90.5	42.1	77.4	87.8	36.9	66.7	88.7	38.0	69.9
Total	86.9	50.8	68.9	79.0	23.8	52.7	84.7	43.6	64.5

Source: Author's calculations based on unit-level data of NSSO 2004–2005.

TABLE A.9 Proportion of Students (As Percentage of Total Population) 2011–2012

Students Proportion 2011–2012

Socio-religious Category	Age Group	Rural			Urban			Total		
		Male	Female	Total	Male	Female	Total	Male	Female	Total
SCs/STs	15–19	58.2	48.8	53.9	67.4	66.7	67.1	60.0	52.2	56.5
	20–24	14.2	7.0	10.6	26.7	18.3	22.4	17.0	9.6	13.2
	25–29	1.3	0.3	0.8	3.8	3.5	3.7	1.9	1.0	1.4
	Total	28.4	19.9	24.3	34.5	29.0	31.9	29.7	21.8	25.9
Hindus	15–19	67.5	56.6	62.6	77.4	75.3	76.4	70.1	61.4	66.2
	20–24	21.9	9.8	15.8	36.6	27.5	32.2	26.4	15.0	20.8
	25–29	2.7	0.5	1.6	4.1	3.1	3.6	3.1	1.3	2.2
	Total	35.2	23.5	29.5	40.5	33.9	37.4	36.8	26.5	31.8
Hindu-OBCs	15–19	70.3	57.8	64.7	77.6	75.2	76.5	72.0	61.9	67.5
	20–24	21.9	8.9	15.6	36.7	24.1	30.7	26.1	13.1	19.8
	25–29	2.5	0.4	1.4	4.1	3.2	3.6	3.0	1.2	2.1
	Total	37.1	24.1	30.8	40.5	32.7	36.8	38.0	26.4	32.4

Group	Age										
UC-Hindus	15–19	78.9	70.0	74.9	84.7	82.4	83.7	81.3	75.1	78.5
	20–24	35.1	17.2	25.9	42.6	38.3	40.6	38.6	26.2	32.5
	25–29	5.7	1.1	3.4	4.6	2.8	3.7	5.2	1.9	3.5
	Total	43.5	29.7	36.8	45.0	39.2	42.3	44.1	33.8	39.2
Muslims	15–19	54.6	42.6	48.8	54.9	51.1	53.2	54.7	45.7	50.5
	20–24	17.4	7.5	12.4	17.4	9.8	13.8	17.4	8.4	13.0
	25–29	1.9	0.3	1.1	1.2	2.7	1.9	1.6	1.2	1.4
	Total	29.6	19.5	24.5	27.5	23.3	25.5	28.7	20.9	24.9
Muslim-OBCs	15–19	58.4	38.4	49.0	52.0	46.2	49.2	56.0	41.4	49.1
	20–24	14.3	6.7	10.4	16.8	8.0	12.7	15.4	7.2	11.4
	25–29	1.5	0.1	0.7	0.6	1.0	0.8	1.1	0.4	0.7
	Total	30.4	16.8	23.6	25.6	20.7	23.3	28.4	18.3	23.5
Muslims-General	15–19	50.4	46.1	48.3	57.6	56.2	56.9	53.3	49.6	51.5
	20–24	20.3	8.1	14.3	17.9	11.4	14.8	19.2	9.5	14.5
	25–29	2.0	0.5	1.2	1.9	4.8	3.2	2.0	2.1	2.0
	Total	28.6	22.1	25.4	29.2	25.9	27.7	28.8	23.6	26.3

(Continued)

TABLE A.9 Proportion of Students (As Percentage of Total Population) 2011–2012

| Socio-religious Category | Age Group | Students Proportion 2011-2012 ||||||||||
| | | Rural ||| Urban ||| Total |||
		Male	Female	Total	Male	Female	Total	Male	Female	Total
Other Minorities	15–19	67.1	64.7	66.0	83.3	86.3	84.6	72.2	70.8	71.5
	20–24	23.2	18.2	20.7	42.0	34.7	38.2	29.9	24.6	27.2
	25–29	2.1	2.2	2.2	6.3	2.8	4.6	3.7	2.5	3.1
	Total	35.4	30.5	33.0	45.2	38.5	41.9	38.8	33.3	36.1
All Population	15–19	65.8	54.9	60.9	73.2	70.7	72.1	67.9	59.3	64.0
	20–24	21.4	9.9	15.6	33.1	24.7	29.0	25.3	14.6	20.0
	25–29	2.6	0.6	1.5	3.8	3.0	3.4	3.0	1.3	2.1
	Total	34.5	23.3	29.0	38.3	32.3	35.4	35.7	26.0	31.0

Source: Author's calculations based on unit-level data of NSSO 2011–2012.

TABLE A.10 Proportion of Students (As Percentage of Total Population) 2004–2005

Students Proportion 2004–2005

Socio-religious Category	Age Group	Rural			Urban			Total		
		Male	Female	Total	Male	Female	Total	Male	Female	Total
SCs/STs	15–19	39.1	27.1	33.6	50.9	46.4	48.9	41.4	30.8	36.6
	20–24	8.8	3.8	6.2	18.0	11.5	14.9	10.8	5.2	7.9
	25–29	0.8	0.2	0.5	2.9	0.9	2.0	1.2	0.3	0.8
	Total	18.5	10.6	14.6	26.8	21.4	24.3	20.2	12.6	16.5
Hindus	15–19	47.8	33.1	41.1	62.9	60.9	62.0	51.6	40.0	46.3
	20–24	10.7	4.0	7.2	24.6	16.6	20.9	14.8	7.2	11.0
	25–29	1.0	0.3	0.6	3.7	1.0	2.4	1.8	0.4	1.1
	Total	22.6	12.9	17.9	31.9	26.5	29.4	25.2	16.4	20.9
Hindu-OBCs	15–19	48.9	31.8	41.0	55.1	56.1	55.5	50.3	37.0	44.2
	20–24	9.8	3.6	6.6	21.5	11.4	16.8	12.8	5.3	9.0
	25–29	0.8	0.2	0.5	3.0	1.1	2.1	1.4	0.4	0.9
	Total	22.9	12.5	17.8	28.5	23.1	26.0	24.3	14.8	19.7

(Continued)

TABLE A.10 *(Continued)*

Students Proportion 2004–2005

Socio-religious Category	Age Group	Rural			Urban			Total		
		Male	Female	Total	Male	Female	Total	Male	Female	Total
UC-Hindus	15–19	60.3	48.3	54.7	79.2	75.8	77.6	67.5	58.9	63.5
	20–24	15.8	6.2	11.1	31.8	24.8	28.5	22.9	14.2	18.7
	25–29	1.7	0.6	1.1	4.8	1.1	3.0	3.1	0.8	2.0
	Total	29.2	19.1	24.3	38.6	33.5	36.2	33.2	25.0	29.2
Muslims	15–19	40.3	26.4	33.6	43.8	40.9	42.4	41.5	31.5	36.7
	20–24	10.7	2.3	6.3	12.0	7.5	10.0	11.2	4.1	7.7
	25–29	0.9	0.3	0.6	0.8	0.6	0.7	0.9	0.4	0.6
	Total	20.8	11.1	15.9	21.6	19.1	20.4	21.1	13.8	17.5
Muslim-OBCs	15–19	42.2	25.8	34.2	47.5	29.4	39.0	44.2	27.1	35.9
	20–24	8.3	2.4	4.9	10.4	5.9	8.4	9.2	3.6	6.2
	25–29	1.3	0.3	0.7	0.9	0.1	0.5	1.2	0.2	0.7
	Total	21.9	10.7	15.9	22.7	13.6	18.4	22.2	11.6	16.8

	Age										
Muslims-General	15–19	39.0	26.2	32.9	42.1	44.6	43.3	40.1	32.6	36.5
	20–24	11.5	2.4	7.0	12.6	8.7	10.8	11.9	4.6	8.4
	25–29	0.7	0.2	0.5	0.6	0.8	0.7	0.7	0.4	0.6
	Total	20.0	11.1	15.6	20.9	20.7	20.8	20.3	14.5	17.5
Other Minorities	15–19	52.6	47.4	50.1	74.6	74.1	74.4	59.8	54.8	57.5
	20–24	12.0	10.3	11.1	27.5	23.7	25.8	17.0	13.9	15.4
	25–29	1.6	1.0	1.3	3.7	2.4	3.1	2.3	1.4	1.8
	Total	23.9	20.4	22.1	38.1	34.3	36.4	28.5	24.3	26.4
All Population	15–19	47.1	33.0	40.6	60.2	57.7	59.0	50.7	39.6	45.6
	20–24	10.8	4.1	7.4	22.6	15.6	19.3	14.4	7.2	10.8
	25–29	1.0	0.3	0.7	3.3	1.0	2.2	1.7	0.5	1.1
	Total	22.5	13.1	17.8	30.6	25.7	28.3	24.9	16.5	20.8

Source: Author's calculations based on unit-level data of NSSO 2004–2005.

TABLE A.11 UR (UPSS) for Various Age Groups 2011–2012

Socio-religious Category	Age Group	UR (UPSS)								
		Rural			Urban			Total		
		Male	Female	Total	Male	Female	Total	Male	Female	Total
SCs/STs	15–19	9.0	4.4	7.6	11.3	15.9	12.2	9.3	5.5	8.2
	20–24	5.1	3.6	4.6	9.0	16.6	10.7	5.8	5.4	5.7
	25–29	1.8	2.4	2.0	4.1	6.6	4.6	2.3	3.0	2.5
	30–34	0.9	0.4	0.7	2.6	4.5	3.0	1.3	0.9	1.1
	35–39	0.1	0.1	0.1	0.6	0.4	0.6	0.2	0.2	0.2
	40–44	0.0	0.1	0.0	0.6	0.2	0.5	0.1	0.1	0.1
	45–49	0.0	0.0	0.0	0.4	1.3	0.6	0.1	0.2	0.1
	50–54	0.0	0.0	0.0	0.2	0.0	0.1	0.0	0.0	0.0
	55–59	0.1	0.0	0.1	0.1	0.0	0.0	0.1	0.0	0.1
	60–64	0.0	0.0	0.0	0.0	0.0	0.0	0.0	0.0	0.0
	Total	1.7	1.1	1.5	3.2	4.7	3.6	2.0	1.5	1.9
Hindus	15–19	8.3	3.4	6.9	12.5	11.5	12.3	9.1	4.6	7.8
	20–24	6.0	5.6	5.9	9.8	19.9	12.1	7.0	8.7	7.4
	25–29	2.1	2.8	2.3	5.2	8.9	6.0	3.1	4.2	3.4

	Age									
	30–34	0.9	0.9	0.9	1.7	4.5	2.2	1.1	1.6	1.3
	35–39	0.2	0.2	0.2	0.4	0.8	0.5	0.3	0.3	0.3
	40–44	0.1	0.2	0.1	0.3	0.4	0.3	0.1	0.2	0.1
	45–49	0.0	0.1	0.0	0.3	0.6	0.4	0.1	0.2	0.1
	50–54	0.0	0.0	0.0	0.6	0.0	0.5	0.2	0.0	0.1
	55–59	0.0	0.4	0.2	0.2	0.0	0.1	0.1	0.4	0.1
	60–64	0.0	0.0	0.0	0.1	0.0	0.1	0.0	0.0	0.0
	Total	1.7	1.3	1.6	2.8	5.3	3.3	2.0	2.1	2.0
Hindu-OBCs	15–19	8.1	2.6	6.5	12.5	8.2	11.4	9.0	3.6	7.4
	20–24	5.9	5.9	5.9	9.7	17.6	11.7	6.8	8.6	7.3
	25–29	2.2	2.6	2.3	4.5	8.6	5.4	2.9	3.9	3.2
	30–34	0.8	0.9	0.9	1.0	4.1	1.7	0.9	1.6	1.1
	35–39	0.3	0.4	0.3	0.4	0.8	0.5	0.3	0.5	0.4
	40–44	0.0	0.1	0.1	0.1	0.3	0.1	0.0	0.2	0.1
	45–49	0.0	0.2	0.1	0.1	0.1	0.1	0.1	0.2	0.1
	50–54	0.1	0.0	0.1	0.1	0.0	0.1	0.0	0.0	0.1
	55–59	0.0	0.9	0.3	0.1	0.0	0.1	0.0	0.8	0.3
	60–64	0.0	0.0	0.0	0.2	0.0	0.1	0.0	0.0	0.0
	Total	1.7	1.3	1.6	2.5	4.8	3.0	1.9	1.9	1.9

(Continued)

TABLE A.11 (Continued)

Socio-religious Category	Age Group	UR (UPSS)									
		Rural			Urban			Total		
		Male	Female	Total	Male	Female	Total	Male	Female	Total
UC-Hindus	15–19	8.8	4.0	7.4	15.3	13.0	14.8	10.8	6.4	9.6
	20–24	8.1	11.5	9.0	11.5	25.8	14.5	9.5	16.7	11.3
	25–29	2.9	4.8	3.3	6.8	10.7	7.6	4.7	7.5	5.3
	30–34	1.1	1.9	1.3	2.0	5.0	2.6	1.5	3.0	1.9
	35–39	0.2	0.0	0.1	0.4	1.3	0.5	0.3	0.4	0.3
	40–44	0.2	0.4	0.3	0.3	0.7	0.4	0.3	0.5	0.3
	45–49	0.0	0.1	0.0	0.4	0.4	0.4	0.2	0.2	0.2
	50–54	0.0	0.0	0.0	1.3	0.0	1.1	0.6	0.0	0.4
	55–59	0.0	0.0	0.0	0.2	0.0	0.2	0.1	0.0	0.1
	60–64	0.1	0.0	0.1	0.0	0.0	0.0	0.1	0.0	0.1
	Total	1.8	2.2	1.9	3.0	6.5	3.7	2.3	3.6	2.6
Muslims	15–19	10.4	12.9	11.1	13.0	9.9	12.4	11.4	12.1	11.6
	20–24	5.3	8.3	5.9	11.1	11.7	11.2	7.8	9.5	8.1
	25–29	2.0	7.0	3.1	2.9	6.4	3.3	2.3	6.9	3.2
	30–34	0.7	1.5	0.9	1.0	3.0	1.3	0.8	1.9	1.1

	Age									
	35–39	0.4	1.4	0.6	0.3	0.4	0.4	0.4	1.1	0.5
	40–44	0.1	0.0	0.1	0.1	0.3	0.1	0.1	0.1	0.1
	45–49	0.0	1.1	0.2	0.2	0.1	0.1	0.1	0.8	0.2
	50–54	0.0	0.1	0.0	0.5	0.2	0.4	0.2	0.1	0.1
	55–59	0.0	0.0	0.0	0.0	0.0	0.0	0.0	0.0	0.0
	60–64	0.0	0.0	0.0	0.9	0.0	0.7	0.2	0.0	0.2
	Total	2.2	4.1	2.6	3.8	4.5	3.9	2.8	4.2	3.1
Muslim-OBCs	15–19	10.3	19.4	12.8	6.6	7.1	6.7	8.8	15.4	10.5
	20–24	4.3	12.4	5.8	8.5	11.0	8.9	6.1	11.9	7.1
	25–29	1.3	9.4	3.0	2.0	4.4	2.3	1.6	7.9	2.8
	30–34	0.8	3.5	1.4	0.8	4.4	1.4	0.8	3.8	1.4
	35–39	0.8	2.9	1.3	0.3	0.0	0.2	0.6	2.1	0.9
	40–44	0.3	0.0	0.2	0.1	0.5	0.2	0.2	0.1	0.2
	45–49	0.0	0.0	0.0	0.0	0.0	0.0	0.0	0.0	0.0
	50–54	0.0	0.0	0.0	0.1	0.2	0.1	0.0	0.1	0.0
	55–59	0.0	0.0	0.0	0.0	0.0	0.0	0.0	0.0	0.0
	60–64	0.0	0.0	0.0	1.4	0.0	1.2	0.5	0.0	0.3
	Total	2.0	5.8	2.9	2.6	4.0	2.8	2.3	5.3	2.9

(Continued)

TABLE A.11 (Continued)

Socio-religious Category	Age Group	UR (UPSS)							Total		
		Rural			Urban			Total		
		Male	Female	Total	Male	Female	Total	Male	Female	Total
Muslims-General	15–19	8.9	8.1	8.7	19.0	13.4	18.0	12.7	9.4	11.9
	20–24	6.5	5.4	6.2	13.7	12.6	13.5	9.7	7.8	9.3
	25–29	2.5	5.1	3.1	3.7	8.8	4.3	3.0	6.0	3.6
	30–34	0.5	0.2	0.4	1.2	1.7	1.3	0.8	0.6	0.7
	35–39	0.0	0.0	0.0	0.4	0.8	0.5	0.2	0.3	0.2
	40–44	0.0	0.0	0.0	0.1	0.0	0.1	0.0	0.0	0.0
	45–49	0.0	2.3	0.4	0.3	0.2	0.3	0.1	1.8	0.4
	50–54	0.0	0.2	0.0	1.0	0.0	0.9	0.3	0.1	0.3
	55–59	0.0	0.0	0.0	0.0	0.0	0.0	0.0	0.0	0.0
	60–64	0.0	0.0	0.0	0.0	0.0	0.0	0.0	0.0	0.0
	Total	2.1	2.7	2.3	5.1	5.0	5.1	3.2	3.3	3.3
Other Minorities	15–19	14.2	8.7	12.8	16.6	48.7	23.0	14.6	14.4	14.6
	20–24	5.3	13.2	7.8	20.3	21.2	20.6	9.7	15.9	11.7
	25–29	4.0	5.6	4.5	4.5	10.6	6.1	4.2	7.1	5.1
	30–34	1.0	4.2	2.2	4.0	3.1	3.7	2.0	3.9	2.7

	Age										
	35–39	0.6	1.2	0.8	0.5	4.1	1.4	0.6	1.9	1.0
	40–44	0.1	0.0	0.1	0.3	0.0	0.2	0.2	0.0	0.1
	45–49	0.0	0.0	0.0	0.2	0.0	0.2	0.1	0.0	0.1
	50–54	0.0	0.0	0.0	0.6	0.0	0.5	0.2	0.0	0.2
	55–59	0.0	0.0	0.0	0.0	0.0	0.0	0.0	0.0	0.0
	60–64	0.0	0.0	0.0	0.0	0.0	0.0	0.0	0.0	0.0
All	Total	2.3	3.4	2.7	3.9	7.1	4.7	2.8	4.4	3.3
Population	15–19	8.9	5.1	7.8	12.8	12.2	12.7	9.8	6.3	8.9
	20–24	5.8	6.3	6.0	10.6	18.8	12.4	7.2	9.2	7.8
	25–29	2.2	3.3	2.5	4.8	8.8	5.6	3.1	4.6	3.5
	30–34	0.9	1.1	0.9	1.7	4.2	2.2	1.1	1.8	1.3
	35–39	0.2	0.4	0.3	0.4	1.0	0.5	0.3	0.5	0.4
	40–44	0.1	0.1	0.1	0.3	0.4	0.3	0.1	0.2	0.1
	45–49	0.0	0.2	0.1	0.3	0.5	0.3	0.1	0.2	0.1
	50–54	0.0	0.0	0.0	0.6	0.0	0.5	0.2	0.0	0.1
	55–59	0.0	0.4	0.1	0.1	0.0	0.1	0.1	0.3	0.1
	60–64	0.0	0.0	0.0	0.2	0.0	0.1	0.1	0.0	0.0
	Total	1.8	1.7	1.7	3.0	5.4	3.5	2.2	2.4	2.2

Source: Author's calculations based on unit-level data of NSSO 2011–2012.

TABLE A.12 UR (UPSS) for Various Age Groups 2004–2005

Socio-religious Category	Age Group	UR (UPSS)								
		Rural			Urban			Total		
		Male	Female	Total	Male	Female	Total	Male	Female	Total
SCs/STs	15–19	5.4	2.1	4.2	16.7	10.1	15.3	7.3	2.7	5.7
	20–24	4.1	3.7	4.0	12.4	13.2	12.6	5.7	4.7	5.3
	25–29	1.2	1.4	1.2	5.1	12.0	6.6	1.9	2.3	2.0
	30–34	0.7	0.7	0.7	3.3	2.4	3.0	1.1	0.8	1.0
	35–39	0.2	0.2	0.2	0.6	1.1	0.8	0.2	0.3	0.3
	40–44	0.1	0.1	0.1	0.3	0.2	0.2	0.1	0.1	0.1
	45–49	0.1	0.2	0.2	0.2	0.0	0.2	0.2	0.2	0.2
	50–54	0.0	0.0	0.0	0.7	0.2	0.6	0.1	0.0	0.1
	55–59	0.2	0.0	0.2	0.1	0.0	0.1	0.2	0.0	0.1
	60–64	0.0	0.3	0.1	0.0	0.0	0.0	0.0	0.3	0.1
	Total	1.5	1.0	1.3	5.1	4.6	5.0	2.1	1.4	1.8
Hindus	15–19	5.5	2.8	4.5	12.5	11.3	12.2	6.8	3.8	5.8
	20–24	4.6	4.6	4.6	11.2	18.1	12.8	6.3	6.9	6.5
	25–29	1.6	2.8	2.1	4.9	12.1	6.4	2.6	4.1	3.1

	Age									
	30–34	0.6	1.3	0.9	2.0	5.4	2.8	1.0	1.9	1.3
	35–39	0.2	0.6	0.4	0.8	3.7	1.6	0.4	1.1	0.6
	40–44	0.2	0.3	0.2	0.4	1.8	0.7	0.2	0.5	0.3
	45–49	0.1	0.2	0.1	0.8	0.8	0.8	0.3	0.3	0.3
	50–54	0.0	0.2	0.1	0.9	0.5	0.9	0.3	0.2	0.2
	55–59	0.1	0.1	0.1	0.4	0.0	0.3	0.2	0.1	0.1
	60–64	0.1	0.3	0.2	0.1	0.1	0.1	0.1	0.3	0.2
	Total	1.5	1.5	1.5	3.7	6.9	4.4	2.1	2.3	2.2
Hindu-OBCs	15–19	5.2	2.7	4.3	9.8	9.1	9.7	6.1	3.5	5.2
	20–24	4.1	4.4	4.2	9.2	16.7	11.0	5.3	6.2	5.6
	25–29	1.3	3.5	2.2	3.4	11.0	5.2	1.9	4.6	2.8
	30–34	0.5	1.4	0.9	1.6	5.2	2.5	0.8	1.9	1.2
	35–39	0.1	0.4	0.2	0.6	4.8	1.8	0.2	1.0	0.5
	40–44	0.1	0.3	0.2	0.3	2.4	0.8	0.2	0.6	0.3
	45–49	0.1	0.2	0.1	0.7	0.9	0.7	0.2	0.3	0.2
	50–54	0.0	0.3	0.1	0.2	0.4	0.3	0.1	0.3	0.1
	55–59	0.0	0.1	0.0	0.6	0.0	0.5	0.1	0.1	0.1
	60–64	0.2	0.4	0.2	0.3	0.1	0.2	0.2	0.3	0.2
	Total	1.4	1.6	1.4	3.1	6.5	3.9	1.8	2.2	1.9

(Continued)

TABLE A.12 (Continued)

Socio-religious Category	Age Group	UR (UPSS)								
		Rural			Urban			Total		
		Male	Female	Total	Male	Female	Total	Male	Female	Total
UC-Hindus	15–19	7.5	5.8	6.9	12.2	16.7	13.6	8.5	8.0	8.4
	20–24	6.4	8.2	7.0	12.9	22.9	15.3	9.0	12.9	10.1
	25–29	3.0	3.9	3.3	6.5	13.6	7.8	4.6	6.5	5.1
	30–34	1.0	2.3	1.5	1.8	7.8	3.0	1.3	3.8	2.1
	35–39	0.5	1.8	1.0	1.0	4.3	1.7	0.7	2.4	1.2
	40–44	0.3	0.8	0.5	0.6	2.0	0.9	0.4	1.1	0.6
	45–49	0.1	0.3	0.2	1.1	1.4	1.2	0.5	0.5	0.5
	50–54	0.0	0.4	0.2	1.5	0.6	1.4	0.7	0.5	0.6
	55–59	0.0	0.3	0.1	0.4	0.0	0.3	0.1	0.3	0.2
	60–64	0.0	0.0	0.0	0.0	0.1	0.0	0.0	0.0	0.0
	Total	2.1	2.7	2.3	3.8	8.9	4.8	2.8	4.2	3.2
Muslims	15–19	6.6	8.1	7.0	9.5	9.4	9.5	7.6	8.5	7.8
	20–24	4.3	11.9	6.0	8.6	20.7	10.4	6.1	14.5	7.7
	25–29	1.5	6.1	2.7	4.1	10.9	5.0	2.5	7.1	3.5
	30–34	1.4	2.7	1.8	0.9	4.4	1.5	1.2	3.1	1.7

	Age									
	35–39	0.2	0.1	0.2	0.4	0.1	0.4	0.3	0.1	0.2
	40–44	0.4	0.6	0.4	0.3	0.0	0.2	0.3	0.4	0.4
	45–49	0.3	0.0	0.2	0.0	0.0	0.0	0.2	0.0	0.2
	50–54	0.1	0.1	0.1	0.4	0.0	0.3	0.2	0.1	0.1
	55–59	0.1	0.0	0.1	0.1	0.0	0.0	0.1	0.0	0.1
	60–64	0.1	0.0	0.1	0.0	0.0	0.0	0.1	0.0	0.1
	Total	2.0	3.7	2.4	3.6	6.4	4.0	2.5	4.4	3.0
Muslim-OBCs	15–19	7.7	8.5	7.9	7.1	12.5	8.3	7.5	9.8	8.1
	20–24	5.8	20.6	9.9	11.2	15.2	11.9	8.2	19.0	10.7
	25–29	1.7	13.0	4.9	3.5	17.0	5.7	2.4	13.9	5.2
	30–34	1.9	4.3	2.7	1.5	7.0	2.5	1.8	4.8	2.6
	35–39	0.5	0.1	0.4	0.2	0.1	0.2	0.4	0.1	0.3
	40–44	0.8	0.0	0.5	0.0	0.0	0.0	0.5	0.0	0.3
	45–49	0.2	0.0	0.1	0.1	0.0	0.1	0.1	0.0	0.1
	50–54	0.0	0.0	0.0	0.0	0.0	0.0	0.0	0.0	0.0
	55–59	0.0	0.0	0.0	0.2	0.0	0.1	0.1	0.0	0.0
	60–64	0.0	0.0	0.0	0.0	0.0	0.0	0.0	0.0	0.0
	Total	2.5	5.7	3.4	3.8	7.4	4.5	2.9	6.1	3.8

(Continued)

TABLE A.12 *(Continued)*

Socio-religious Category	Age Group	UR (UPSS)									
		Rural			Urban			Total		
		Male	Female	Total	Male	Female	Total	Male	Female	Total
Muslims-General	15–19	5.8	8.0	6.3	11.1	6.8	10.3	7.6	7.7	7.6
	20–24	3.6	5.0	3.9	6.7	24.3	9.0	4.8	10.4	5.7
	25–29	1.4	1.8	1.5	4.4	6.0	4.6	2.5	2.6	2.5
	30–34	0.6	1.2	0.8	0.6	2.4	0.9	0.6	1.5	0.8
	35–39	0.1	0.0	0.1	0.5	0.1	0.4	0.3	0.0	0.2
	40–44	0.2	1.1	0.4	0.5	0.0	0.4	0.3	0.8	0.4
	45–49	0.4	0.0	0.3	0.0	0.0	0.0	0.2	0.0	0.2
	50–54	0.1	0.2	0.1	0.7	0.0	0.5	0.3	0.2	0.2
	55–59	0.2	0.0	0.2	0.0	0.0	0.0	0.2	0.0	0.1
	60–64	0.2	0.0	0.2	0.1	0.0	0.0	0.2	0.0	0.1
	Total	1.6	2.2	1.8	3.4	5.4	3.7	2.3	3.0	2.4
Other Minorities	15–19	12.5	9.7	11.5	19.9	12.5	17.7	13.9	10.2	12.6
	20–24	7.7	13.2	10.0	18.8	34.4	22.8	10.8	16.5	13.0
	25–29	2.6	6.8	4.2	7.6	19.2	10.3	4.2	9.0	5.9
	30–34	1.2	2.5	1.8	1.3	10.4	4.7	1.2	4.3	2.5

	Age									
	35–39	0.2	1.1	0.6	0.1	6.4	1.7	0.2	2.0	0.9
	40–44	0.4	1.0	0.6	0.4	2.0	0.9	0.4	1.2	0.7
	45–49	0.0	0.1	0.1	3.1	0.3	2.5	1.0	0.2	0.7
	50–54	0.0	0.9	0.3	1.4	0.0	1.1	0.4	0.7	0.5
	55–59	0.2	0.0	0.1	0.5	0.0	0.4	0.3	0.0	0.2
	60–64	0.8	0.0	0.5	0.0	5.1	1.1	0.6	0.5	0.6
	Total	2.8	4.2	3.3	5.4	10.5	6.8	3.5	5.4	4.2
All Population	15–19	5.9	3.6	5.1	12.0	11.0	11.8	7.2	4.6	6.4
	20–24	4.7	5.7	5.1	11.1	19.4	13.0	6.5	8.1	7.0
	25–29	1.7	3.2	2.2	5.0	12.5	6.4	2.6	4.6	3.3
	30–34	0.7	1.5	1.0	1.8	5.8	2.8	1.0	2.1	1.4
	35–39	0.2	0.6	0.4	0.7	3.6	1.4	0.3	1.1	0.6
	40–44	0.2	0.4	0.3	0.4	1.6	0.7	0.2	0.6	0.4
	45–49	0.1	0.2	0.1	0.8	0.7	0.8	0.3	0.3	0.3
	50–54	0.0	0.2	0.1	0.9	0.4	0.8	0.3	0.3	0.3
	55–59	0.1	0.1	0.1	0.4	0.0	0.3	0.2	0.1	0.1
	60–64	0.1	0.3	0.2	0.1	0.4	0.2	0.1	0.3	0.2
	Total	1.6	1.8	1.7	3.8	7.1	4.5	2.2	2.6	2.4

Source: Author's calculations based on unit level data of NSSO 2004–2005.

TABLE A.13 UR (UPSS) for Different Levels of Education 2011–2012

Socio-religious Category	Level of Educational Attainment	Rural			Urban			Total		
		Male	Female	Total	Male	Female	Total	Male	Female	Total
SCs/STs	Not-literate	0.4	0.1	0.3	0.8	0.6	0.7	0.5	0.2	0.3
	Below primary	0.5	0.2	0.4	2.1	1.6	2.0	0.7	0.4	0.6
	Primary	2.1	0.2	1.6	2.6	1.0	2.3	2.2	0.3	1.7
	Middle	2.0	2.0	2.0	3.0	3.0	3.0	2.2	2.1	2.2
	Secondary	2.2	9.4	3.6	3.5	5.2	3.8	2.6	8.5	3.7
	Higher secondary	4.8	10.6	5.7	3.7	11.8	4.9	4.4	11.0	5.5
	Diploma/Certificate	10.7	17.5	12.0	8.0	12.7	8.8	9.4	15.2	10.4
	Graduate	9.3	19.6	11.0	6.1	22.5	9.3	7.7	21.2	10.1
	PG and above	15.2	22.5	16.1	6.3	16.9	9.3	10.5	18.1	12.1
	Total	1.7	1.1	1.5	3.2	4.7	3.6	2.0	1.5	1.9
Hindus	Not-literate	0.4	0.1	0.3	0.8	0.4	0.6	0.5	0.1	0.3
	Below primary	0.5	0.1	0.4	1.8	1.9	1.8	0.7	0.4	0.6
	Primary	1.3	0.3	1.1	1.3	1.5	1.4	1.3	0.5	1.1
	Middle	1.7	1.6	1.7	1.9	2.6	2.0	1.8	1.8	1.8

	Secondary	1.8	5.4	2.4	2.1	5.2	2.5	1.9	5.3	2.4
	Higher secondary	3.0	7.6	3.7	3.9	8.5	4.5	3.4	8.0	4.0
	Diploma/Certificate	8.6	19.0	10.4	4.3	10.6	5.3	6.5	14.9	7.9
	Graduate	7.0	17.0	8.4	4.9	13.7	6.5	5.7	14.8	7.2
	PG and above	8.5	18.4	10.5	4.5	11.8	6.4	5.7	13.4	7.5
	Total	1.7	1.3	1.6	2.8	5.3	3.3	2.0	2.1	2.0
Hindu-OBCs	Not-literate	0.5	0.1	0.3	0.7	0.0	0.4	0.5	0.1	0.3
	Below primary	0.4	0.0	0.3	1.2	1.8	1.4	0.5	0.3	0.5
	Primary	0.9	0.5	0.8	0.6	0.2	0.5	0.8	0.4	0.7
	Middle	1.8	2.2	1.9	1.4	1.8	1.5	1.7	2.1	1.8
	Secondary	1.9	4.1	2.3	1.6	6.9	2.4	1.8	4.8	2.3
	Higher secondary	2.5	6.3	3.0	4.2	9.6	4.9	3.1	7.4	3.7
	Diploma/Certificate	11.1	21.9	13.4	4.5	13.2	5.8	7.9	18.5	9.9
	Graduate	7.3	13.6	8.3	5.6	15.6	7.5	6.3	14.8	7.8
	PG and above	8.4	20.5	11.0	5.2	13.7	7.1	6.4	16.0	8.5
	Total	1.7	1.3	1.6	2.5	4.8	3.0	1.9	1.9	1.9
UC-Hindus	Not-literate	0.1	0.1	0.1	1.0	0.8	0.9	0.3	0.2	0.3
	Below primary	1.1	0.0	0.8	2.7	2.4	2.7	1.5	0.4	1.2
	Primary	1.0	0.2	0.8	1.2	5.1	1.9	1.1	1.1	1.1

(Continued)

TABLE A.13 *(Continued)*

UR (UPSS) and Level of Education 2011–2012

Socio-religious Category	Level of Educational Attainment	Rural			Urban			Total		
		Male	Female	Total	Male	Female	Total	Male	Female	Total
	Middle	1.0	0.4	0.8	2.2	3.1	2.3	1.4	1.1	1.3
	Secondary	1.2	3.9	1.6	1.9	3.1	2.0	1.5	3.7	1.8
	Higher secondary	2.6	7.6	3.3	3.7	6.4	4.1	3.1	7.0	3.7
	Diploma/Certificate	4.0	8.9	4.5	2.7	6.4	3.3	3.3	7.1	3.8
	Graduate	5.8	19.7	7.7	4.4	10.6	5.5	4.9	12.8	6.2
	PG and above	6.1	16.4	8.3	3.8	10.1	5.4	4.3	11.3	6.1
	Total	1.8	2.2	1.9	3.0	6.5	3.7	2.3	3.6	2.6
Muslims	Not-literate	0.8	1.3	0.9	0.7	1.0	0.8	0.8	1.2	0.9
	Below primary	2.2	2.0	2.2	4.2	0.0	3.5	2.9	1.3	2.6
	Primary	1.5	1.1	1.4	2.6	2.1	2.5	1.9	1.3	1.8
	Middle	2.7	11.6	4.0	3.0	8.8	3.6	2.8	10.8	3.8
	Secondary	4.7	9.4	5.4	3.3	9.0	3.7	4.1	9.3	4.6
	Higher secondary	4.2	20.2	7.3	8.8	12.2	9.2	6.7	17.1	8.3
	Diploma/Certificate	1.6	27.6	8.2	8.2	0.2	7.2	5.7	16.6	7.6

	Graduate	7.0	36.3	11.6	11.2	20.6	12.4	9.8	26.8	12.1
	PG and above	6.7	13.9	8.2	6.7	9.8	7.7	6.7	10.9	7.9
	Total	2.2	4.1	2.6	3.8	4.5	3.9	2.8	4.2	3.1
Muslim-OBCs	Not-literate	0.9	2.0	1.3	0.5	0.0	0.4	0.8	1.5	1.0
	Below primary	1.7	0.0	1.4	1.1	0.0	0.9	1.5	0.0	1.2
	Primary	1.2	1.2	1.2	3.4	4.3	3.5	2.0	2.0	2.0
	Middle	2.6	16.5	4.5	1.7	1.0	1.7	2.3	11.9	3.4
	Secondary	5.3	16.1	6.8	3.3	13.6	4.0	4.3	15.4	5.5
	Higher secondary	4.7	25.8	9.4	3.1	10.5	4.2	3.8	19.0	6.5
	Diploma/Certificate	2.1	39.8	14.8	4.2	0.0	3.9	3.6	28.7	7.8
	Graduate	3.4	28.0	9.6	11.9	27.4	14.1	9.3	27.7	12.6
	PG and above	4.0	14.1	6.6	4.3	17.5	8.1	4.2	16.2	7.5
	Total	2.0	5.8	2.9	2.6	4.0	2.8	2.3	5.3	2.9
Muslims-General	Not-literate	0.5	0.6	0.5	1.1	2.0	1.4	0.6	1.0	0.7
	Below primary	2.7	3.2	2.8	7.1	0.1	6.2	4.1	2.5	3.9
	Primary	1.1	1.0	1.1	1.8	0.1	1.6	1.3	0.8	1.2
	Middle	3.0	7.2	3.6	3.9	16.3	5.1	3.4	10.4	4.3
	Secondary	4.3	2.1	4.0	3.3	2.9	3.2	3.8	2.3	3.7
	Higher secondary	3.9	15.6	5.8	13.9	14.4	13.9	9.1	15.2	9.9

(Continued)

TABLE A.13 *(Continued)*

UR (UPSS) and Level of Education 2011–2012

Socio-religious Category	Level of Educational Attainment	Rural			Urban			Total		
		Male	Female	Total	Male	Female	Total	Male	Female	Total
	Diploma/Certificate	1.2	0.0	1.0	16.4	0.0	13.2	8.9	0.0	7.3
	Graduate	8.8	47.9	13.1	11.1	15.4	11.7	10.3	26.1	12.2
	PG and above	8.5	13.6	9.4	8.8	4.8	7.6	8.8	6.0	8.0
	Total	2.1	2.7	2.3	5.1	5.0	5.1	3.2	3.3	3.3
Other Minorities	Not-literate	0.0	0.0	0.0	0.0	0.0	0.0	0.0	0.0	0.0
	Below primary	0.7	0.0	0.5	0.0	0.1	0.0	0.6	0.0	0.4
	Primary	2.1	1.1	1.8	2.1	0.6	1.6	2.1	1.0	1.7
	Middle	3.0	2.3	2.8	5.2	1.3	4.4	3.6	2.2	3.2
	Secondary	0.9	5.7	2.2	0.9	18.0	3.9	0.9	8.7	2.8
	Higher secondary	5.6	10.1	6.7	5.7	7.6	6.1	5.7	9.1	6.4
	Diploma/Certificate	9.1	16.7	11.0	10.4	11.3	10.7	9.8	13.6	10.8
	Graduate	7.2	19.7	11.1	6.1	9.8	7.3	6.5	12.9	8.5
	PG and above	9.3	30.2	19.1	2.8	8.5	4.6	4.1	15.3	8.1
	Total	2.3	3.4	2.7	3.9	7.1	4.7	2.9	4.4	3.3

All Population										
	Not-literate	0.5	0.2	0.3	0.8	0.5	0.7	0.5	0.2	0.4
	Below primary	0.7	0.3	0.6	2.4	1.4	2.2	1.1	0.4	0.9
	Primary	1.4	0.4	1.1	1.7	1.5	1.7	1.5	0.6	1.3
	Middle	1.9	2.4	2.0	2.2	3.2	2.4	2.0	2.6	2.1
	Secondary	2.0	5.7	2.6	2.2	6.6	2.8	2.1	5.9	2.7
	Higher secondary	3.2	9.0	4.1	4.6	8.7	5.2	3.8	8.9	4.6
	Diploma/Certificate	8.3	19.4	10.3	5.2	10.1	6.0	6.7	14.8	8.1
	Graduate	7.0	18.6	8.8	5.5	13.5	7.0	6.0	15.2	7.7
	PG and above	8.5	19.7	10.9	4.5	11.4	6.3	5.7	13.4	7.6
	Total	1.8	1.7	1.7	3.0	5.4	3.5	2.2	2.4	2.2

Source: Author's calculations based on unit-level data of NSSO 2011–2012.

TABLE A.14 *UR (UPSS) for Different Levels of Education 2004–2005*

UR (UPSS) for Different Levels of Education 2004–2005 (15–64 Years)

Socio-religious Category	Educational Attainment	Rural			Urban			Total		
		Male	Female	Total	Male	Female	Total	Male	Female	Total
SCs/STs	Not-literate	0.4	0.2	0.3	1.4	0.6	1.0	0.5	0.2	0.4
	Below primary	0.6	0.7	0.6	4.0	2.7	3.8	1.1	0.9	1.1
	Primary	1.3	1.3	1.3	3.8	3.2	3.7	1.8	1.6	1.7
	Middle	1.9	3.2	2.2	7.1	7.8	7.2	3.1	3.9	3.3
	Secondary	4.2	8.2	4.9	5.9	12.5	6.8	4.7	9.3	5.5
	Higher secondary	7.2	19.5	9.5	5.7	15.3	7.4	6.8	18.4	8.9
	Diploma/Certificate	6.2	15.8	8.7	16.5	9.5	14.6	10.7	12.9	11.3
	Graduate	10.2	27.5	12.5	10.0	26.4	13.2	10.1	26.9	12.8
	PG and above	7.8	23.4	10.2	10.3	24.3	13.6	8.8	23.9	11.8
	Total	1.5	1.0	1.3	5.1	4.6	5.0	2.1	1.4	1.8
Hindus	Not-literate	0.4	0.2	0.3	1.0	0.6	0.8	0.5	0.3	0.4
	Below primary	0.9	1.2	1.0	2.5	3.1	2.6	1.1	1.5	1.2
	Primary	1.1	1.0	1.1	2.2	3.1	2.4	1.3	1.4	1.3
	Middle	1.4	2.8	1.7	4.1	7.8	4.6	2.1	3.8	2.4

	Secondary	3.0	8.7	4.0	4.2	12.2	5.3	3.4	9.6	4.5
	Higher secondary	4.5	13.0	5.8	4.0	13.7	5.4	4.3	13.3	5.7
	Diploma/Certificate	7.2	21.0	10.3	7.4	15.7	9.1	7.3	18.2	9.6
	Graduate	6.0	29.1	9.0	5.8	16.9	8.0	5.9	20.6	8.4
	PG and above	5.3	22.4	8.1	4.4	16.3	7.4	4.8	17.9	7.6
	Total	1.5	1.5	1.5	3.7	6.9	4.5	2.1	2.3	2.2
Hindu-OBCs	Not-literate	0.4	0.2	0.3	0.5	0.7	0.6	0.4	0.3	0.3
	Below primary	1.0	1.1	1.0	1.2	4.5	2.1	1.0	1.6	1.2
	Primary	1.1	0.7	1.0	1.5	1.4	1.5	1.2	0.8	1.1
	Middle	1.0	3.0	1.4	2.7	6.2	3.2	1.4	3.5	1.9
	Secondary	2.7	9.1	3.9	4.0	15.8	5.6	3.1	10.7	4.4
	Higher secondary	4.1	13.6	5.6	3.3	21.2	5.7	3.8	15.9	5.6
	Diploma/Certificate	7.3	24.7	11.5	8.4	18.0	10.1	7.9	21.8	10.8
	Graduate	4.9	36.4	8.8	8.2	24.2	11.5	6.5	28.9	10.2
	PG and above	4.9	27.9	8.5	3.8	18.5	7.1	4.3	22.2	7.8
	Total	1.4	1.6	1.4	3.1	6.5	3.9	1.8	2.2	1.9
UC-Hindus	Not-literate	0.4	0.4	0.4	1.2	0.0	0.7	0.5	0.4	0.4
	Below primary	1.0	2.2	1.4	2.0	0.3	1.6	1.2	1.9	1.5
	Primary	0.6	1.2	0.8	1.7	6.1	2.6	0.9	2.0	1.2

(Continued)

TABLE A.14 *(Continued)*

UR (UPSS) for Different Levels of Education 2004–2005 (15–64 Years)

Socio-religious Category	Educational Attainment	Rural			Urban			Total		
		Male	Female	Total	Male	Female	Total	Male	Female	Total
	Middle	1.6	2.1	1.7	4.0	9.4	4.8	2.4	3.6	2.7
	Secondary	2.8	8.4	4.0	3.9	8.3	4.5	3.3	8.4	4.2
	Higher secondary	3.5	10.5	4.6	4.2	9.7	5.0	3.8	10.1	4.8
	Diploma/Certificate	8.2	17.0	9.9	5.2	15.3	7.2	6.2	15.8	8.1
	Graduate	5.8	22.0	8.0	4.4	13.1	6.1	4.8	15.2	6.7
	PG and above	4.8	16.7	6.8	4.0	15.0	6.8	4.2	15.3	6.8
	Total	2.0	2.7	2.3	3.8	8.9	4.8	2.7	4.2	3.2
Muslims	Not-literate	0.4	0.8	0.5	1.2	0.2	0.9	0.6	0.7	0.6
	Below primary	1.6	0.8	1.4	0.8	1.1	0.9	1.3	0.9	1.3
	Primary	2.2	2.7	2.3	2.8	3.9	2.9	2.4	3.0	2.5
	Middle	3.5	11.2	4.7	4.7	7.4	5.0	4.0	10.0	4.8
	Secondary	5.4	19.4	7.5	4.4	27.2	6.0	4.9	21.8	6.7
	Higher secondary	3.9	48.5	10.7	8.4	25.4	10.6	6.3	37.4	10.6
	Diploma/Certificate	9.0	41.9	19.2	8.0	12.1	9.1	8.4	23.5	12.6

	Graduate	8.1	44.1	13.5	7.3	31.8	11.4	7.6	35.9	12.2
	PG and above	16.2	28.4	17.7	10.8	16.1	12.1	12.0	17.5	13.3
	Total	2.0	3.7	2.4	3.6	6.4	4.0	2.5	4.4	3.0
Muslim-OBCs	Not-literate	0.4	0.5	0.4	2.0	0.0	1.4	0.8	0.4	0.7
	Below primary	1.5	1.7	1.5	1.3	2.5	1.5	1.4	1.9	1.5
	Primary	2.6	2.3	2.6	2.3	0.3	2.1	2.5	1.6	2.4
	Middle	5.6	22.7	8.4	4.7	17.6	6.3	5.2	21.2	7.7
	Secondary	5.9	28.2	10.4	8.4	49.5	12.8	7.1	34.7	11.5
	Higher secondary	3.7	59.8	15.6	9.3	40.2	14.3	6.5	51.6	15.0
	Diploma/Certificate	9.6	45.9	23.3	2.2	21.6	8.0	5.7	35.5	15.9
	Graduate	7.4	45.8	16.1	7.7	16.2	9.3	7.6	31.0	12.4
	PG and above	21.5	97.9	28.5	17.6	10.4	16.3	19.2	32.2	21.1
	Total	2.5	5.7	3.4	3.8	7.4	4.5	2.9	6.1	3.8
Muslims-General	Not-literate	0.4	1.1	0.6	0.6	0.3	0.5	0.4	1.0	0.6
	Below primary	1.6	0.4	1.4	0.5	0.0	0.4	1.3	0.3	1.2
	Primary	1.9	2.9	2.1	2.8	6.4	3.2	2.2	3.7	2.4
	Middle	1.9	0.9	1.8	4.5	1.1	4.1	3.1	1.0	2.8
	Secondary	5.4	11.0	6.0	2.7	5.3	2.8	4.0	9.2	4.4
	Higher secondary	4.1	35.9	7.8	8.1	14.4	8.8	6.3	24.2	8.3

(Continued)

TABLE A.14 *(Continued)*

UR (UPSS) for Different Levels of Education 2004–2005 (15–64 Years)

Socio-religious Category	Educational Attainment	Rural			Urban			Total		
		Male	Female	Total	Male	Female	Total	Male	Female	Total
	Diploma/Certificate	8.4	8.2	8.4	11.3	4.9	9.7	10.7	5.2	9.5
	Graduate	6.1	49.7	10.8	7.7	34.7	12.2	7.1	38.3	11.7
	PG and above	12.8	1.4	11.1	9.4	17.0	11.4	10.0	15.5	11.4
	Total	1.6	2.2	1.8	3.4	5.4	3.7	2.3	3.0	2.4
Other Minorities	Not-literate	0.6	0.0	0.3	1.1	0.0	0.6	0.6	0.0	0.3
	Below primary	0.9	0.6	0.8	0.2	0.2	0.2	0.7	0.6	0.7
	Primary	0.7	1.4	1.0	1.4	3.9	2.1	0.8	1.8	1.2
	Middle	2.7	3.8	3.0	5.5	9.8	6.4	3.4	4.9	3.9
	Secondary	5.3	11.0	6.9	5.3	14.3	7.3	5.3	11.8	7.0
	Higher secondary	8.5	29.6	15.6	3.1	19.8	6.9	5.9	26.2	11.7
	Diploma/Certificate	10.9	24.3	16.2	12.1	16.6	13.5	11.5	21.5	15.0
	Graduate	10.5	19.7	13.5	10.0	15.1	11.3	10.1	16.7	11.9
	PG and above	6.7	32.1	17.2	5.0	16.7	8.6	5.3	20.8	10.4
	Total	2.8	4.2	3.3	5.4	10.5	6.8	3.5	5.4	4.2

All Population										
Not-literate	0.4	0.3	0.3	1.0	0.5	0.8	0.5	0.3	0.4
Below primary	0.9	1.2	1.0	2.0	2.7	2.2	1.1	1.4	1.2
Primary	1.2	1.2	1.2	2.2	3.3	2.4	1.4	1.5	1.5
Middle	1.6	3.4	2.0	4.2	7.9	4.8	2.4	4.3	2.8
Secondary	3.3	9.5	4.5	4.3	13.4	5.5	3.7	10.5	4.9
Higher secondary	4.7	17.1	6.8	4.3	15.3	5.9	4.6	16.4	6.5
Diploma/Certificate	7.8	23.1	11.7	7.9	15.5	9.5	7.8	19.2	10.5
Graduate	6.4	28.8	9.6	6.2	17.5	8.5	6.3	21.0	8.9
PG and above	5.8	23.8	9.0	5.0	16.3	7.8	5.3	18.2	8.2
Total	1.6	1.8	1.7	3.8	7.1	4.5	2.2	2.6	2.4

Source: Author's calculations based on unit-level data of NSSO 2011–2012.

TABLE A.15 Result of Logistic Regression for Participation in Employment 2004–2005 and 2011–2012

Nature of Variable	Broad Category		Variable Name	Logistic Results			
				NSSO 61st Round		NSSO 68th Round	
				Coef**.	P > z	Coef**.	P > z
Independent	Individual characteristics	Location	Rural/urban	.5170621	0.00	.6601713	0.00
		Gender	Male/female	.9203213	0.00	.635321	0.00
		Age	Age	1.876442	0.00	2.427261	0.00
		Age	Age squared	.7661252	0.00	.9954623	0.00
		Education	Primary education	1.105498	0.00	1.000032	0.00
			Secondary education	.8875094	0.00	1.174806	0.00
			Higher secondary/diploma	.5127161	0.00	.6401671	0.00
			Graduate & above	.4989084	0.00	.5233007	0.00

Socio-religious status	SCs/STs	1.086934	0.00	1.32469	0.00
	Hindu-OBCs	1.430359	0.00	1.527604	0.00
	Muslim-OBCs	1.306112	0.00	1.226254	0.00
	Muslims-General	.6704933	0.00	.8305236	0.00
	Other minorities	.6901863	0.00	.9127489	0.00
Household characteristics	Edu. of household head	Ownership of land	1.355831	0.00	1.33644	0.00
		Primary education	.8371579	0.00	.8310935	0.00
		Secondary education	.618252	0.00	.7030684	0.00
		Higher secondary/diploma	.5302209	0.00	.6603821	0.00
		Graduate & above	.4379089	0.00	.4573041	0.00

Source: Author's own calculations based on unit level data of NSSO (61st and 68th rounds).

Note: ** $p < 0.05$.

References

Abras, A., Hoyos, A., Narayan, A., & Tiwari, S. (2013). Inequality of opportunities in the labor market: Evidence from life in transition surveys in Europe and Central Asia. *IZA Journal of Labor & Development, 2*(7). doi: 10.1186/2193-9020-2-7

Adnett, N. (1996). *European labour markets: Analysis and policy.* Harlow: Prentice Hall.

Ahmad, A. (1993). *Indian Muslims: Issues in social and economic underdevelopment.* New Delhi: Khama Publishers.

Akerlof, G. (1976). The economics of caste and of rat race and other woeful tales. *Quarterly Journal of Economics, 90*(4), 599–617. doi: 10.2307/1885324

———. (1980). The theory of social customs of which unemployment may be one of the consequences. *Quarterly Journal of Economics, 94*(4), 749–773. doi: 10.2307/1885667

Ali, I., & Sikand, Y. (2006, 9 February). *Survey of socio-economic conditions of Muslims in India.* Retrieved from www.countercurrents.org

Ambedkar, B. R. (1936). *Annilhilation of caste.* Columbia, SC: Columbia Center for New Media Teaching and Learning. Retrieved from ccnmtl.columbia.edu/projects/mmt/ambedkar/web/readings/aoc_print_2004.pdf

———. (1987a). Philosophy of Hinduism. In Vasant Moon (Comp.), *Dr. Babasaheb Ambedkar writings and speeches,* Vol. 3 (pp. 3–94). New Delhi: Dr. Ambedkar Foundation. Retrieved from http://www.mea.gov.in/Images/attach/amb/Volume_03.pdf

Ambedkar, B. R. (1987b). The Hindu social order—Its essential features. In Vasant Moon (Comp.), *Dr. Babasaheb Ambedkar writings and speeches*, Vol. 3 (pp. 95–115). New Delhi: Dr. Ambedkar Foundation. Retrieved from http://www.mea.gov.in/Images/attach/amb/Volume_03.pdf

———. (1987c). The Hindu social order—Its unique features. In Vasant Moon (Comp.), *Dr. Babasaheb Ambedkar writings and speeches*, Vol. 3 (pp. 116–129). New Delhi: Dr. Ambedkar Foundation. Retrieved from http://www.mea.gov.in/Images/attach/amb/Volume_03.pdf

Amemia, T. (1985). *Advanced econometrics*. Cambridge, MA: Harvard University Press.

Anker, R., Malkas, H., & Korten, A. (2003). *Gender-based occupational segregation in the 1990's* (pp. 1–6). Geneva: ILO. Retrieved from http://www.ilo.org/public/libdoc/ilo/2003/103B09_287_engl.pdf

Appadorai, M. G. A. (Ed). (1934, 4 July). Reservation of posts for minorities and backward classes (resolution; pp.116–117). In *Speeches and documents on the Indian constitution, 1921–1947*, Vol. I. New Delhi: Ministry of Home Affairs, Government of India.

Arneson, R. J. (1989). Equality and equal opportunity for welfare. *Philosophical Studies: An International Journal for Philosophy in the Analytic Tradition*, 56(1), 77–93.

———. (1990). Liberalism, distributive subjectivism, and equal opportunity for welfare. *Philosophy & Public Affairs*, 19(2), 158–194.

———. (1999). Equality of opportunity for welfare defended and recanted. *Journal of Political Philosophy*, 7(4), 488–491.

Asimov, M. S., & Bosworth, C. E. (Eds). (1998). History of civilizations of Central Asia, Vol. 4. *The age of achievement*. Retrieved from http://unesdoc.unesco.org/images/0011/001116/111664eo.pdf

Atkinson, A. B., Trinder, C. G., & Maynard, A. K. (1983). *Parents and children: Incomes in two generations*. London: Heinemann Educational Books.

Awad, I. (2009). *The global economic crisis and migrant workers: Impact and response* (No. 433612). International Labour Organization.

Azariadis, C., & Drazzen, A. (1990). Threshold externalities in economic development. *Quarterly Journal of Economics*, 105 (2), 501–526. doi: 10.2307/2937797

Bancroft, G. (1958). American labor force. New York, NY: Wiley.

Banerjee, A. (1990). Comparative curfew: Changing dimensions of communal politics in India. In D. Vaas (Ed), *Mirrors of violence: Communities, riots, and survivors in South Asia*. New Delhi: Oxford University Press.

Barro, R. J., & Sala-I-Martin, X. (1992). Convergence. *Journal of Political Economy, 100*(2), 223–251. doi: 10.1086/261816

———. (1995). *Economic growth*. New York, NY: McGraw-Hill.

Barros, R. P., Ferreira, F., Vega, J. R. M., & Saavedra, J. (2009). *Measuring inequality of opportunities in Latin America and the Caribbean*. Washington, DC: World Bank.

Barros, R. P., Vega, J. R. M., & Saavedra, J. (2010). Measuring progress toward basic opportunities for all. *Brazilian Review of Econometrics, 30*(2), 335.

Basant, R. (2012). *Education and employment among Muslims in India: An analysis of patterns and trends* (WP No. 2012-09-03). Ahmedabad: Indian Institute of Management. Retrieved from https://www.iimahd.ernet.in/assets/snippets/.../12051717332012-09-03.pdf

Basant, R., & Shariff, A. (2010). The state of Muslims in India: An overview. In Rakesh Basant & Abusaleh Shariff (Eds.), *Handbook of Muslims in India: Empirical and policy perspectives* (pp. 1–23). New Delhi: Oxford University Press.

Becker, G. S. (1962). Investment in human capital: A theoretical analysis. *Journal of Political Economy, 70*(5), 9–49. doi: 10.1086/258724

———. (1964). *Human capital: A theoretical and empirical analysis, with special reference to education*. New York, NY: Columbia University Press.

Becker, S. O., & Woessmann, L. (2009). Was Weber wrong? A human capital theory of protestant economic history. *Quarterly Journal of Economics, 124*(2), 531–596.

Behrman, J. R., & Wolfe, B. L. (1984). The socioeconomic impact of schooling in a developing country. *The Review of Economics and Statistics, 66*(2), 296–303.

Bhaumik, S. K., & Chakraborty, M. (2010). Earnings inequality: The impact of the rise of caste and religion-based politics. In Rakesh Basant & Abusaleh Shariff (Eds), *Handbook of Muslims in India: Empirical and policy perspectives* (pp. 235–253). New Delhi: Oxford University Press.

Bjørkhaug, H., & Øyslebø Sørensen, S. (2012). Feminism without gender? Arguments for gender quotas on corporate boards in Norway. In F. Engelstad & M. Teign (Eds), *Firms, boards and gender quotas: Comparative perspectives* (pp. 185–209). Emerald Group Publishing Limited.

Blauner, R. (1964). Alienation and freedom: The factory worker and his industry. Oxford, England: The University of Chicago Press.

Borooah, V. K. (2005). Caste, inequality and poverty in India. *Review of Development Economics, 9*(3), 399–414. doi:10.111 1/j.1467-9361.2005.00284

———. (2010). On the risks of belonging to disadvantaged groups: A Bayesian analysis of labour market outcomes. In Rakesh Basant & Abusaleh Shariff (Eds), *Handbook of Muslims in India: Empirical and policy perspectives* (pp. 199–220). New Delhi: Oxford University Press.

Borooah, V. K., & Iyer, S. (2005). Vidya, Veda and Varna: The influence of religion and caste on education in rural India. *Journal of Development Studies, 41*(8), 1369–1404. doi: 10.1080/00220380500186960

Borooah, V. K., Dubey, A., & Iyer, S. (2006). Has job reservation been effective? Caste, religion, and economic status in India. *Development and Change*.

Bossert, W. (1995). Redistribution mechanisms based on individual characteristics. *Mathematical Social Sciences, 29*(1), 1–17.

Boulding, K. E. (1970). *Beyond economics: Essays on society, religion, and ethics*. Ann Arbor, MI: University of Michigan.

Bourguignon, F., Ferreira, F. H., & Menendez, M. (2007). Inequality of opportunity in Brazil. *Review of Income and Wealth, 53*(4), 585–618.

Bowles, S. (1972). Schooling and inequality from generation to generation. *Journal of Political Economy, 80*(3), 19–51.

Bowles, S., & Gintis, H. (2002). The inheritance of inequality. *Journal of economic Perspectives, 16*(3), 3–30.

Bowles, S., & Nelson, V. I. (1974). The 'inheritance of IQ' and the intergenerational reproduction of economic inequality. *The Review of Economics and Statistics, 56*(1), 39–51.

Brad Shuck, M., Rocco, T. S., & Albornoz, C. A. (2011). Exploring employee engagement from the employee perspective: Implications for HRD. *Journal of European Industrial Training, 35*(4), 300–325.

Breman, J. (1996). *Footloose labour: Working in India's informal economy*. Cambridge: Cambridge University Press.

Brenner, R., & Kiefer, N. M. (1981). The economics of the diaspora. Discrimination and occupational structure. *Economic*

Development & Cultural Change, 29(3), 517–534. Retrieved from http://www.jstor.org/stable/1153707

Bry, G. (1959). The average workweek as an economic indicator (Occasional Paper No. 69). New York: National Bureau of Economic Research.

Bulutay, T. (1996). *Education and the labor market in Turkey*. In proceedings of a seminar, State Institute of Statistics, Ankara.

Campbell, G. (1893). *Memoirs of my Indian career*, Vol. 2. London: Macmillan.

Cantoni, D. (2010). *The economic effects of the protestant reformation: Testing the Weber Hypothesis in the German lands* (Universitat Pompeu Fabra Working Paper, 1260).

Cassel, D., & Cichy, U. (1986). Explaining the growing shadow economy to East and West: A comparative systems approach. *Comparative Economic Studies, 28*(1), 20–41.

Castells, M., & Portes, A. (1989). World underneath: The origins, dynamics, and effects of the informal economy. In A. Portes, M. Castells, & L. Benton (Eds), *The informal economy: Studies in advanced and less developed countries* (pp. 11–37). Baltimore, MD: Johns Hopkins Press.

Chand, R., & Srivastava, S. K. (2014). Changes in the rural labour market and their implications for agriculture. *Economic & Political Weekly, 49*(10), 47–54.

Chandra, N., & Pratap, S. (2001). Organising informal sector workers. In Amitabh Kundu & A. N. Sarma (Eds.), *Informal sector in India*. New Delhi: Institute for Human Development.

Checchi, D., & Peragine, V. (2010). Inequality of opportunity in Italy. *The Journal of Economic Inequality, 8*(4), 429–450.

Chen, M. A. (2007). *Rethinking the informal economy: Linkages with the formal economy and the formal regulatory environment* (DESA Working Paper No. 46). New York: UNDESA.

Chiswick, B. R. (1983a). An analysis of the earnings and employment of Asian-American men. *Journal of Labor Economics, 1*(2), 197–214. doi: 10.1086/298010

———. (1983b). The earnings and human capital of American Jews. *Journal of Human Resources, 18*(3), 313–336. Retrieved from http://www.jstor.org/stable/pdfplus/145204

———. (1985). The labor market status of American Jews: Patterns and Determinants. In Milton Himmelfarb & David Singer (Eds), *American Jewish yearbook*, Vol. 85 (pp. 131–153). New York: The American Jewish Committee.

Ciccone, A. (1994). *Human capital and technical progress: Stagnation, transition and growth*. Stanford, CA: Department of Economics, Stanford University.

Clark, R., Ramsbey, T. W., & Adler, E. S. (1991). Culture, gender, and labor force participation: A cross-national study. *Gender and Society*, 5(1), 47–66. Retrieved from http://www.jstor.org/stable/189929

Coase, R. H. (1937). The nature of the firm. *Economica*, 4(16), 386–405. doi: 10.1111/j.1468-0335.1937.tb00002.x/full

Cohen, G. A. (1989). On the currency of egalitarian justice. *Ethics*, 99(4), 906–944.

Coser, L. A. (1957). Social conflict and the theory of social change. *The British Journal of Sociology*, 8(3), 197–207.

Das, M. B. (2008). *Minority status and labor market outcomes: Does India have minority enclaves?* Washington, DC: World Bank. doi:10.1596/1813-9450-4653

Dasgupta, P., & Goldar, B. (2005). *Female labour supply in rural India: An econometric analysis*. Delhi: Institute of Economic Growth.

Dejong, E. (2011). Religious values and economic growth: A review and assessment of recent studies. In Gerrieter Haar (Ed), *Religion and development. Ways of transforming the world* (pp. 111–140). New York, NY: Columbia University Press.

DeMaris, A. (1992). Logit modeling: Practical applications. *Sage University Paper Series on Quantitative Applications in the Social Sciences*, Vol. 999 (pp. 7–86). Newbury Park, CA: SAGE Publications.

Desai, S. B., Dubey, A., Joshi, B. L., Sen, M., Shariff, A., & Vanneman, R. (2010). *Human development in India: Challenges for a society in transition* (p. 178). New Delhi: Oxford University Press.

Desai, S., & Jain, D. (1994). Maternal employment and changes in family dynamics: The social context of women's work in rural South India. *Population and Development Review*, 20(1), 115–136.

Desai, S., & Kulkarni, V. (2008). Changing educational inequalities in India: In the context of affirmative action. *Demography*, 45(2), 245–270.

DeSoto, H. (1989). The other path. New York, NY: Harper and Row Publishers Inc.

Dhulipala, V. (2015). *Creating a new Medina*. New Delhi: Cambridge University Press.

Dilnot, A., & Morris, C. (1981). What do we know about the black economy? *Fiscal Studies*, *2*(1), 58–73. doi: 10.1111/j.1475-5890.1981.tb00457.x

Doeringer, P. B., & Piore, M. J. (1971). *Internal labor markets and manpower analysis*. Lexington, MA: Heath/Lexington Books. Retrieved from http://files.eric.ed.gov/fulltext/ED048457.pdf

Douglas, P. (1934). *The theory of wages*. New York, NY: Macmillan.

Dunlop, J. T. (1957). The task of contemporary wage theory. In J. T. Dunlop (Ed.), *The theory of wage determination* (pp. 3–27). London: Palgrave Macmillan.

Durand, J. D. (1948). *The Labor Force in the United States, 1890–1960*. New York, NY: Social Science Research Council.

Dutt, R. C. (1893). *A history of civilisation in ancient India, based on Sanskrit literature*, Revised edition. London: Kegan Paul, Trench, Trübner & Company. Retrieved from http://www.isec.ac.in/History_%20of_%20civilisation_%20in_%20ancient_%20India.pdf

Dworkin, R. (1981a). What is equality? Part 1: Equality of welfare. *Philosophy & Public Affairs*, *10*(3), 185–246. Retrieved from http://www.jstor.org/stable/2264894

———. (1981b). What is equality? Part 2: Equality of resources. *Philosophy & Public Affairs*, *10*(4), 283–345. Retrieved from http://www.jstor.org/stable/2265047

Edgerton, D. L., Assarsson, B., Hummelmose, A., Laurila, I. P., Rickertsen, K., & Vale, P. H. (2012). *The econometrics of demand systems: With applications to food demand in the Nordic countries*, Vol. 34. New York, NY: Springer Science & Business Media.

Elliot, H. M. (2006). *History of India, as told by its own historians: The Muhammadan period*. London: Forgotten Books.

Elliott, J. R. (2001). Referral hiring and ethnically homogeneous jobs: How prevalent is the connection and for whom? *Social Science Research*, *30*(3), 401–425.

Elson, D. (1999). Labor markets as gendered institutions: Equality, efficiency and empowerment issues. *World Development*, *27*(3), 611–627.

Fadayomi, T., & Olurinola, I. O. (2014). Determinants of labour force participation in Nigeria: The influence of household structure. *Journal of Economics and Development Studies*, *2*(2), 169–190.

Fazal, T. (2013a). *Millennium development goals and Muslims of India*. New Delhi: Oxfam India.

Fazal, T. (2013b). *Muslims of India: Vulnerabilities and needs* (Oxfam India Working Paper No. OIWPS-XIII). New Delhi: Oxfam India.

Fazal, T., & Kumar, R. (2013). Muslims in India: A study of socio-economic and educational levels in four focus states. In Mushirul Hasan, Zoya Hasan, & Council for Social Development (Eds), *Indian social development report 2012: Minorities at the margin*. New Delhi: Oxford University Press.

Feige, E. L. (1990). Defining and estimating underground and informal economies: The new institutional economics approach. *World Development, 18*(7), 989–1002. doi: 10.1016/0305-750X(90)90081-8

Ferman, P. R., & Ferman, L. A. (1973, 1 January). The structural underpinnings of the irregular economy. *Asia Pacific Journal of Human Resources, 8*(1), 1–17. doi: 10.1177/103841117300800101

Ferreira, F. H. G., & Gignoux, J. (2011). *Measurement of educational inequality: Achievement and opportunity*. Washington, DC: World Bank.

Ferreira, F. H. G., Gignoux, J., & Aran, M. (2011). Measuring inequality of opportunity with imperfect data: The case of Turkey. *The Journal of Economic Inequality, 9*(4), 651–680. doi: 10.1007/s10888-011-9169-0

Fields, G. S., Leary, J. B., & López-Calva, L. F. (1998). *Education's crucial role in explaining labor income inequality in urban Bolivia*. Harvard Institute for International Development, Harvard University.

Finegan, T. A. (1962). Hours of work in the United States: A cross-sectional analysis. *Journal of Political Economy, 70*(5, Part 1), 452–470.

Fleurbaey, M. (1994). On fair compensation. *Theory and Decision, 36*(3), 277–307.

———. (2008). *Fairness, responsibility, and welfare*. Oxford: Oxford University Press.

Fleurbaey, M., & Maniquet, F. (1997). Implementability and horizontal equity imply no-envy. *Econometrica: Journal of the Econometric Society*, 1215–1219.

Fogel, R. W. (1990). *The conquest of high mortality and hunger in Europe and America: Timing and mechanisms* (NBER Working Paper Series on Historical Factors in Long-run Growth, No. 16). Cambridge, MA: National Bureau of Economic Research.

Frey, B., Weck, H., & Pommerehene, W. W. (1982). Has the shadow economy grown in Germany, An exploratory study. *Review of World Economics, 118,* 524. doi: *10.1007/BF02706263*

Gallie, D., White, M., Cheng, Y., & Tomlinson, M. (1998). Restructuring the employment relationship. *OUP Catalogue.*

Gangl, M. (2000). *Education and labour market entry across Europe: The impact of institutional arrangements in training systems and labour markets* (Working Paper No. 25). Mannheim: Mannheim University.

———. (2001). European patterns of labour market entry. A dichotomy of occupationalized vs. non-occupationalized systems? *European Societies, 3*(4), 471–494.

Gayer, L., & Jaffrelot, C. (2012). *Muslims in Indian cities: Trajectories of marginalisation.* New York, NY: Columbia University Press.

Gellerman, S. W. (1963). *Motivation and productivity.* New York, NY: American Management Association.

Ghosh, J. (1995). Employment and labour under structural adjustment–India since 1991. *The Indian Journal of Labour Economics, 38*(4), 567–576.

Glewwe, P. (1996). The relevance of standard estimates of rates of return to schooling for education policy: A critical assessment. *Journal of Development economics, 51*(2), 267–290.

Gockel, G. L. (1969). Income and religious affiliation: A regression analysis. *American Journal of Sociology, 74*(6), 632–649. doi: 10.1086/224714

Goldberg, J., & Smith, J. (2008). The effects of education on labor market outcomes. *Handbook of research in education finance and policy (688-708).* New York, NY: Routledge.

Government of India. (2006). *Report of prime minister's high level committee on social, economic and educational status of Muslim community in India.* New Delhi: Cabinet Secretariat.

———. (2011a). *India human development report 2011: Towards social inclusion.* New Delhi: Institute of Applied Manpower Research.

———. (2011b). *Population by religious communities census of India.* New Delhi: Ministry of Home Affairs.

Greene, W. H. (1997). *Econometric Analysis,* 3rd ed. Englewood Cliffs, NJ: Prentice Hall.

Greif, A. (1994). Cultural beliefs and the organization of society: A historical and theoretical reflection on collectivist and individualist societies. *Journal of Political Economy, 102*(5), 912–950.

Grier, R. (1997). The effect of religion on economic development: a cross national study of 63 former colonies. *Kyklos, 50*(1), 47–62.

Guiso, L., Paola, S., & Luigi, Z. (2003). People's opium? Religion and economic attitudes. *Journal of Monetary Economics, 50*(1), 225–282. doi: 10.1016/S0304-3932(02)00202-7

Gutmann, P. M. (1977). The subterranean economy. *Financial Analysts Journal, 33*(6), 23–29. doi: 10.2469/ccb.v2007.n6.4818

Hajari, N. (2015), *Midnight's furies: The deadly legacy of India's partition*. Boston, MA: Houghton Mifflin Harcourt Publishing Company.

Harding, P., & Jenkins, R. (1989). *The myth of the hidden economy: Towards a new understanding of informal economic activity*. Milton Keynes: Open University Press.

Hardy, P. (1972). *The Muslims of British India*. Cambridge: Cambridge University Press.

Hart, K. (1973). Informal income opportunities and urban employment in Ghana. *Journal of Modern African Studies, 11*(1), 61–89. doi: 10.1017/S0022278X00008089

Hasan, M., & Hasan, Z. (2013). *Social development report*. New Delhi: Oxford University Press.

Hasan, Z., & Menon, R. (2004). *Unequal citizens: A study of Muslim women in India*. New Delhi: OUP.

Hatløy, A., Kebede, T., Zhang, H., & Bjørkhaug, I. (2012). *Perceptions of good jobs: Analytical report—Port Loko and Freetown, Sierra Leone*. Washington, DC: World Bank.

Hauser, R. M. (2002). *Meritocracy, cognitive ability, and the sources of occupational success*. Madison, WI: Center for Demography and Ecology, University of Wisconsin.

Hay, J. (2006). *Hinduism*. Farmington Hills, MI: Greenhaven Press.

Heckman, J. J., & Hotz, V. J. (1986). An investigation of the labor market earnings of Panamanian males: Evaluating the sources of inequality. *Journal of Human Resources, 21*(4), 507–542.

Heckman, J. J., Killingsworth, M., & MaCurdy, T. (1981). Empirical evidence on static labour supply models: A survey of recent developments. In Z. Hornstein, J. Grice & A. Webb (Eds.), *The economics of the labour market* (pp. 75–122). London: Her Majesty's Stationery Office.

Hicks, J. (1932). *The theory of wages*. London: Macmillan.

Hild, M., & Voorhoeve, A. (2004). Equality of opportunity and opportunity dominance. *Economics & Philosophy, 20*(1), 117–145.

Hirway, I. (2012). Missing labour force: An explanation. *Economic & Political Weekly, 47*(37), 67–72.

Hoekman, B. M., & Kostecki, M. M. (2009). *The political economy of the world trading system: the WTO and beyond*. Oxford: Oxford University Press.

Hornstein, A. (2013). Why labor force participation (usually) increases when unemployment declines. *Economic Quarterly, 99*(1), 1–23. Retrieved from https://www.richmondfed.org/~/media/richmondfedorg/publications/research/economic_quarterly/2013/q1/pdf/hornstein.pdf

Hosmer, D. W., & Lemeshow, S. (1989). *Applied logistic regression*. New York, NY: Wiley.

———. (2000). *Applied logistic regression*, 2nd Edition. New York, NY: John Wiley & Sons, Inc. doi:10.1002/0471722146

Houston, J. F. (1987). The underground economy: A troubling issue for policy makers. *Business Review*, (September), 3–12.

Hoyos, A., & Narayan, A. (2011). *Inequality of opportunities among children: How much does gender matter?* Washington, DC: World Bank. Retrieved from https://openknowledge.worldbank.org/handle/10986/27452

Hunter, W. W. (1876). *The Indian Musalmans*, 3rd ed. London: Trübner.

Hurley, D. T. (2003). Horizontal and vertical intra-industry trade: The case of ASEAN trade in manufactures. *International Economic Journal, 17*(4), 1–14.

Iannaccone, L. (1998). Introduction to the economics of religion. *Journal of Economic Literature, 36*(3), 1465–1495. doi: 10.1016/j.religion.2008.01.006

Ibbetson, D. C. J. (1881). *Report on the census of the Punjab*, Vol. 1 (p. 7; Calcutta, 1883; as quoted by Hardy Peter).

ILO. (1972). *Employment, income and equality: A strategy for increasing productive employment in Kenya*. Geneva: International Labour Office.

———. (2012). *Global employment trends 2012: Preventing a deeper jobs crisis*. Retrieved from http://www.ilo.org/global/research/global-reports/global-employment-trends/WCMS_171571/lang–en/index.htm

———. (2018). *World employment and social outlook: Trends 2018*. Retrieved from https://www.ilo.org/wcmsp5/groups/public/—dgreports/—dcomm/—publ/documents/publication/wcms_615594.pdf

Israeli, O. (2007). A Shapley-based decomposition of the R-square of a linear regression. *The Journal of Economic Inequality, 5*(2), 199–212.

Jamison, D. T., & Lau, L. J. (1982). *Farmer education and farm efficiency*. Baltimore, MD: Johns Hopkins University Press.

Jencks, C., & Tach, L. (2006). Would equal opportunity mean more mobility? In S. Morgan, D. Grusky, & G. Fields (Eds), *Mobility and inequality: Frontiers of research from sociology and economics*. Stanford, CA: Stanford University Press.

Jevons, W. S. (1888). *The theory of political economy*. London: Macmillan.

Johnston, J. (1984). *Econometric methods*, 3rd edn. New York, NY: McGraw-Hill.

Johnston, J., & DiNardo, J. (1997). *Econometric methods*. New York, NY: MacGraw-Hill.

Jones, C. O. (1961). Representation in congress: The case of the house agriculture committee. *American Political Science Review, 55*(2), 358–367.

Kannan, K. P., & Raveendran, G. (2012). Counting and profiling the missing labour force. *Economic & Political Weekly, 47*(6), 77–80.

Kapadia, K. (1995). The profitability of bonded labour: The gem-cutting industry in rural South India. *The Journal of Peasant Studies, 22*(3), 446–483.

Kasnakoglu, Z., & Dayioglu, M. (1996). Education and the labor market participation of women in Turkey. In T. Bulutay (Ed.), *Education and the Labor Market in Turkey*. Turkey: SIS Publication.

Keeley, M. C. (2013). *Labor supply and public policy: A critical review*. Elsevier.

Kemp, M. C., & Wan Jr., H. Y. (1986). Gains from trade with and without lump-sum compensation. *Journal of International Economics, 21*(1–2), 99–110.

Kennedy, S., & Hedley, D. (2003). *A note on educational attainment and labour force participation in Australia* (No. 2003-03). The Treasury, Australian Government.

Kern, H., & Schumann, M. (1990). *The impact of technology on job content and work organization*. In Conference on Technology and the Future of Work, Stanford University, Stanford, California, March (Vol. 28, p. 29).

Kerr, C. (1954). The balkanization of labor markets. In E. Wight Bakke (Ed), *Labor mobility and economic opportunity*. New York, NY: John Wiley & Sons.

Kerr, C., Harbison, F. H., Dunlop, J. T., & Myers, C. A. (1960). Industrialism and industrial man. *Int'l Lab. Rev.*, *82*, 236.

Khalidi, O. (2006). *Muslims in the Indian Economy*. Gurgaon: Three Essays Collective.

Khan, S. (1989). Muslim decline in India. In Iqbal A. Ansari (Ed), *The Muslim situation in India* (pp. 73–79). New Delhi: Sterling Publishers.

Kijima, Y. (2006). Why did wage inequality increase? Evidence from urban India 1983–99. *Journal of Development Economics*, *81*(1), 97–117.

Killingsworth, M. R. (1983). *Labor supply*. Cambridge: Cambridge University Press.

King, C. R. (1994). *One language, two scripts: The Hindi movement in nineteenth century North India* (pp. 135–137, 173). New Delhi: Oxford University Press.

Klasen, S., & Pieters, J. (2012). Push or pull? Drivers of female labor force participation during India's economic boom. IZA Discussion Paper No. 6395. Institute for the Study of Labor (IZA), Bonn.

Kleinbeck, U., & Fuhrmann, H. (2000). Effects of a psychologically based management system on work motivation and productivity. *Applied Psychology*, *49*(3), 596–610.

Kmenta, J. (1985). *Elements of econometrics*. New York, NY: Macmillan.

Knights, D., & Willmott, H. (Eds.). (2016). *Labour process theory*. Springer.

Kosters, M. H. (1966). *Income and substitution effects in a family labor supply model* (no. P-3339). Santa Monica, CA: Rand Corp.

Kuran, T. (1995). Islamic economics and the Islamic subeconomy. *Journal of Economic Perspectives*, *9*(4), 155–173.

———. (1997). Islam and underdevelopment: An old puzzle revisited. *Journal of Institutional and Theoretical Economics (JITE) (Zeitschrift für die gesamte Staatswissenschaft)*, 41–71.

———. (1997). The genesis of Islamic economics: A chapter in the politics of Muslim identity. *Social Research*, 301–338.

Lal, D. (1988). *Hindu equilibrium, cultural stability and economic stagnation*, Vol. 1. Oxford: Clarendon Press.

Lapierre, D., & Collins, L. (1995). *Esta noche, la libertad* (Freedom at Midnight) (No. 954 L313e). Plaza & Janés.

Lefranc, A., Pistolesi, N., & Trannoy, A. (2008). Inequality of opportunities vs. inequality of outcomes: Are Western societies all alike? *Review of income and wealth*, 54(4), 513–546.

Lelyveld, J. (1968, 28 October). India's 55 million Muslims living in rejection and isolation. *New York Times*, p. 6.

Levin, J. S. (1994). Religion and health: Is there an association, is it valid, and is it causal? *Social Science and Medicine*, 38(11), 1475–1482. doi: 10.1016/0277-9536(94)90109-0

Lincoln, J. R., & Kalleberg, A. L. (1996). Commitment, quits, and work organization in Japanese and US plants. *ILR Review*, 50(1), 39–59.

Lockheed, M. E., Jamison, T., & Lau, L. J. (1980). Farmer education and farm efficiency: A survey. *Economic development and cultural change*, 29(1), 37–76.

Long, C. D. (1958). The labor force under changing income and employment. National Bureau of Economic Research, General Series No. 65, Princeton University Press.

Long, J. S. (1997). Regression models for categorical and limited dependent variables. *Advanced quantitative techniques in the social sciences*, Vol. 7. Thousand Oaks, CA: SAGE Publications.

Lord Dufferin. (1888, 11 November). Dufferin's Minute of November 1888 on Provincial Councils, enclosed with letter dated 11 November 1888 to Viscount Cross, Secretary of State for India, *Letters from Dufferin to Cross*, Vol. 5, Papers of the First Viscount Cross, India Office Library, EUR E 243.

Lucas Jr., R. E. (1988). On the mechanics of economic development. *Journal of Monetary Economics*, 22(1), 3–42. doi: 10.1016/0304-3932(88)90168-7

———. (1993). Making a miracle. *Econometrica*, 61(2), 251–272. doi: 10.2307/2951551

Lund, C., De Silva, M., Plagerson, S., Cooper, S., Chisholm, D., Das, J., ... & Patel, V. (2011). Poverty and mental disorders: breaking the cycle in low-income and middle-income countries. *The lancet*, 378(9801), 1502–1514.

Mahmood, S. T. (2006, 19 November). From William Hunter to Rajinder Sachar: Reports & reports but no results. *Milli Gazette*. Retrieved from http://www.milligazette.com/dailyupdate/2006/200611195_condition_muslims_india.htm

Mallah, S. (2007, 7 May). Two-nation theory exists. *Pakistan Times*. Retrieved from http://pakistantimes.net/2007/05/07/-oped2.htm

Malhotra, A., Vanneman, R., & Kishor, S. (1995). Fertility, dimensions of patriarchy, and development in India. *Population and Development Review, 21*(2), 281–305.

Malhotra, I., & Linden, J. J. (1973). *What ails the Indian Muslims?* Islamabad: Khursheed Printers.

Mangeloja, E. (2005). Economic growth and religious production efficiency. *Applied Economics, 37*(20), 2349–2359. doi: 10.1080/00036840500217531

Mankiw, N. G., Romer, D., & Weil, D. N. (1992). A contribution to the empirics of economic-growth. *Quarterly Journal of Economics, 107*(2), 407–437. doi: 10.2307/2118477

Margolis, D. N., & Simonnet, V. (2003). Educational track, networks and labor market outcomes. IZA Discussion Paper No. 699.

Marshall, S. E. (1985). Development, dependence, and gender inequality in the Third World. *International Studies Quarterly, 29*, 217–240.

Marx, K. (1859). *A contribution to the critique of political economy*. Moscow: Progress Publishers.

———. (1859). Preface to a contribution to the critique of political economy. *The Marx-Engels Reader, 2*, 3–6.

———. (1933). *Wage–labour and capital* (pp. 19–20). New York, NY: International Publishers.

———. (1995[1887]). Capital: A critique of political economy, Chapter 6, Vol. 1, Book One: *The process of capitalist production* (pp. 119; Online version: Marx/Engels Internet Archive marxists.org). Retrieved from https://archive.org/stream/capitalcritiqueo00marx/capitalcritiqueo00marx_djvu.txt

———. (1996). *Capital: A critique of political economy*, Vol. 1 (p. 178). London: Lawrence & Wishart.

Maslow, A. H. (1962). Some basic propositions of a growth and self-actualization psychology. In A. W. Combs (Ed.), *Perceiving, behaving, becoming: A new focus for education* (pp. 34–49). Washington, DC, US: National Education Association.

McGregor, P. P., & Borooah, V. K. (1992). Is low spending or low income a better indicator of whether or not a household is poor: some results from the 1985 Family Expenditure Survey. *Journal of Social Policy, 21*(1), 53–69.

Mehrotra, S., Gandhi, A., & Sahoo, B. K. (2013). Estimating India's skill gap: On a realistic basis for 2022. *Economic and Political Weekly, 48*(13), 102–111.

Mehrotra, S., Parida, J., Sinha, S., & Gandhi, A. (2014). Explaining employment trends in the Indian economy: 1993-94 to 2011-12. *Economic & Political Weekly, 32*, 49–57.

Mehrotra, S., Sinha, S., Parida, J. K., & Gandhi, A. (2014). *Why a jobs turnaround despite slowing growth?* New Delhi: Institute of Applied Manpower Research, Planning Commission, Government of India. Retrieved from http://www.iamrindia.gov.in/writereaddata/UploadFile/turnaround.pdf

Menard, S. (1995). Applied logistic regression analysis. *Sage University Paper Series on Quantitative Applications in the Social Sciences* (pp. 7–106). Thousand Oaks, CA: SAGE Publications.

Meng, R., & Sentance, J. (1984). Religion and the determination of earnings: Further results. *Canadian Journal of Economics, 17*(3), 481–488. doi: 10.2307/135187

Metcalf, T. R. (1965). *The aftermath of revolt: India 1857–1870.* Princeton, NJ: Princeton University Press.

Mincer, J. (1958). Investment in human capital and personal income distribution. *Journal of political economy, 66*(4), 281–302.

———. (1974). Schooling, Experience, and Earnings. *Human Behavior & Social Institutions, 2.*

———. (1962a). *Labor force participation of married women.* In Conference of the Universities-National Bureau Committee for Economic Research, Aspects of Labor Economics, Princeton University Press, Princeton, New Jersey.

———. (1962b). On-the-job training: Costs, returns, and some implications. *Journal of Political Economy, 70*(5), 50–79. doi: 10.1086/258725

Misra, B. B. (1986). *The government and bureaucracy in India, 1947–1976.* New Delhi: Oxford University Press.

Mondal, S. R. (1992). Economic and social situations among Muslims of West Bengal: Some empirical observations. In F. R. Faridi & M. M. Siddiqi (Eds), *The social structure of Indian Muslims* (pp. 108–116). New Delhi: Institute for Objective Studies.

Morrison, A., Raju, D., & Sinha, N. (2007). *Gender equality, poverty and economic growth.* Policy Research Working Paper No. WPS 4349. Washington, DC: World Bank.

Naughton, B. (2007). *The Chinese economy: Transitions and growth.* Cambridge, MA: MIT Press.

Naik, A. K. (2009, 23–26 September). *Informal sector and informal workers in India.* Paper presented at Special IARIW-SAIM Conference on 'Measuring the Informal Economy in Developing Countries' Kathmandu, Nepal.

National Commission for Women. (1988). *Shram Shakti report of the National Commission on self-employed women and women in the informal sector.* New Delhi: Shastri Bhawan, Department of Women and Child Development.

Noland, M. (2005). Religion and economic performance. *World Development, 33*(8), 1215–1232. doi: 10.1016/j.worlddev.2005.03.006

Noll, H. H. (2011). The Stiglitz-Sen-Fitoussi-report: Old wine in new skins? Views from a social indicators perspective. *Social Indicators Research, 102*(1), 111–116.

Norton, A. (2013). *On the Muslim question.* Princeton, NJ: Princeton University Press.

Nozick, R. (1974). *Anarchy, state, and utopia.* New York, NY: Basic Books.

North-Western Provinces Government Gazette. (1861, 24 December). Allahabad: North-Western Provinces Government Gazette.

NSSO (National Sample Survey Organisation). (2011). Employment and unemployment situation in India 2009–10.

———. (2011). *Key indicators of employment and unemployment in India 2009–2010.* NSS 66th Round. New Delhi: NSSO.

Oakley, A. (1974). *Women's work.* New York, NY: Vintage Books.

Obermeyer, C. M. (1992). Islam, women, and politics: The demography of Arab countries. *Population and Development Review, 18*(1), 33–60.

OECD. (2012). How does education affect employment rates? In *Education at a Glance 2012: Highlights.* Paris: OECD. doi: 10.1787/eag_highlights-2012-11-en

Offe, C., & Keane, J. (1985). *Disorganized capitalism: Contemporary transformations of work and politics* (p. 16). Cambridge: Polity.

Ooghe, E., & Schokkaert, E. (2007). Equality of opportunity versus equality of opportunity sets. *Social Choice and Welfare, 28*(2), 209–230.

Panigrahi, D. (2004). *India's partition: The story of imperialism in retreat.* London: Routledge.

Papola, T. S. (1981). *Urban informal sector in a developing economy.* New Delhi: Vikas Publishing House.

———. (2005). Social exclusion and discrimination in hiring practices: The case of Indian private industry. In Sukhadeo Thorat, Aryama & Prashant Negi (Eds), *Reservation and Private Sector—Quest for Growth and Equal Opportunity* (pp. 101–108). New Delhi and Jaipur: Rawat Publications.

Pascarella, E. T., & Terenzini, P. T. (2005). *How college affects students: A third decade of research*, Vol. 2. Indianapolis, IN: Jossey-Bass.

Parliamentary Paper. (1865). Papers relating to the administration of Oude (No. 62; pp. 71–72).

Parthasarthi, G. (1985). Nehru to chief ministers, 20 sept. 1953. In *Jawaharlal Nehru: Letters to chief ministers, 1947–1964*, Vol. 3 (pp. 376–377). New Delhi: Rekha Printers Private Limited.

Peragine, V. (2004). Ranking income distributions according to equality of opportunity. *The Journal of Economic Inequality, 2*(1), 11–30.

Phelps Brown, E. H. (1962). Seven centuries of the prices of consumables compared with builders wage rates. *Economic History, 2.*

Phillips, P. C. (1987). Towards a unified asymptotic theory for autoregression. *Biometrika, 74*(3), 535–547.

Piore, M. J., & Sabel, C. F. (1984). *The second industrial divide: possibilities for prosperity*, Vol. 4. New York: Basic books.

Planning Commission. (2011). *Report of the expert group to review the methodology for estimation of poverty* (No. id: 4531).

Polanyi, K. (1957). *The great transformation. The political and economic origins of our time* (pp. 72–73). Boston, MA: Beacon Press.

———. (1994). Karl Polanyi as socialist. In K. McRobbie (Ed.), *Humanity, Society, and Commitment: On Karl Polanyi* (pp. 115–134). Montreal: Black Rose.

Psacharopoulos, G., & Tzannatos, Z. (1989). Female labor force participation: An international perspective. *The World Bank Research Observer, 4*(2), 187–201.

———. (1991). *Female labor force participation and education.* Washington, DC: The World Bank.

Quarterly National Household Survey. (2011). *Central statistics office.* Retrieved from http://www.cso.ie/en/media/csoie/releasespublications/documents/labourmarket/2011/qnhs_q12011.pdf

Rakowski, C. A. (1994). The informal sector debate, Part 2: 1984–1993. In C. A. Rakowski *(Ed.), Contrapunto: The informal sector debate in Latin America* (pp. 31–50). Albany: State University of New York Press.

Rawls, J. (1971). *Theory of justice.* Cambridge, MA: Harvard University Press.

Ray, S. (1983). *Freedom movement and Indian Muslims.* New Delhi: The People's Publishing House.

Reddy, R. (2003, 7 August). *Deprivation affects Muslims more.* Retrieved from https://www.countercurrents.org/comm-reddy070803.htm

Robbins, L. (1930). On the elasticity of demand for income in terms of effort. *Economica, 29,* 123–129. doi: 10.2307/2548225

Roemer, J. E. (1998). *Equality of opportunity.* Cambridge, MA: Harvard University Press.

———. (1993). A pragmatic theory of responsibility for the egalitarian planner. *Philosophy & Public Affairs, 22*(2), 146–166.

Romer, P. M. (1986). Increasing returns and long-run growth. *Journal of Political Economy, 94*(5), 1002–1037. Retrieved from http://www.jstor.org/stable/1833190

———. (1990). Endogenous technological change. *Journal of Political Economy, 98*(5), S71–S102. Retrieved from http://www.jstor.org/stable/2937632

Römer, K. (2001, October). *Time synchronization in ad hoc networks.* In Proceedings of the 2nd ACM international symposium on Mobile ad hoc networking and computing (pp. 173–182). ACM.

Russel, W. H. (1860). *My diary in India in the years 1858–9,* Vol. 2 (p. 239). Farington Street, London: Routledge, Warne and Routledge.

Sachar Committee. (2006). *Social, economic and educational status of the Muslim community of India: A report.* New Delhi: Prime Minister's High Level Committee.

Sainath, P. (1996). *Everybody loves a good drought: Stories from India's poorest districts.* London: Review.

Salazar-Xirinachs, J. M., Nübler, I., & Kozul-Wright, R. (Eds) (2014). *Transforming economies: Making industrial policy work for growth, jobs and development.* Geneva: ILO/UNCTAD.

Sastre, M., & Trannoy, A. (2002). Shapley inequality decomposition by factor components: Some methodological issues. *Journal of Economics, 77*(1) 51–89.

Schneider, F., & Enste, D. H. (2000). Shadow economies: Size, causes, and consequences. *Journal of Economic Literature, 38*(1), 77–114. doi: 10.1257/jel.38.1.77

Schoenberg, E. H., & Douglas, P. H. (1937). Studies in the supply curve of labor: The relation in 1929 between average earnings in American cities and the proportions seeking employment. *Journal of Political Economy, 45*(1), 45–79.

Schultz, T. (1961). Investment in human capital. *The American Economic Review, 51*(1), 1–17. Retrieved from http://www.jstor.org/stable/1818907

———. (1963). *The economic value of education*. New York, NY: Columbia University Press.

Schultz, T. W. (1961). Investment in human capital. *The American economic review, 51*(1), 1–17.

Scoville, J. G. L. (1991). Towards a model of caste economy. In James G. Scoville (Ed.), *Status Influences in Third World labour markets: Caste, gender and custom*. Berlin; New York: Walter de Gruyter.

———. (1985). *Commodities and capabilities*. Amsterdam: North-Holland.

Sen, A. (1980). Description as choice. *Oxford Economic Papers, 32*(3), 353–369.

———. (1984). Development: Which way now. In A. Sen (Ed.), *Resources Values and Development* (p. 485). Oxford: Blackwell, and Cambridge, MA: Harvard University PRess.

Sen, A. K. (1985). Well-being, agency and freedom: The Dewey lectures 1984. *Journal of Philosophy, 82*, 169–221.

Sethuraman, S. V. (1976). *Jakarta urban development and employment*. Geneva: International Labour Organization.

Sethuraman, S. V. (1998). *Gender, informality and poverty: A global review. Gender Bias in Female Informal Employment and Incomes in Developing Countries*. Geneva/Cambridge, MA/Washington, DC: Women in Informal Employment Globalising and Organising (WIEGO)/World Bank.

Shariff, A. (1999). *India: Human development report, a profile of Indian states in the 1990s*. New Delhi: NCAER & OUP.

Shariff, A., & Azam, M. (2004). *Economic empowerment of Muslims in India*. New Delhi: Institute of Objective Studies.

Shorrocks, A. F. (2013). Decomposition procedures for distributional analysis: A unified framework based on the Shapley value. *The Journal of Economic Inequality, 11*(1), 99–126.

Simon, H. A. (1951). A formal theory of the employment relationship. *Econometrica, 19*(3), 293–305. doi: 10.2307/1906815

Simson, C., & White, A. (1982). *Beating the system: The underground economy*. Boston, MA: Auburn House Publishing Company.

Singh Sarila, N. (2005). *The shadow of the great game*. Noida: HarperCollins.

Smith, A. (1776). *The wealth of nations*. New York, NY: The Modern Library.

———. (1776 [1937]). An inquiry into the nature and causes of the wealth of nations, Modern Library Edition, edited by Edwin Cannan and with an introduction by Max Lerner. New York: Random House, Inc.

Solon, G. (1992). Intergenerational income mobility in the United States. *American Economic Review, 82*(3), 393–408.

———. (1999). Intergenerational mobility in the labor market. In O. Ashenfelter & D. Card (Eds), *Handbook of labor economics*, Vol. 3 (pp. 1761–1800). Amsterdam: Elsevier.

Steen, T. P. (1996). Religion and earnings: Evidence from the NLS youth cohort. *International Journal of Social Economics, 23*(1), 47–58. doi: 10.1108/03068299610108872

Stewart, R. B., & Sanchez Badin, M. R. (2006). The World Trade Organization and global administrative law. In Christian Joerges & Ernst-Ulrich Petersmann (Eds), *Constitutionalism, multilevel trade governance and social regulation* (pp. 9–71). Oxford and Portland: Hart Publishing.

Stokey, N. L. (1988). Learning by doing and the introduction of new goods. *Journal of Political Economy, 96*(4), 701–717. doi: 10.1086/261559

System of National Accounts. (1993). *System of National Accounts 1993*. Brussels/Luxembourg: Commission of the European Communities. Retrieved from https://unstats.un.org/unsd/nationalaccount/docs/1993sna.pdf

Tansel, A. (1996). Self employment, wage employment and returns to education for urban men and women in Turkey. In T. Bulutay (Ed.), *Education and the Labor Market in Turkey* (pp. 175–208). Turkey: SIS Publication.

Tansel, A., & Tasci, H. M. (2004). Determinants of unemployment duration for men and women in Turkey.

Thorat, S., & Newman, K. S. (2010). *Blocked by caste: Economic discrimination in modern India* (p. 20). New Delhi: Oxford University Press.

Thorat, S., Mahamallik, M., & Venkatesan, S. (2007). *Human poverty and socially disadvantage groups in India*. New Delhi: UNDP.

Tomes, N. (1983). Religion and the rate of return on human capital: Evidence from Canada. *Canadian Journal of Economics, 16*(1), 122–138. doi: 10.1080/13504851.2011.608635

———. (1984). The effects of religion and denomination on earnings and the returns to human capital. *Journal of Human Resources, 19*(4), 472–488. doi: 10.2307/145943

———. (1985). Religion and the earnings function. *The American Economic Review, 75*(2), 245–250.

UNESCO. (2013). *Educational attainment and employment outcomes: Evidence from 11 developing countries*. Retrieved from http://unesdoc.unesco.org/images/0022/002263/226333e.pdf

United Nations. (2015). *Millennium development goals report 2015*. New York, NY: United Nations Publications.

United States Department of Labor. (1992). *Occasional paper series on the informal sector* (Occasional paper No. 2). Washington, DC: US Government Publishing Office.

Unni, J. (2010). Informality and gender in the labour market for Muslims: Has education been a route out of poverty. In R. Basant & A. Shariff (Eds), *Handbook of Muslims in India: Empirical and Policy Perspectives* (pp. 221–234). New Delhi: Oxford University Press.

Unni, J., & Rani, U. (2008). *Flexibility of labour in globalizing India: the challenge of skills and technology*. New Delhi: Tulika Books.

Upadhyay, V. (2007). *Employment and earnings in urban informal sector—A study on Arunachal Pradesh*. Noida: V. V. Giri National Labour Institute.

Van de gaer, D. (1993). *Equality of opportunity and investment in human capital* (Doctoral dissertation). Leuven: Catholic University of Leuven.

Verick, S. (2014). *Female labor force participation in developing countries*. Bonn: Institute for the Study of Labor (IZA).

Vroom, V. H. (1964). *Work and motivation*, Vol. 54. New York, NY: Wiley.

Weber, M. (1904) *The protestant ethic and the spirit of capitalism* (Translated by S. Kalberg). New York: Oxford University Press.

———. (1930). *The Protestant ethic and the spirit of capitalism*. New York, NY: Scribner/Simon & Schuster.

Weber, M. (1958). *The protestant ethic and the spirit of capitalism* (Translated by Talcott Parsons). New York, NY: Charles Scribner's Sons.
Welch, F. (1970a). Education in production. *Journal of Political Economy*, *78*(1), 35–39. doi: 10.1086/259599
———. (1970b). Education in production. *Journal of Political Economy*, *78*(1), 35–59. Retrieved from http://www.jstor.org/stable/1829618
Whitehead, A. (2007, 8 August). Sixty bitter years after partition. *BBC News*. Retrieved from http://news.bbc.co.uk/1/hi/world/south_asia/6926057.stm
WHO, UNICEF, UNFPA and The World Bank. (2012). *Trends in maternal mortality: 1990–2010*. Retrieved from www.unfpa.org/webdav/site/global/shared/documents/publications/2012/Trends_in_maternal_mortality_A4-1.pdf
Wood, J. C. (1988). William Stanley Jevons: Critical Assessments.
Wooldridge, M. J. (2009). *An introduction to multiagent systems*, 2nd ed Hoboken, NJ: John Wiley & Sons, Inc.
World Bank. (2006). *World development report 2006: Equity and development*. Washington, DC: World Bank.
———. (2013). *Global financial development report 2014: Financial inclusion*, Vol. 2. Washington, DC: World Bank Publications.
———. (2014). *World development indicators 2014*. Washington, DC: World Bank.
———. (2015). Annual Report
Woytinsky, W. S. (1940). *Additional workers and the volume of unemployment in the depression*, Vol. 1. Committee on Social security, Social Science Research Council.
Zakaria, R. (1995). *The widening divide: An insight into Hindu–Muslim relations*. New Delhi: Penguin Books.
Zimmerman, D. J. (1992). Regression toward mediocrity in economic stature. *American Economic Review*, *82*(3), 409–429.

Index

activity status, 18

Bengali Muslim, 54
British vengeance role in 1857, 66

capabilities, 115
colonial economy
    artisans, 57
    spatial analysis, 57
colonial legacy, 74
confiscation of property and land, 62
current daily status, 18

Deccan Muslim, 57
decomposition of D-index, 124
Delhi Durbar, 60
demographic characteristics
    description, 12
dissimilarity index, 124

earnings inequality, 120
economics of religion
    studies, 6
education level, 21

employment and unemployment surveys, 15
    data sets of NSSO, 128
equality of opportunity, 116

fears of Muslims, 75
fictive commodity, 29

Ghaznavid hegemony, 55
Gopal Singh Commission Report (GSCR) of the 1980s, 77

household characteristics
    description, 12
Human Opportunity Index (HOI), 116, 129
    conceptual framework, 151
    employment controlled for SRC status, 151
    employment
        age group 15–24 years, 134
        age group 25–39 years, 136–138

age group 40–64 years, 139–142
levels of educational attainment, 142–150

impact of post-1857, 74
Indian Civil Services (ICS), 65
Indian labour market
  Muslims, 42
    caste structure, 43
    Dalits, 46
    discrimination, 44
    discrimination, evidence point, 45
    education endowment, 47
    enrolment rates, marginal impact, 43
    study in Surat, 45
    substantial proportion, 44
    WPR, 47
Indian Muslims
  employment, 76
  socio-economic and development status, 75
Indo-Gangetic plain, 55
inequality
  measurement and quantification, 113
informal activity, 35
informal economy, 35
  employment, 37
International Labour Organization (ILO)
  definition of informality, 35
Islamic civilization, 54
isolation female labour force, 109

Kundu Committee Report (KCR), 77

labour, 28
labour force, 20
labour force participation rate (LFPR), 78–79, 108
  age, 79–83
  education, 83–85
labour force
  activity, 17
  participation rate, 20
labour markets, 2, 26, 27, 28
  Catholics, 41
  developing world, 34
  emphasis, 30
  epidemiological studies, 40
  genuine commodities, 29
  human capital
    concept and its role, 30
  inequality of opportunity, 122
  mechanism, 27
  positioning of Muslims, 28
  religious tradition, comparison, 39
  self-employed
    employers, 16
    own account workers, 16
    activity status, 16
    casual wage labour, 16
    helper in household enterprise, 16
    regular salaried/wage employee, 16
  studies, 39
  transactions, 34
labour supply curve
  wage slope, 33
labour supply theory, 27
labour
  academic investigation, 30
  emphasis, 30
  genuine commodities, 29

human capital
  concept and its role, 30
  supply and demand, 32
Linear Probability Model (LPM), 22
logistic model, 22–25
lower labour force, 109

material life
  mode of production, 1
Ministry of Home Affairs (MOHA), 77
Mughal Empire
  degeneration, 60
Muslim backwardness, 75
Muslim community
  informal rule of reservation, 68
Muslim employment, 63, 70, 72
  artisans, 57
  population in west region, 58
  spatial analysis, 57
Muslim pension holders, 62
Muslim population in Punjab
  distribution and size, 55
Muslim sultanate
  Malda, 55
Muslim women
  skill gaps and reproductive, 109
Muslims in India, 51
  British rule, 52, 53
    mutiny in 1857, 53
    transformation, 53
  demoralization thesis, 71
  educational attainment, 60
  employment data, 63
  marginalization, 65
  scant data, 51
  suspicion theory, 65
  mutiny of 1857, 61

Nawabs of Bengal, 56
North-Western Provinces, 62

own account enterprise (OAE), 37

Pakistan
  geographical scenarios, 67
  ideology, 67
people's capacities to carry out work, 28
plight of Muslims, 70
post-Partition era
  Muslims in, 71

Rawalsian intervention, 112
religious affiliation
  Catholics, 41
  epidemiological studies, 40
  studies, 39
  tradition comparison, 39

Sachar Committee Report (SCR), 3, 4, 77
segmentation theory, 27
segmented labour markets (SLM) theory, 27
Shapley decomposition method, 127
socio-religious community (SRC), 78, 108, 110
student enrolment rate (SER), 78, 94–96

The East India Company, 56
The Protestant work ethic, 1
The Theory of Wages, 33

unemployment rate (UR), 78
  age and education, 96–99
Usual Principal and Subsidiary
  Activity Status (UPSS),
  128

victory of labour party in
  England, 67

worker population ratio
  (WPR), 47, 85

worker
  economic activity, 19
workforce participation rate
  (WFPR), 20, 85
  age, 90–91
  data analysis, 86
  education, 91–94
  Muslim women, 88
  rural–urban comparisons, 88
  transition phase, 89
  women participation, 89

About the Author

Javaid Iqbal Khan is a young economist born and brought up in Halmatpora village in the border district of Kupwara in the Indian state of Jammu and Kashmir. He has a doctorate degree in economics from the Department of Economics, University of Kashmir at Hazratbal, Srinagar, where he is currently working as Senior Assistant Professor. Apart from teaching microeconomic theory and Indian economic policy, Dr Khan is working in the area of labour market segmentation and economics of conflict. His areas of research are frontiers of economics, political philosophy and economic history. With focus on religious minorities in labour market, Dr Khan is currently involved in studying effects of religious affiliation on labour market outcomes. He has also extensively published research on the microeconomic dimension of armed conflict with special focus on Jammu and Kashmir.

Apart from publishing research papers and delivering public talks on issues of topical importance and contemporary relevance, Dr Khan has published two edited volumes: *Critical Reflections and Explorations in Regional Development: Insights from North-West India* in 2018 and *Perspectives on Jammu and Kashmir Economy* in 2017. He also authored *A Text Book of Economics* in 2014.